GUIDE TO

MOZAMBIQUE

GUIDE TO

MOZAMBIQUE

MIKE SLATER

STRUIK

Struik Publishers (Pty) Ltd
(a member of The Struik Publishing Group (Pty) Ltd)
Cornelis Struik House
80 McKenzie Street
Cape Town 8001
Reg. No.: 54/00965/07

Reproduction by cmyk Prepress, Cape Town
Printed and bound by South China Printing Co.,
Hong Kong

First edition 1994
Second edition 1997
ISBN 1 86872 013 6

Copyright © in published edition
Struik Publishers (Pty) Ltd 1994, 1997

Editor: Lesley Hay-Whitton
Designer: Darren MacGurk
Cover designers: Neville Poulter and Janice Evans
Cartographers: John Loubser (colour map) and
Paul Marais (black and white maps)
Illustrator: Richard Pooler
Proofreader and indexer: Sandie Vahl
Text © Mike Slater 1994, 1997
Photographs © as credited below 1997
Illustrations © Struik Publishers, 1994, 1997
Maps © Struik Publishers 1994, 1997

PHOTOGRAPHIC CREDITS: Andrew Bannister, 65, 70 (bottom), 72, 74 (top) [Anthony Bannister Photo Library], 79, 146 (top and bottom), 150 (top), 155, 157 (top and bottom), 158. **Mike Coppinger,** 159 (top and bottom). **Daniel Erasmus,** 154 (top). **Peter Kirchhoff,** back cover, 66 (top), 67, 68, 69 (top), 70 (top), 150 (bottom), 152, 153 (top and bottom). **Jackie Murray,** 71, 74 (bottom). **Jackie Nel,** 69 (bottom), 73 (bottom) [both Photo Access]. **Phillip Richardson,** 73 (top) [Anthony Bannister Photo Library]. **Cleeve Robertson,** 149 (top and bottom). **Mike Slater,** cover (spine and back flap), 66 (bottom), 75, 76, 80 (bottom), 147, 148, 151, 154 (bottom), 156, 160 (top and bottom). **David Steele,** front cover (main picture) [Photo Access], 77 (top and bottom) [Photo Access], 78 (bottom) [Photo Access], 80 (top) [courtesy of Benguela Island Lodge], 145 [Photo Access]. **Koos van der Linde,** 78 (top) [courtesy of Benguela Island Lodge]. **Patrick Wagner,** front cover (inset).

The travel, accommodation and other facilities in this book represent a large proportion of those available at the time of going to press in 1997. The tourist world, however, is by its nature subject to rapid change. While every effort has been made to ensure that the most recent information has been supplied, some of the details will inevitably become outdated. Prospective travellers are advised to consult Mozambique Tours and Travel in Johannesburg before setting out on their journey. Contact telephone numbers appear at the end of the first chapter. The publishers would appreciate comments from readers relating to new, upgraded or defunct facilities, for incorporation in future editions. Please write to: The Editor, *Guide to Mozambique*, Struik Publishers, P.O. Box 1144, Cape Town 8000.

Contents

AUTHOR'S PREFACE

As a South African born and bred in Johannesburg, Mozambique was always out of bounds to me, partly due to internal conflict and partly because apartheid policies made South Africans unwelcome travellers. Nelson Mandela is now president of South Africa and the conflict in Mozambique has ended. I am delighted to have spent thirteen fascinating months in Mozambique, researching this guide and learning some Portuguese.

When Mozambique gained independence from Portugal in 1975, it might have become a viable, developing country but for the fact that Rhodesians and bitter ex-Mozambicans in South Africa formed and supported the rebel Renamo movement, causing untold misery in its campaign to make Mozambique ungovernable. When the cease-fire was signed in October 1992, I was in Pemba. On my return in September 1993, the jubilation and renewed confidence of the people were obvious: farmers were preparing to plant the first crop in over a decade; markets were transformed into bustling, noisy displays of fruit, seafood, freshly baked bread, woven baskets, hats and furniture, and intricate Makonde sculptures; musicians were playing marimbas, dancers invoking the spirits of the ancestors with energetic movements, and sailors offering trips in stately dhows.

This book was made possible by the generous, resilient people of Mozambique. It is a tribute to their lively, forgiving nature, despite the untold horrors of seventeen years of civil war. Many have helped me with their time, hospitality, knowledge and advice. Although it may embarrass some, I would like to mention a few names: Victor Zaccarius and Joaquim Domingos of the National Directorate for Tourism were very supportive, as was the United Nations in Mozambique, allowing me on their planes and providing invaluable information on road conditions, land mines and the process of reconstruction in Mozambique. Angela Self of the South African Foreign Trade Organization supplied details of trade and industry. Paul Dutton of the World Wildlife Fund, Bob Langeveld of the Mozambican Department of Nature Conservation and Don Beswick of the Endangered Wildlife Trust briefed me on conservation and wildlife in Mozambique.

Dries Loots of ESKOM and Senhor Tonim of HCB supplied details of the Cahora Bassa hydro-electricity project. Ollie and Bonny in Beira, Stef Meier in Pemba, Senhor Whitey of Hotel Central, Tony of Inhaca Protea Hotel and the Karos Polana Hotel provided magnificent accommodation. To Mozambique Island Tours (Bazaruto), the folks at Polana Tours, Mrs Robertson of Ilha Magaruque and Christiane Alary of the Panthera Azul bus service I extend my thanks. Ross Douglas and Chris Malouney filled gaps in my knowledge of the southern coastline, Assilmane Ndergomang and his dhow crew took me through the Querimba islands, and Chun Sik (Senhor Suki) in Pangane showed me his old Portuguese naval charts.

Jeremy Duvenage shared his experiences of the difficulties of crossing the Zambezi at Caia. Peter Green, Karin Reusch and Peter Kirchhoff were fellow adventurers during sections of my journey. My parents, George and Sue, as well as all my friends, were there whenever I needed to take advantage of their generosity. Tine, Roger and Shauna showed me Pemba's nightlife. Many other individuals and organizations deserve formal recognition. I wish I had more space, but this is a guidebook, not a telephone directory.

This, my first book, is dedicated to the memory of Gus Cox, Kirsten Klingenberg, Wayne Cleminson and Duncan Longmore.

Mike Slater
Johannesburg, July 1994; updated July 1996.

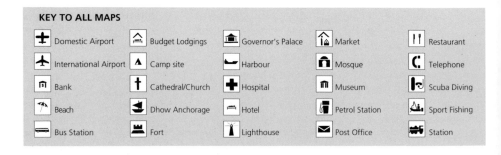

KEY TO ALL MAPS

✈ Domestic Airport	⌂ Budget Lodgings	🏛 Governor's Palace	Market	Restaurant
✈ International Airport	▲ Camp site	Harbour	Mosque	Telephone
Bank	Cathedral/Church	Hospital	Museum	Scuba Diving
Beach	Dhow Anchorage	Hotel	Petrol Station	Sport Fishing
Bus Station	Fort	Lighthouse	Post Office	Station

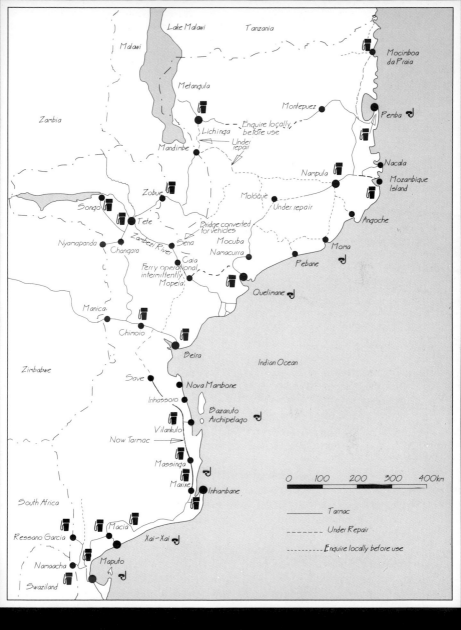

Mozambique

Introduction

The Land

Overview of Mozambique

Mozambique is a maritime country. Most of its citizens live in small, traditional fishing villages, tucked away in dune forests along its 2 500-kilometre-long coastline. The dhow, an ancient vessel of Arab origin with its characteristic gaff-rigged cotton sail, is still the most common form of transport between coastal towns. Fishing is a major sector of the workforce and fish an important source of protein. Portuguese is widely spoken, but other languages encountered range from English (spoken by Maputo street children who grew up in refugee camps in Malawi) to Arabic, echoing from Mozambique Island schools, and Makonde and Swahili in Cabo Delgado. There are also ten major vernaculars.

Mozambique has borders to the south with South Africa and Swaziland; to the west is Zimbabwe, and to the north-west Malawi. Mozambique's northern border along the Rovuma River is Tanzania, while to the east the country has an Indian Ocean coastline.

Each of Mozambique's ten provinces is presided over by a governor, housed in grand style near the centre of each capital city. During the Socialist/Marxist era of the 1980s, movement between provinces required the written approval of the governors of both provinces, but this is no longer the case. Much bureaucratic red tape has fallen away, and officials have been instructed to be courteous and co-operative towards visitors, in order to encourage reconstruction and development through tourism. Mozambique was avoided by even the most intrepid of adventurers before the conclusion of hostilities between the forces of rebel Renamo and the governing Frelimo in October 1992. Since then, the transformation has been swift and successful. The once devastated infrastructure has been one of the first sectors to benefit. Today all major towns are served by a satellite telephone system, which is rapidly expanding. Almost all important roads (both tarred and gravel) have been cleared of land mines and are being upgraded. Transport has been greatly improved by the introduction of minibus and bus companies, offering reliable services throughout Maputo, Inhambane, Sofala, Gaza and Manica provinces. They are expanding into the rest of Mozambique.

The mighty Zambezi River is still a formidable obstacle to movement between northern and southern Mozambique, but the sabotaged bridge at Vila de Sena and the once inoperable ferry at Caia have been repaired. If reliable, these will expand the country's overland travel routes and opportunities significantly. The international and domestic airline L.A.M. (Linhas Aéreas de Moçambique) links Inhambane, Beira, Tete, Quelimane, Nampula, Pemba and Lichinga to the outside world, via Maputo International Airport. Cargo ships and the odd, rare passenger boat ply the Mozambique Channel, off-loading provisions and imported luxuries, and loading up produce at the harbours of Maputo, Inhambane, Beira, Quelimane, Nacala and

Pemba. Mozambique is a fascinating blend of the world's major cultures and religions, and an unrivalled beach destination. Although parts of the lush tropical coastline and islands, with their white beaches and rows of coconut, papaya and cashew trees, have been exploited by developers, other areas remain untouched, with no electricity, telephones or motorboats to detract from a serene and timeless atmosphere.

While it may be difficult to tear yourself away from the sunshine and palm trees of Mozambique's beaches, the interior is not without rewards. Mountaineers will enjoy the challenge of its mountains, from the 2 500-metre-high, contorted sandstones of Chimanimani and Binga in Manica Province, to the towering granite domes of Gorongosa in Sofala, Namuli in Zambezia and Unango in Niassa. Rock climbers will be interested to know that Unango peak is surrounded by what may be the world's longest sheer pitches. For bird-watchers there is the promise of many endemic bird species. Although they were devastated by poaching and forest clearing during the civil upheaval, game reserves are receiving attention. The Maputo Elephant Reserve is likely to be the first to welcome day visitors from Maputo. The Gorongosa National Park was particularly ravaged, as it was once the base of the Renamo movement. International groups have begun to rehabilitate this reserve and it may be open to special interest groups by mid-1997.

The ten provinces

There are ten provinces (excluding Maputo city, which is defined as a separate province for statistical purposes). The latest information available was gathered in 1980.

MAPUTO PROVINCE. The Incomati is the most important river in the province. Other minor rivers are the Umbelúzi, Matola, Tembe, Maputo and Futi.

The climate along the coast is humid tropical, while the interior is dry tropical. Annual rainfall ranges from 400 to 800 mm, falling mainly from November to March. December is the wettest month, and August usually completely dry. Temperatures rarely drop below 20 °C or rise above 30 °C. November is the hottest month and July the coldest. Vegetation ranges from coastal thicket to open broad-leafed woodland and acacia savanna.

The population of one million are mainly Shangaan and Ronga tribespeople. Three quarters are engaged in subsistence agriculture, while in the past 7% were migrant workers on South African mines and other important sectors of industry and administration. Maputo harbour is a major source of income for the government. The main commercial crops used to be cashews, citrus and beans. Maputo was previously the main beefproducer of Mozambique.

GAZA PROVINCE. Gaza's annual rainfall is generally below 600 mm; the Pafúri area receives the least (300 mm), and Xai-Xai the most (1 200 mm). Temperatures range from highs of 18 °C in June to 30 °C in December. The vegetation is mainly acacia savanna and brachystegia (miombo) deciduous woodland. The Limpopo, southern Mozambique's largest river, runs through Gaza.

The Shangaans comprise over 90% of the population and the Chope the balance. In 1980 82,6% of the 500 000 inhabitants were engaged in subsistence agriculture, 1,3% were fishermen and 6,2% were migrant mine workers. Cashews and rice were the main commercial crops, with cotton grown extensively on the Limpopo flood plain. Small amounts of citrus were also produced.

INHAMBANE PROVINCE. Apart from the Save River on the border with Sofala Province, the only other river of note is the Govuro.

The climate ranges from humid tropical within 100 kilometres of the coastline to dry tropical in the interior. January and February are the wettest months (about 120 mm of rain falls during each), while the months from May to October each receive less than 20 mm. The hottest period is December and January, when average temperatures are in the region of 30 °C. Temperatures during June to August may drop to 20 °C.

There are dense, tangled dune forests along the coastal fringe and on the islands of the Bazaruto Archipelago. Deciduous and semi-deciduous dry forests are found sporadically among miombo woodland throughout the province. Mangrove swamps occur along the edges of the bays of Inhambane and Vilankulo and at the mouth of the Rio Save (Sabi River). Meadows and mopane savannas occur along the banks of the Save.

In 1980, the Tswa tribe comprised 65% of the population of 700 000, while the Chope and Bitonga made up 17% each. About 88,2% of the people were engaged in subsistence agriculture and 5% in the industrial and mining sectors. Today a high proportion are engaged in fishing activities.

Inhambane was once the most important citrus-producing region of Mozambique and the second most important cashew growing area (after Nampula). It still has extensive coconut plantations, which have not been exploited on a commercial basis recently. Inhambane Province has also in the past been a significant cattle-, goat- and pig-raising region.

SOFALA PROVINCE. Several channels drain the swamps around the Buzi, Gorongosa, Muda, Púngoe, Urema and Zangue rivers. The deltas of the Save, Buzi, Púngoe and Zambezi rivers are along the coast of Sofala province.

Beira (the capital city of Sofala) experiences rainfall above 250 mm during December, January and March. This drops to less than 50 mm per month from June to October. Average temperatures at Beira are highest from December to February, when they approach 30 °C, while temperatures from June to August may drop below 20 °C.

Along the coast south of Beira, there are extensive mangrove swamps. The interior north and west of Beira is covered in extensive dry and humid deciduous forests. The coastal dunes are blanketed by dense dune thickets. Parallel to this is a belt of palm savanna islands, surrounded by swampland. The areas which become inundated annually along the river banks and in the Zambezi delta are characterized by herbaceous or wooded meadows and savannas. Acacia savannas occur along the border with Manica province.

In 1980, around 60% of the province's population of 750 000 was made up of Sena (along the Zambezi valley) and 40% Shona (in and around Beira) tribes with a smattering of Chuabo people in the Zambezi delta. Approximately 71% of the population were engaged in subsistence agriculture, 12% in industry, 6% in administration, 4% in each of the commerce and communication sectors and the rest were engaged in fishing, construction or education. Sofala was once an important area for the production of cashews, citrus and livestock.

MANICA PROVINCE. Mount Binga (2 436 m) is Mozambique's highest point. Most of Manica is defined by the drainage basins of the Buzi and Púngoè rivers, with the rest of the province's runoff ending up in the Zambezi. The Revué river is dammed near Chicamba, forming Lake Chicamba Real.

Generally Manica's climate is moderated by its altitude, with average highs of 25 °C in December and January. During June and July temperatures often drop to 15 °C at night. Rainfall reaches a peak of 250 mm in December and January, while the months from May to October each experience less than 20 mm.

Most of the province is covered in high-rainfall miombo woodland. The southern region has acacia savanna and dry miombo woodland, with a thin belt of mopane savanna along the banks of the Save. The central and eastern parts of Manica Province have extensive montane evergreen forests and humid semi-deciduous timberlands.

Approximately 60% of the 1980 population of 400 000 were Shona and 30% Sena, with the rest classified as Nyungwe. About 87% of the population were engaged in subsistence agriculture, with the most important other economic sectors being administration, industry and commerce.

Manica was once an important citrus producing region, and livestock also played a fairly important role.

ZAMBEZIA PROVINCE. Mounts Namuli (2 419 m) and Chiperone (2 054 m) are Mozambique's second and third highest points respectively. The Zambezi drains a fifth of the province. Other major basins are drained by the Licungo, Melela, Molócuè and Ligonha.

Apart from the far west of the province on the Malawi border (dry tropical) and the area around Mount Namuli, the rest of Zambezia is classified as humid tropical. Average temperatures are between 25 °C and 30 °C, with November to March the hottest, and April to June the coldest. Precipitation ranges from 250 mm in January and February, to less than 15 mm in August.

The vegetation ranges from the western open savannas and the swampland meadows of the Zambezi delta, to the lowland deciduous miombo woodlands of the west and the highland miombos of the interior plateau. There are extensive mangrove swamps along the coast, especially around Quelimane, Paiva, Pebane and Moebase. Slightly inland are semi-deciduous humid forests with evergreen montane forests in the inland high-lying areas.

The population in 1980 was about 1,5 million, made up of 40% Lomwe, 30% Chuabo, 20% Marende and 10% Sena, with around 90% engaged in subsistence agriculture.

Zambezia used to be the main coconut and tea producing area, with citrus and cashews also cultivated. Livestock was also an important source of revenue.

NAMPULA PROVINCE. The Meluli, Monapo, Mecubúri and Lúrio (on the border of Cabo Delgado province) rivers drain Nampula Province. Temperatures reach the high thirties from November to March. The period from May to August is the coolest, during which readings may drop to below 20 °C at night. Precipitation reaches 250 mm in January and drops to 10 mm by August.

Mangrove swamps occur along long stretches of the coastline in the region of Angoche, Mogincual and Memba. The greater part of the province consists of deciduous miombo woodland. Dry deciduous forests occur in the eastern half of the province, and evergreen montane forests in the mountainous regions.

In 1980 there was a total population of approximately 1,5 million, making Nampula Mozambique's most densely peopled province. The population was made up almost exclusively of the Makua tribe. Roughly 90% of the province's population were engaged in subsistence agriculture, industry and administration absorbing most of the remainder of the workforce.

Nampula is the cashew capital of Mozambique and, although the number of trees have diminished since the high of 30 million in 1971 (due to neglect and tropical cyclones in 1981 and 1994), the processing plant at Monapo is still operating. The province was once a significant producer of citrus and coconuts. Sheep, cattle and goats also contributed to the economy in the past.

CABO DELGADO PROVINCE. The Megaruma, Montepuez and Messalo rivers drain most of Cabo Delgado. The northern and north-western sector of the province is drained by the Lugenda and Rovuma rivers. Rainfall is highest between January and April and lowest from July to November, with a peak of 260 mm in January and a low of 5 mm in July. Average temperatures are close to 30 °C from November to March. June to September is the coolest period, but the mercury rarely drops below the 25 °C mark.

The coastal wooded dune thickets are at their most extensive in this province and baobab tree forests occur almost on top of some of the beaches, such as Wimbe near Pemba. Mangrove swamps occur extensively on the edge of the shallow coastal bays and between the islands of Ibo and Querimba. Tree and shrub savannas occur just inland of the dune strip west of Pemba. The rest of the province is covered by open miombo woodland, ranging from semi-deciduous and high rainfall to dry deciduous and large leaf.

There were about 600 000 people in Cabo Delgado in 1980, of whom 70% were Makua, 20% Makonde (Cabo Delgado is the only province where the Makonde, famous for their bizarre carvings, live) and 10% Mwani. About 92% of the population were engaged in some form of agriculture, and fishing and industry were other important employers.

Cashews and coconuts were important commercial crops before the civil upheaval, and a coconut plantation on Querimba Island has continued to operate uninterruptedly on the mainland.

NIASSA PROVINCE. At an average altitude of about 700 m above sea level, Niassa is the highest of the ten provinces of Mozambique. The Lichinga Plateau, which comprises about one quarter of the province, lies 1 000 m above sea level and reaches over 1 500 m in places. In the far north-western corner of Niassa, Mount Txitonga (1 848 m) is the highest point in the province.

The province is drained almost exclusively by the Lugenda and Rovuma rivers, while the western edge of Niassa, along the shores of Lago Niassa (Lake Malawi), is actually part of the huge Zambezi River drainage basin.

At Lichinga, deep in the heart of the tropics, temperatures are modified markedly by altitude. Average temperatures may reach 25 °C during November and December. The mercury can drop below the 10 °C mark in the night from May to August.

Monthly rainfall at Lichinga is over 200 mm between December and March. Rainfall above 300 mm is often reported during March itself. August and September generally receive no rainfall.

Apart from the open and wooded acacia savannas around Mandimba, Niassa is covered by the full range of miombo woodland. Evergreen montane forests cover the slopes of the mountains.

With a population of only 300 000 in 1980 and an area larger than any of the other nine provinces, Niassa is the most sparsely peopled region of Mozambique. About half of the population were Makua, 40% Yao and 5% Nyanja.

Approximately 90% of the 1980 population were involved in agriculture, while the rest of the economically active sector were employed by the industrial and administrative sectors.

TETE PROVINCE. Apart from the base of the Zambezi River valley, which drops to below 100 metres, altitudes in the province are generally in the 300-metre to 700-metre range, while the Angonia and Marávia plateaux rise to well above 1 000 metres. Notable mountain peaks are Dómuè (2 095 m), Maconcoè (1 665 m) and Ulongwé (1 416 m). The whole of Tete Province is drained by the Zambezi River.

From October to March Tete town has an average temperature above 32 °C, with a maximum above 45 °C in November. Even during June and July, the temperature rarely drops below 25 °C. Contrast this with readings at Chiputo on the Marávia Plateau, where the average temperature is only 25 °C in November and 15 °C in July.

Tete town receives rain from December to March, with February being the wettest (160 mm) and April to October receiving almost no rain.

Chiputo usually experiences 340 mm of rain in January (the highest rainfall in the whole country). Rainfall during February and December also approaches the 300 mm mark, and monthly falls from May to October average around 15 mm.

With acacia and mopane savanna, the full range of miombo types as well as mountain pastures, Tete province has the widest variety of vegetation.

The population in 1980 was some 500 000, 40% of whom were Nyanja, 35% Nyungwe and 25% Sena. About 90% of Tete's people were involved in some form of agriculture. Administrators and business people comprised the balance of the workforce.

Great herds of livestock once roamed its pastures, but were decimated by banditry.

Climate

The hot, rainy season is from October to March. The best time to visit Mozambique is during the winter months (from April to September) which, while drier, less humid and cooler, can still be very hot, especially in the north along the coast.

History in brief

Mozambique (Moçambique in Portuguese) has had a long, colourful and sometimes troubled history since the Portuguese explorer Pero da Covilhã anchored off Sofala, near modern-day Beira, in 1487. Mozambique was the only country on the coast of East Africa colonized by the Portuguese. The name Mozambique is apparently derived from the name of one of the early Arab traders, a Sultan Mussa Ben Mbiki. While the Portuguese may have been the first Europeans to reach this part of the East African coastline, Arabs had in fact been trading with the native tribes since AD 600.

Today Catholic cathedrals vie with mosques in towns and villages throughout Mozambique, which can be ascribed to a trading rivalry between the Portuguese and Arabs dating back over 500 years.

At the time of the Portuguese arrival off the shores of Mozambique, all ports on the East African coast were firmly under Arab control. By 1510 the Portuguese were in possession of all former Arab ports along the coast. The Chinde mouth of the Zambezi was discovered in 1889, prior to which vessels entered the treacherous, shallow, sand-barred mouth alongside Ilha Conceição. Under a convention of 1891, a British concession was granted in Chinde and for many years it was the main route to Nyasaland (now Malawi). The concession lapsed only in 1922 when a railway line was completed between Beira and Malawi. Chinde was almost destroyed by a cyclone in 1922 and the old village has almost disappeared due to the action of the sea. Chupanga (formerly Shupanga), just upstream from the old sugar-growing centre of Marromeu, was where Mary Moffat, wife of missionary and explorer David Livingstone, died in 1862. She is buried in the Chupanga mission churchyard.

13

In 1934 the railway bridge at Sena was constructed and the first train crossed on its way to Malawi in 1935. The bridge incorporates a footpath and is a remarkable feat of engineering. Spanning a staggering 3 660 metres, it was the longest bridge in the world when it was built.

During the conflict in Mozambique, Renamo rebels (at the instigation of the then Rhodesian secret service) sabotaged two spans of the bridge. A plan to repair and convert the bridge for road traffic, to facilitate the transport of relief aid to Zambezia province, has now come to fruition.

Mozambique today

Its vast coastline extending for more than 2 500 kilometres makes this a unique nation of seafaring traders and fishermen, with a lively, friendly Latin temperament. Most places that are worth visiting are located on or near to the coast, where the dhow is still the predominant form of local transport.

For 17 years Mozambique was devastated by civil war. General elections were successfully held in October 1994.

The historic signing of the Nkomati Accord in 1985 ended (in theory anyway) the hostilities which had existed between the Frelimo government and the former South African government.

This Nkomati Accord also marked the departure point of the Mozambique government from its former alignment with the Soviet economic bloc towards closer ties with the West and a free market economy. In fact, in 1990 the Congress of the ruling party formally departed from its Marxist-Leninist ideology and announced plans to privatize state institutions and hold multiparty elections.

Following United Nations-brokered talks in Rome in 1990 and in Lisbon in 1991 and 1992, a comprehensive peace agreement was finally signed by Renamo and Frelimo in October of 1992. ONUMOZ peace monitors arrived shortly afterwards and managed to repatriate millions of refugees from neighbouring states, demobilize most of the opposing armed forces and begin the training of a new united army well before the October 1994 elections.

Thanks largely to ONUMOZ, Mozambique today is transformed. The media are no longer censored and newspapers are filled with information and debate. International investors are renovating old lodges and hotels and building new ones, and the road system has been extensively overhauled. Rehabilitation of transport and infrastructural links is progressing and it is already possible to travel widely in two-wheel-drive vehicles. Even in the most far-flung corners of the country, schools and hospitals are being rebuilt and buses and taxis are transporting hundreds of thousands of Mozambicans between villages, towns and cities to reopen links between friends and relatives which had been broken by conflict for up to 17 years.

Since the Peace Accord of October 1992, people have been busy rebuilding their lives and are fast regaining their former reputation as being among the friendliest folk in the world.

Perhaps the single most significant indicator of Mozambique's newly found status as a safe, prospering, developing country is the visitors who are flocking to experience the warmth of the people and climate and the splendour of the beaches, coral reefs, landscapes and historic settlements. Inhambane province's beaches are crowded with fishermen, scuba and snorkel divers, sun-worshippers and overland travellers during the Zimbabwe and South African school holidays. The coral wonderland surrounding the Bazaruto Archipelago attracts adventurers

14

from all over the world, looking for new, exciting fishing and diving destinations. Small, intimate, thatch and reed lodges dot the southern coastline, offering personalized service and kilometres of African tropical beaches at their finest.

Government

Since the general election in 1994, the government of Mozambique has entered what may best be viewed as an interim period. Renamo and ruling party Frelimo are involved in constant talks regarding the country's future. This may take the form of a government of national unity, whereby all political parties with sufficient support will be granted interim cabinet posts.

Economy

Due to the disruption of transport links and the destruction of the infrastructure during the years of civil strife in Mozambique, economic activities decreased drastically or came to a complete standstill in many areas. Most skilled workers left at the time of independence from Portugal in 1975, leaving behind a country unable to maintain its industries, farms, roads, railways, harbours and communication links. Soviet and East German 'advisers' and technicians were sent to fill the void left by the departing Portuguese. They managed to contribute very little. Instead they appeared to aggravate the situation, by over-exploiting Mozambique's fish, agricultural, wildlife and hardwood resources. When they left, few Mozambicans lamented and fewer could claim to have benefited from their presence.

Today the processing of food, petroleum refining and commercial fishing remain the leading foreign currency earners. Urgent efforts are being made to rehabilitate the agricultural (particularly cashews, copra and tea) and mining sectors, as well as the transmission of power from Cahora Bassa to South Africa. Even though the value of local production has declined to less than half the levels of 1973, recent developments at the Pande gas fields, the South Africa–Maputo development corridor and in the tourism industry throughout the country augur well for the future.

Education

Despite past constraints on curricula and rebel attacks on schools and teachers, the revitalization of education is gaining ground, mainly through the efforts of both local and foreign non-govermental organizations (NGOs). Koranic schools managed to function along the coast, despite upheavals. Eduardo Mondlane University in Maputo has continued to operate, despite enormous obstacles. However, from a low of only sixteen secondary schools functioning throughout the country, mostly in Maputo and Beira, in 1992, education has a long way to go.

Health

Trained health workers joined the 1975 exodus and the country has not yet been able to train enough doctors, nurses and rural orderlies to fill the gap left by them. Although much has been attained through programmes instituted by the United Nations and foreign aid agencies, health facilities remain desperately inadequate, with the result that outbreaks of diseases related to poor hygiene (such as cholera and dysentery) occur regularly in the slum areas of cities such as Beira. In urban areas, state hospitals are usually staffed by foreign-trained doctors, but they are overworked and unable to provide care approaching internationally acceptable standards.

Private clinics operate in Maputo and generic medicines are available cheaply over the counter at state pharmacies, although they may have reached the end of their shelf life. Until the situation improves, visitors should take sensible precautions such as malaria prophylaxis, drinking bottled water and taking out cover from a medical evacuation insurance policy (South Africa's medical facilities, for example, are excellent).

The United Nations

Mozambique is one of the more recent and significant success stories for this world body. The U.N. ground operations began in October 1992 and, under the guidance of U.N. troops and officials, Mozambique has been pulled back from the edge of oblivion. The first task of ONUMOZ was to secure the Tete and Beira corridors for the passage of essential goods, eg. food, fuel and raw materials. This operation was extended to encompass the whole country and was assisted by the removal of land mines on roads, under bridges and around almost every strategic structure (such as wells, lighthouses, electricity pylons and warehouses).

By mid-1994, almost all Mozambique's most important roads had been cleared of mines, and the opening up of the countryside was being tackled. ONUMOZ also addressed the enormous task of repatriating over two million refugees and demobilizing the opposing armed forces, while at the same time training them for civilian life and beginning the formation of a new united army. ONUMOZ facilitated the registration of voters and made final arrangements to ensure that the October 1994 election took place successfully. Transport, to allow canvassing in remote areas, as well as to ensure that all voters reached the polls, was arranged and provided through branches of the U.N. These include the Children's Fund (UNICEF), the World Health Organization (WHO), the High Commissioner for Refugees (UNHCR) and the World Food Programme (WFP), who have been working through NGOs to bring housing, food, seeds, tools, medical care, education, reconstruction and redevelopment to the people. This combination of international efforts, as well as the determination of the people to maintain peace and secure their future, an exciting and splendid natural environment being opened up to visitors and the prospects of a government of national unity, certainly justify the hopes and supports the views of people both inside the country and from neighbouring states that Mozambique has a very positive future.

People

Population

In 1986 the population of Mozambique was 15 000 000: 1 000 000 people in Maputo, 250 000 in Beira, 120 000 in Nampula, and 70 000 in Quelimane and Tete.

Art and architecture

The architecture of the mosques, churches and palaces in Mozambique's towns and cities is rich, sometimes bizarre, always intriguing to tourists who enjoy looking beyond the colourful markets, stunning beaches and endless coral reefs. Manueline villas and Victorian mansions stand side by side. Just across intricate mosaic pavements you might see the spire of a Catholic cathedral vying for attention with the minarets of a meticulously maintained mosque. Even boats used for fishing and transport between villages and tiny coral islands display craftsmanship originating in far-off corners of the world: the dhows of the Middle East, bamboo one-person platforms with a collapsible mast originating in the East, high-bowed rowing boats reminiscent of Scottish 'dories' and the local version of modern ski boats crafted in mahogany, with inboard diesel engines.

The environment

National parks

While Mozambique has four national parks (Banhine in Gaza, Zinave in Inhambane, the Bazaruto Archipelago and Gorongosa in Sofala) and four nature reserves (Maputo Elephant in Maputo province, Marromeu in Sofala, Gili in Zambezia and Niassa in Niassa), only Bazaruto Archipelago, Gorongoso and Maputo Elephant Reserve can receive and accommodate visitors.

Maputo Elephant Reserve, the first mainland park to be rehabilitated, was open to day guests at the time of writing. Many will be keen to visit Gorongosa, so popular before the civil war. It was once the base of Renamo and, while the wildlife was decimated, Chitengo Camp now has basic facilities. Ask at 'Mariners' in Beira (see page 121) before visiting this area and even then do not venture off well-used roads.

An exciting plan, the Gaza Peace Park, has been drawn up by South African conservation groups, but its implementation is being held up by the threat of poaching. Also known as the Kruger-Banhine cross-border project, this would fulfil a long-held dream to re-open the South Africa/ Mozambique frontier to the ancient migratory routes of big game such as elephant and buffalo. The park would mirror the Kruger in Mozambique's Gaza province, as far east as the Limpopo River. This is only the beginning of an extended objective which is to include Mozambique's Parques Nacional de Banhine e Zinave and the coastal Pomene convervancy, as well as Zimbabwe's Gonarezhou and Malapati reserves. Thus a reserve would be created offering elephant, lion, buffalo, rhino, leopard and whales - the Big Six! Find out the latest position by contacting Maritz Wahl or Deon Marais at South Africa's Department of Environmental Affairs and Tourism, tel. Pretoria (012) 30 3426.

Fauna and flora

Mozambique was once home to large herds of elephant, rhino and buffalo, prides of lion, leopard and cheetah and many smaller animal species. The plant life, although better able than the animal life to weather the ravages of war, is threatened by continued illegal forestry and 'slash and burn' subsistence agriculture.

There is a dire need for conservation efforts in Mozambique to be supported by the international community. Contact Dr Milagre Cezerilo of the Direção Nacional de Flora e Fauna Bravia in Maputo at tel. 43 1789 for more information. Other organizations that are presently involved include the Endangered Wildlife Trust (see page 49) and the South African National Parks Board.

Bird-watching in Mozambique

Due to the unique combination of coastal, riverine, swamp, mountain, forest and grassland habitats which occur especially in the central region of Mozambique, the birdlife is correspondingly rich in variety. Upwards of 900 species have been documented south of the Zambezi River, while the Gorongosa region in particular holds great rewards for serious bird-watchers and ornithologists.

Birds which are found in the Mozambique, and particularly the Gorongosa area, but are difficult to find anywhere else in southern Africa, include the following species: greenheaded oriole, bluethroated sunbird, chestnutfronted helmetshrike, blackcap tchagra, Livingstone's flycatcher, Mozambique batis, Vanga flycatcher, singing cisticola, blackheaded apalis, redwinged warbler, moustached warbler, Eastern saw-wing swallow, mascarene martin, Nyasa seedcracker, oliveheaded weaver, whitebreasted alethe, green tinker barbet, Böhm's bee-eater and sooty tern.

Marine parks

Apart from the reefs around the Bazaruto Archipelago (Parque Nacional de Bazaruto), no marine environments off Mozambique's shores had at the time of writing received formal recognition. Conservation groups, as well as the government, are taking the threat to undersea ecosystems seriously, paying particular attention to the Quirimba Archipelago, parts of which are earmarked for future declaration as a protected area.

Coral reefs

Mozambique's coral reefs rank with the world's richest and most extensive. They are all protected by laws prohibiting any surface water sport, fishing, spear fishing or shellfish and lobster collecting activities on or near coral reefs. Boaters caught anchoring on coral or breaking other regulations are liable to have their boat and other vehicles seized, and face the possibility of arrest and stiff fines. A simple guideline if you intend to enjoy the privilege of snorkelling or scuba diving on Mozambique's corals is hands (and feet) off! Remember that, even if you so much as touch these delicate micro-organisms, millions may die, quite apart from the ramifications of killing reef fish and collecting shells. If you want a shell to take home with you, please buy it from the recognized dealers in Maputo, Quelimane or at Wimbe beach near Pemba.

Deep-sea fishing

The Mozambique Channel is well known among big-game fishermen for its record-sized marlin and billfish. The most popular spots are off Ponta do Ouro, Inhaca Island, Praia de Xai-Xai, Inhambane, Bazaruto Archipelago, Nacala and Pemba. Although it is illegal to drive on any of Mozambique's beaches, launching points are designated at certain spots and, where there is no formal arrangement, boaters may launch their craft and must then remove vehicles from the beach. Inspectors are being trained by the World Wildlife Fund (W.W.F.) and the Endangered Wildlife Trust (E.W.T.) to enforce these regulations, but it is up to fishing clubs to educate their members.

Scuba diving and snorkelling

There are popular dive sites off Ponta Malongane, Inhaca and Portuguese islands, Praia de Xai-Xai, Pandane and Tofinho near Inhambane, Morrungulo, Bazaruto Archipelago, Pebane, Moebase (Ilha do Fogo), Angoche Archipelago, Wimbe beach near Pemba and dozens of spots along the Quirimba Archipelago in the far north.

The lodges on Magaruque, Bazaruto and Benguerra offer the longest-established diving operations, including dive masters and the latest equipment and boats (as do Pontas do Ouro and Malongane). Other locations offer varying facilities. Some are likely to be upgraded in the future, so make enquiries before you decide on where your diving holiday will take place.

Snorkelling is excellent at most dive sites, as the depth of the reefs usually varies from a few metres at low tide to around 15 metres at high tide. The nearest decompression chambers are in South Africa, at Richards Bay and Johannesburg.

At remote sites, chances of rescue may be slight, while other, more established operations have reliable systems to evacuate casualties to South Africa and Zimbabwe. It is recommended that all visitors to Mozambique take out insurance with an organization such as Med-Rescue International, Criticare or Dive-Evac (see page 48–50).

Whether by using high-tech scuba equipment, a simple snorkel and goggles or from the top of a sleek surfboard skimming down rolling breakers, the exploration of the thousands of kilometres of untouched coral reefs and seashore is difficult to match

Legend:

Accommodation: Hotel = H, Lodge = L, Camp = C, Private cottages = P

Facilities: Electricity = E, Water = W, Sanitation = S, Petrol = P, Vehicle/Boat repair = V, Shops = S

Fishing: Launch: – Surf = S, – Protected = P; Gamefish = G; Bottomfish = B; Distance to grounds = Dist

Destination	Distance ex Maputo (Approx km)	Accommodation H	L	C	P	Facilities E	W	S	P	V	S	Fishing S	P	G	B	Dist (km)
Ponta do Ouro	150	•	•	•		•	•				•	•	•	•	•	5 – 25
Ponta Malongane	150	•	•	•		•	•				•	•	•	•	•	5 – 25
Inhaca Island	35	•	•	•	•	•	•	•					•	•	•	5 – 15
Bilene (San Martino)	160	•	•	•	•	•	•	•	•		•	•		•	•	5 – 10
Xai-Xai	215	•		•	•	•	•	•	•	•	•		•	•	•	1 – 15
Závora	350		•			•	•	P V S available at Inhambane					•	•	•	1 – 10
Jangamo	480	•	•					•	P V S available at Inhambane				•	•	•	1 – 10
Tofo	460	•		•	•	•	•	•	P V S available at Inhambane				•	•	•	1 – 15
Ponta da Barra	470		•	•		•	•	•	P V S available at Inhambane				•	•	•	1 – 20
Pandane	470		•			•							•	•	•	1 – 20
Morrungulo	520	•	•			•	•	•					•	•	•	5 – 10
Pomene	650												•	•	•	1 – 10
Vilankulo	800	•	•	•	•	•	•	•	•	•	•		•	•	•	20 – 30
Inhassoro	875	•		•	•	•	•	•		•			•	•	•	40 – 60
Santa Carolina	By sea/air	•		•		•	•	•					•	•	•	10 – 25
Benguerra	from	•				•	•	•					•	•	•	5 – 35
Bazaruto	Vilankulo	•				•	•	•					•	•	•	5 – 25
Magaruque	only	•		•		•	•	•					•	•	•	3 – 20

Table reproduced (with alterations) from the May/June 1994 issue of Ski-Boat magazine.

anywhere in the world. Dive where few (if any) have been before, from the comfort of boats operated from luxurious, secluded lodges, or swim from a deserted beach to reefs which are almost exposed at low tide and may be only five metres below the surface at high tide. Catch your meal from the ocean's bounteous pantry or join the ranks of the world's big-game fishermen who capture, photograph, tag and then release these magnificent beasts back into the depths. Generally calm waters, a very gradually dipping continental shelf and opposing currents create spots throughout the Mozambique Channel which saltwater fly-fishermen consider world class.

1

Getting by in Mozambique

General

This chapter contains ways to avoid possible pitfalls and frustrations of travelling in a country where distances between places of interest are great, public transport is limited, credit cards are rarely accepted and your trusty dog-eared French phrase-book, so useful in West Africa, will only elicit baffled expressions from Moçambicanos.

Visas and other formalities

Passport
Passports of all member nations of the United Nations are recognized by Mozambique. Your passport must be valid to a date six months after your intended return, or your visa application will be refused.

Visas
Whether you plan to arrive by air, rail or motor vehicle, the first bureaucratic obstacle to be negotiated before you spend thousands on expensive scuba gear or state-of-the-art birding binoculars, is applying for a visa. The government of Mozambique understandably views visas as a way of obtaining much-needed foreign exchange and all passport holders, even citizens of Portugal, must apply (and pay) for a visa.

Bureaucratic wheels usually take a long time to turn in Mozambique, so it is prudent to apply for your visa at least two weeks (the minimum time required is eight days, unless you are prepared to pay for an 'emergency' visa) before your intended visit. Validity (30 days for the standard visa) will commence on the date of arrival. If you intend to do business or need a multiple entry visa, you will require a fax or letter from a company registered in Mozambique to present along with your application. Transit visas valid for three days from time of entry are also sometimes issued.

COST OF VISAS. Visas cost from R100 to R350, depending on type (tourist, visitor, business), length of validity, whether multiple or single entry, whether you use a visa service and how urgently you need it to be processed (this ranges from two weeks to 24 hours). The cost of visas also varies according to where they are obtained.

WHERE TO GET YOUR VISA. Visas are obtainable from the Mozambican diplomatic or consular missions in the main cities of all of Mozambique's neighbours, as well as in many countries around the world.

Visas are not usually issued at the border, and must be applied for from the Mozambican Visa Section in Johannesburg, Cape Town, Durban or Nelspruit (South Africa), Mbabane (Swaziland), Harare (Zimbabwe), Blantyre and Lilongwe (Malawi), Dar es Salaam (Tanzania) or the Mozambique mission in the capital city of your country.

In South Africa, contact the Mozambique Consulate and Visa Section in Pretoria at (012) 343 0957 and ask about the office nearest to you, or phone Mozambique Tours and Travel in Johannesburg (011) 339 7275.

VALIDITY. Unless you make a particular point of ensuring otherwise, your visa will be valid for 30 days from the date of arrival.

Whether your visa is valid for 30 days or six months, it will need to be extended every month at an immigration office while in Mozambique. It is cheapest to pay for visa extensions in rands, Zimbabwe dollars or Malawi Kwacha, but United States dollars (in cash) may be required. A stay of up to three months is permitted on a tourist visa as long as you extend it each month.

EXTENDING YOUR VISA. Once in Mozambique you are likely to be so enchanted by the lifestyle and smiles that you will want to stay longer. If you require a visa extension, just hand in your passport at the local immigration office (Imigração) before your present visa expires. There's one in the capital of each province. Fees are often negotiable and a new visa can be issued in as little as a day if you are willing to pay extra.

Insurance and emergencies

Ask your insurance broker whether your policies cover you in Mozambique. Motorists are advised that the M.V.A. or third party insurance sold at the borders provides you with just U.S.$200 in coverage, and it would be advisable to supplement this with an additional policy. As the possibility of theft is fairly high in Mozambique, take care to insure your personal belongings and your vehicle comprehensively for all risks.

Inform your consulate in Maputo (see page 48) of your arrival and departure dates as well as detailed travel plans. This will ensure you of up-to-date advice and assistance in the event of your falling foul of the law, or some other unforeseen mishap. South Africans, for example, can visit their embassy in Maputo on the corner of Av. Eduardo Mondlane and Av. Julius Nyerere, or telephone Maputo (01) 49 2096.

Health, comfort and safety

Inoculations

No inoculations for smallpox, cholera or yellow fever are required (unless you are coming from an infected area). This may change due to unforeseen circumstances.

Inoculations against typhoid, cholera, hepatitis and T.B. (tuberculosis) are also not required (unless you have come from an infected area), but may be advisable if you intend to spend more than a week in the country, or if you are an adventurous traveller who will often come into contact with the general population.

Staying healthy

Consult your doctor about preventive measures for malaria, dysentery, cholera, bacterial infection and hepatitis. Malaria and polluted drinking water form the main health risks in Mozambique. Malaria, which is prevalent throughout Mozambique, is at its worst during the November to May rainy season. Chloroquine- and Pyrimethamine-resistant strains are rife. Consult a doctor experienced in tropical diseases about measures against malaria, bearing in mind that drugs such as Mefloquine (Larium) and Halofantrine (Halfan) may be more effective than those commonly prescribed. Ask your doctor about their side effects. Wear long clothes and a repellent at night and sleep under a mosquito net.

21

Mozambique is considered a high-risk country as far as AIDS is concerned. In order to avoid infection, **all forms of unprotected sexual contact** (i.e. without a condom) **should be avoided**, as well as any other situations in which exchange of body fluids could take place (for example sharing razors or toothbrushes). It is a good idea to carry your own medical supply kit, including sterile needles and syringes.

Boil all water if you intend to drink it (or simply stick to tea and coffee), or drink only bottled water which is available in most large towns. If travelling away from tourist spots, bring a chemical water-purifier such as Chlor-Floc or a good filter, such as a pocket 'Katadyn', as it may not always be possible to boil your drinking water. It may be prudent to avoid fresh salads in the cheaper restaurants unless you are sure that they were washed in safe water. If food arrives cold, send it back and ensure that it is not merely re-heated. Fruit and vegetables that have been peeled or well cooked are safe.

Meat, fish and poultry should always be approached with healthy suspicion and eaten while still hot. Fresh fish will have bulging, shiny eyes. Do not buy frozen food, as it may have thawed and been re-frozen a few times.

Long trousers and shirts, mosquito nets and insect repellents are your first line of defence against mosquitoes, so bring these along with you.

Medical services
Medical facilities in Mozambique are generally very basic and there is no formal ambulance or rescue service.

Hospitals and pharmacies (farmácias) are usually state-run and very cheap if you have the time to wait and are prepared to run the risk of unhygienic conditions. Drugs such as antibiotics and anti-malaria tablets are sold without prescription but may have expired. It is simple to avoid many diseases by taking preventive measures, such as by drinking only boiled or bottled water. In all warm, wet places insect bites, cuts, grazes and scratches tend to become infected very easily. Avoid getting tropical ulcers (which often lead to hospitalization) by disinfecting every lesion, no matter how minor. Don't walk barefoot on shorelines where there is dried coral on the beach. Even in a First World medical environment, ailments such as malaria, cholera, hepatitis and tropical ulcers are likely to put you in hospital for a week or two.

Medical emergencies should be prepared for by taking out insurance with an evacuation organization like M.R.I. (Med-Rescue International); call toll-free inside South Africa 0800 11 9911. 'Clinica de Sommershield', Av. Kim Il Sung, tel. 49 3924/5/6. Contact the 'special clinic' at the Maputo Central Hospital at 42 4633. Charges are in advance in rands or United States dollars.

Crime
Petty thieving is rife in Mozambique and, although it may be safe to trust the little fellows who will attempt to befriend you or offer to help you all over the country for a small fee, don't be too surprised if your penknife, shoes or odd items of clothing go missing. This is usually only applicable in and around the larger urban areas. A few guidelines:
• Beware of thieves, pickpockets, conmen and bogus policemen, especially in Maputo and Beira.
• In cities, take a taxi at night and don't walk along badly lit roads after dark. Carry what you need in a money belt under your clothes.
• Keep away from crowds as they provide excellent opportunities for muggers and pickpockets to practise their trade on the unsuspecting tourist.

Armed hijackings (especially of new 4x4 vehicles) are a real threat, particularly in Maputo. so keep your driving to a minimum in this city.

Land mines

While clearing operations are progressing, land mines and booby traps remain a deadly serious threat. There are apparently millions lying around everywhere, so don't step off the beaten track, and always find out locally which areas are safe. Assume that all man-made structures outside of the towns, such as bridges, wells, pylons, lighthouses, pump stations, abandoned vehicles, footpaths and reservoirs are mined. Keep out of places where the locals don't go. Land mines may have been cleared from most main and many minor routes, but still don't go off the beaten track without first enquiring locally.

The overall security situation in Mozambique was satisfactory at the time of writing, but it is still not advisable to travel after dark, due to the presence of people, animals, broken-down trucks and vehicles without lights on the pot-holed roads.

Hygiene

The climate is generally tropical with a correspondingly high incidence of insect- and water-borne disease, for instance malaria and cholera. Consult a doctor who has had experience in dealing with cases of malaria about the most suitable type of prophylaxis, bearing in mind that strains that are resistant to Chloroquine and Pyrimethamine occur throughout the country.

Apart from at the better restaurants and hotels, toilet facilities are poor in Mozambique, so always carry a toilet roll and carton of wet gauze wipes. Prevent possible skin cancer by wearing a waterproof sunblock, long light cotton clothing and a broad-brimmed hat during the day. Make sure that you have sufficient supplies of any medications you use to last the duration of your trip – and a little extra as you may not be able to buy many prescription drugs in Mozambique.

Food

Along the coast there is always fish to be had, and vegetarians will never go hungry, as long as they are prepared to live on potatoes, tomatoes, coconuts, cassava (mandioca), bananas, pineapples and little else at times. People who can't survive without their daily slab of tender steak will not be able to venture far out of Maputo and Beira, where the more expensive restaurants offer beef imported from South Africa and Zimbabwe.

If you are cooking for yourself and intend to shop at the markets, carry a fish scale and a selection of herbs and spices. Even if you plan to eat out all the time, most restaurants do not offer a good range of condiments, so bring salt, pepper and lemon juice. Service is often slow and your waiter may consider two hours a reasonable time in which to prepare your meal and will regard it as a personal insult if you complain, and ignore you henceforth.

Clothing and culture

Mozambique is economically a desperately poor country which nevertheless has a rich heritage of colourful cultures and wonderfully diverse scenery.

Although what you wear on the beach is usually entirely your own concern, women should wear skirts or kapelanos (sarongs) while shopping, as stallholders at the markets (mercados) are often followers of the Muslim faith and might be offended by immodest displays of feminine flesh. Men should not wander off the beach without first putting on a shirt. After dark, dress at restaurants and clubs is smart-casual, while ties and jackets are seldom seen, even at the more elite restaurants.

Even midsummer evenings can become quite cool, so pack an anorak or sweater, especially if you intend to visit the higher-lying areas around Chimoio and Lichinga in winter. (See also page 26.)

The law and your rights

While the previously socialist economy has been revised for the better since Samora Machel announced the demise of Marxism in Mozambique in 1985, the same cannot be said for the laws of the land. If you do fall foul of the law, don't hand over your passport, don't lose your temper and don't expect a lawyer to come swooping in to your aid. Do send someone to report your circumstances, as well as the name and ranks of the officers involved, both to your embassy and to your family.

If you get locked up, you will be at the mercy of the police until someone raises enough money to 'ransom' you. For example, if you knock down a child who runs into the road and then do the decent thing by stopping to report the accident to the police, the circumstances will be irrelevant and you are likely to be held in custody until compensation to the relatives as well as a 'fine' is paid. The safest response to a scenario such as this is to seek refuge at your embassy in Maputo (if possible) and to communicate with the authorities from this sanctuary.

The role of the police appears to be limited to stopping motorists both on urban and rural roads with a view to extracting a 'fine' for an imaginative and expanding list of 'misdemeanours'. These can be lumped together under the heading documentos or papers, i.e. your passport, visa and visitor's card (cartão do viajante) – not issued at all border posts – and, if you are a driver, your third-party insurance (seguros), temporary import permit (licença da importação) and driver's licence (carta da condução). Military areas and the Governor's Quarter in each town are very sensitive zones, so do not stop here, and walk on the other side of the road if you are exploring the urban landscape on foot.

If you are a motorist and wish to avoid being fined, make sure your car is road-worthy, wear your seat belt and don't drive on beaches. Note that the law requires your vehicle to be equipped with two reflective warning triangles (one fixed to your front bumper if towing), and you will be fined if you are unable to produce these. The police are likely to stop you at some stage and, if your documents are not in order, do not expect any sympathy from people who cannot speak your language, but certainly understand the universal language of the mighty dollar. Two options are now open to you: you can either offer to turn around and go back to the border to obtain the missing papers, or you can good-naturedly (anger is pointless) begin to negotiate (use a calculator) how much your fine should be.

The amount you will eventually pay is inversely proportional to the length of time you are willing to spend haggling. Chances are good that, if you keep your cool and wait for long enough, the police will wave you on, as they will soon realize that they may be missing out on easier pickings, in the form of some other less patient drivers.

Accommodation

As acceptable accommodation is at a premium throughout Mozambique, attempt wherever possible to make all bookings in advance. You can always move to a more suitable hotel or pensão once you have got your bearings and a room in the establishment of choice becomes vacant.

Note that, unless you are staying in a hotel which has air-conditioned rooms, a mosquito net is an absolute necessity. As these are usually compact and light, it is easiest and best to carry your own net with you. (See page 21.)

Attitudes and expectations

Although geographically part of southern Africa, this former Portuguese colony has a history and culture that is more closely associated with north-eastern Africa, which makes it decidedly different from neighbouring states.

Whether you enter the country overland from one of these six countries (Tanzania, Malawi, Zambia, Zimbabwe, South Africa and Swaziland), by boat through one of the many harbours or by air into the capital city Maputo, you will immediately be faced with the challenging and often humorous prospect of communicating with people who may speak very little English. Arrangements for accommodation and transport, bargaining at the markets, exchanging money and border formalities will be exercises in sign language, gesticulation and a chance for you to practise the little Portuguese you may already know.

Moçambicanos value good manners and courtesy very highly, so a friendly, relaxed and unhurried attitude is the secret to gaining co-operation from officials and making friends with the people.

While poverty remains an obvious feature of society in Mozambique and you can expect to be pestered by beggars and street children in the towns and cities, trust the right people to be your guides or interpreters and you will soon be accepted as a friend to be protected from unwelcome advances or harassment.

Bear in mind that some streets (mainly in the cities of Maputo and Beira) are the realm of the homeless and if you adopt an aggressive attitude towards them your stay is likely to become an unpleasant, and perhaps dangerous, experience.

Please be aware that Mozambican officials are extremely poorly paid, have little understanding of tourists and may be intimidated and a little suspicious when confronted by well-heeled travellers. Remember that to them your possessions represent huge wealth, and, rather than attempting to extract bribes, officials are often simply curious when they ask to look inside your vehicle. Humour them with a smile and you will soon be on your way once more.

Mozambique is a fascinatingly different country, with a cultural blend reminiscent of a cross between Brazil, India and Arabia – a welcome variation from neighbouring English-speaking African states. Mozambicans may be very poor, but they remain courteous and proud, something to be borne in mind, especially when dealing with official bureaucrats.

If your documents are stolen

Always carry a photocopy of all your essential documents, e.g. passport, vehicle papers, etc. with you (in a different place from the original). If the original should be stolen, take the photocopy to a police station and ask for a declaração or written statement that the originals (same word in Portuguese) of the relevant copies have been roubados or stolen by a ladrão (thief). This declaration, as long as it is stamped, will be accepted at roadblocks and border posts and will also facilitate the speedy re-issuing of your passport in Maputo. (See page 48, Consulates in Maputo.)

What to bring with you

WATER: Tap water is not safe in Mozambique. Bottled water is fairly expensive, so bring along your own supply if you are travelling by car. Boil all water and add purification tablets if you can stand the chlorine taste.

FOOD: Powdered or long-life milk, tea bags, jam, cereals, dried fruit, condiments, cheese, soups, chocolates and sweets. Outside of Maputo and Beira, all processed foods are in short supply.

CLOTHES: The weather is usually warm enough for you to be comfortable with a thin sweater even in the middle of the night (so leave behind your bulky down sleeping bag and get yourself a light cotton sheet). The cyclone season is from November to May; the uncomfortably hot (unless you are on a beach) season from October to May and the mosquitoes reach their peak along the coast between January and June.

The sun is very fierce, so bring along a bucket-load of sun-screen. It can get quite cold in parts of Niassa province or around the Chimanimani mountains, so, if you might end up in these areas, carry warm trousers and a coat.

Many visitors require nothing but their swimming costume and kapulano (otherwise known as sarong, kikoyi, kanga and zambia) during the day. Lightweight cotton clothing is most sensible, with the addition of a raincoat for summer and a warm jacket and tracksuit for the winter. Think along the lines of protecting yourself from the sun by day, and from the mosquitoes by night. A sarong is standard worn over your swimming costume during the day, while light long-sleeved shirts and long pants help keep the mozzies off at night. Slipslops and a beach umbrella will be handy and do bring along a few semi-formal outfits for the nightclubs and more exclusive restaurants.

MEDICAL: Anti-malaria tablets, mosquito repellent, mosquito net, antihistamine cream, antibiotic cream, diarrhoea pills, fungal cream, air-freshener (for some of the loos), baby powder, plasters, scissors, tweezers and clinical thermometer (to be used whenever you feel down, as it may be the first signs of malaria).

REFUSE BAGS: There is a shortage of dustbins around Mozambique, so bring your own refuse bags with you and drop off your litter in the towns.

Carry with you

IN A DAY BACKPACK: This guide, a small amount of meticais in cash, toilet paper, pen and paper, calculator to aid bargaining and exchanging cash, a small scale for weighing fish when buying them on the beach.

IN A MONEY BELT (only if you cannot leave them anywhere safer): Foreign currency, traveller's cheques, passport, driver's licence and car keys. Wear your money belt **under your clothes** at all times.

Remember that cameras, bags and backpacks attract attention from thieves, so beware of crowds and badly lit areas. Never leave your possessions out of your sight, particularly in the cities of Maputo, Beira and Nampula.

Accommodation

Accommodation standards in Mozambique are generally low in comparison with the prices that you are expected to pay. With the exception of the hotels Polana and Cardoso in Maputo and the Bazaruto Island Lodge, decent lodgings are often fully booked. A tent may be a godsend, as you can usually negotiate for permission to camp in the grounds of a dirty hotel if you wish to avoid lumpy mattresses, bedbugs and mosquitoes.

Unless you will be staying only in hotels which are air-conditioned, always carry your own mosquito net if you balk at the idea of lugging around a tent. That way you'll avoid making malaria the main entry in your Mozambique diary. Ablution facilities range from good to appalling, while running water is a luxury.

HOTELS, PENSÕES AND POUSADAS. The grading system applicable to hotels, which operated before independence, followed the star system, with one star being basic and five stars denoting the full range of luxury facilities and services.

Some hotels (such as the Polana) have maintained the standards as denoted by their star grading, but standards have generally declined due to a lack of funds for maintenance.

Pensão (boarding house) gradings follow a numerical rating from one to four and, while most pensões may claim to have a rating of four, this has long ceased to be an informative system for the visitor. The difference between a hotel and a pensão in Mozambique normally relates to the number of beds that are on offer, with pensões being smaller than hotels. Pousadas (inns) fill the grey area between hotels and pensões and are found with less frequency throughout Mozambique.

Generally pensões are cheapest, pousadas reasonably priced, and hotels the most expensive form of accommodation.

CAMPING. Camping away from the larger cities in remote areas is sometimes free, but make sure you consult the locals who will help protect you from land mines, thieves and bogus government officials.

Camping sites are more expensive in the southern parts of Mozambique – upwards of Mt60 000 per site (the exchange rate in October 1996 was approximately Mt2 500 to the rand, Mt12 000 to the U.S.$). As you may not be able to pay per person, it is worthwhile getting a group together to share a site.

Localities (usually on beaches) favoured by visitors in the past may have an official assigned to patrol the area and to charge a (highly negotiable) camping fee. If he is a legitimate government official, he will have a receipt book and will also often be a source of useful information and advice.

Eating and drinking
Food is usually more spicy in Mozambique when compared with other countries in southern Africa. The compelling combination of Arab, Indian, Chinese and Portuguese dishes allows the visitor interesting choices when it comes to filling a hole in the stomach. With a coastline that is over 2 500 kilometres long, seafood naturally forms a major part of the local diet, and freshly caught fish is sold on the beaches and at the markets of all the coastal villages and towns. The availability of fruit and vegetables is dictated by season as well as by regional climatic influences and soil type.

From Inhambane northwards coconut groves dominate the landscape, while Zambezia province is famous for its pineapples, Nampula for its cashews and Cabo Delgado for its papayas. As a general rule, the prices of food increase the further south you go, while the variety increases in the opposite direction.

Delicious freshly baked white bread is available even in the most out of the way places; so, as long as you always carry something tasty to spread on that warm loaf, you need never go hungry.

Mozambique imports almost all of its manufactured and processed goods and food, making these more expensive than in neighbouring countries. Sugar, tea, breakfast cereals, milk and other dairy produce, fresh meat, sweets and chocolates, plastic bags and containers and disposable nappies (diapers) are usually in short supply.

There are well-stocked but expensive supermarkets in the larger towns, while the open-air markets may also sell an unlikely array of imported and local products.

Although prices at restaurants and cafés are generally reasonable, it is much less expensive to purchase fresh produce at one of the many markets (which are far cheaper than supermarkets) and to prepare meals yourself. Alternatively, try some of the wholesome simple dishes on offer at small kiosks at the market places.

If you are cooking for yourself, all meat, poultry and fish should be bought alive and then well cooked to avoid stomach bugs. Fresh milk must be boiled. Fresh fish will have eyes that bulge and are shiny, and look out for cysts in meat. Remember too that shellfish, fruit, vegetables and salads that are cleaned in infected water can be responsible for transmitting hepatitis.

Carry your own cooking pot, plate, mug and eating utensils if you are planning to travel away from the larger towns.

If you consider that the average wage in Mozambique (for the few who have jobs) is Mt120 000 per month, you will realize that it must be possible to thrive on a food budget of around Mt15 000 per day.

Municipal water in Maputo may be 'officially' safe to drink, but it is still good practice to boil all water, or to buy bottled water, which is slightly cheaper than drinking cool drinks. Inquire locally outside Maputo as some camp sites may supply boiled or chlorinated drinking water. Beer and cool drinks are available everywhere: there is scarcely a corner of the country where you won't find small boys selling cold cans from cooler boxes.

Cans cost Mt8 000 (about R4) upwards, while the locally produced bottled refrescos are cheaper but more difficult to find. The word for beer in Portuguese is cerveja and local brands nacional.

Prices for a 340 ml can or bottle of beer range from Mt8 000 for Laurentina Export at the Hotel Central near the railway station, to U.S.$3 for a Castle Lager at the Hotel Polana ón Av. Julius Nyerere.

Money matters

Apart from the Hotel Polana and some restaurants in Maputo (ask when booking or before sitting down to a meal), your credit card will be of little use. The B.C.M. (Banco Comercial de Moçambique) (1965 Av. 25 de Setembro, Maputo) , will give the meticais equivalent of U.S.$100 per day against a credit card. Banco Internacional de Moçambique (773 Av. 24 de Julho) have installed Maputo's first automatic tellers.

Traveller's cheques in U.S. dollars are safe and recommended. Cash dollars will attract the best rate, but, because of a proliferation of forgeries, $50 and $100 notes may be rejected. There is an insignificant currency black market, but it is a matter of personal discretion whether you use it. If you fall foul of officials, polite ignorance is best. You may well get the best rate at the secondary exchange bureaux anyway.

Meticais, the local currency, are accepted throughout Mozambique, even at places that advertise their charges in U.S. dollars, but expect a poor rate of exchange.

It may be possible to obtain foreign currency using your card at certain banks, but this will at best be laborious and at worst ultimately futile. American Express traveller's cheques in U.S. dollars are readily exchanged at banks and hotels, and you can use them to pay for your meal or accommodation if prices are quoted in U.S. dollars. If you are planning to travel away from the provincial capitals, carry sufficient cash in U.S. dollars or South African rands.

Avoiding being overcharged

Unsuspecting tourists are ripe for the rip-off all over the world, and Mozambique is no exception. Apart from the unlikely event of the payment of fines and 'official' government taxes and duties covered under 'The law and your rights' (see page 24),

shopping is the most important arena in which you will be confronted by inflated prices. You may well feel that, as a 'rich' visitor, it is part of your civic duty to alleviate poverty, in your own small way, by paying, without complaining, prices at the markets and kiosks that you know are above the normal going rate. Unfortunately while your motives might be admirable, the effect of this approach is inevitably a general increase in prices and a growing reluctance on the part of vendors to sell to the local people who cannot afford to pay any more. Basically the bottom line is that the poor do not benefit from the misguided charity of well-meaning visitors. Rather donate money directly to an organization working with the destitute.

As the metical is a very weak currency, the price of even basic items such as a cup of tea and a bun (bolo) reaches thousands of meticais. Familiarize yourself with the prices of basic items that are quoted in this chapter (bearing in mind an inflation rate of about 5% per month). When shopping at markets or supermarkets or ordering food in a restaurant, you will notice that prices are often not displayed and may not be written on the menu. It is here that a notepad and a pocket calculator come into their own. Point at the item and ask the waiter or vendor to write down (escrever) its price. If you suspect you are being overcharged, show the page to a Mozambican shopper or patron of the eating house. The calculator will facilitate an otherwise laborious process of offer and counter-offer when haggling over items ranging from tomatoes and prawns by the kilogram (use your own scale) to Makonde carvings.

Avoiding paying bribes

Tourists are still a novelty here, so be prepared to encounter some corrupt officials who see you as an opportunity to boost their meagre salary. Avoid turning Mozambique into yet another 'rip-off stop' by politely refusing to pay bribes and insisting on what you reasonably consider to be value for money.

Don't become angry with officials, but always ask to be shown where the regulation (regulamento) states what fees (if any) are due and insist on official receipts. Patience is not only a virtue, but it will confound unscrupulous officials.

Currency

The unit of currency is the metical (Mt), its plural meticais (pronounced 'metti-caaysh'). One thousand meticais are referred to as a mil or quanto/quantos (pronounced 'conto/conch'). **Expect a compound rate of inflation of 5 percentage points per month.** Meticais are acceptable even at hotels and restaurants which advertize prices in foreign currency, but the exchange rate will be very poor.

United States dollars (U.S.$) in cash are the most useful, as these are most easily exchanged, and are sometimes the only currency accepted by officials. South African rands are also very useful, as some fees (e.g. for visa extensions) are cheaper at the rand rate. If you are asked for dollars, point out that you are from South Africa, and thus cannot be expected to carry other currency.

As a rule of thumb, the closer to Maputo you are, the better the rate offered by banks and other official money changers.

The following are approximate exchange rates applicable in October 1996:

U.S.$1 = Mt12 000
South African R1 = Mt2 500
Zimbabwe $1 = Mt1 100
Malawi Kwacha = Mt760
British £1 = Mt16 000

Note that any bank transactions involving pounds sterling attract an automatic £20 handling charge. Avoid U.S.$50 and $100 notes, as they can be difficult to exchange, due to a proliferation of forgeries.

The 'black market'

The legal situation regarding foreign exchange transactions is fairly vague. You should not deal with any 'chancers' who approach you in the street or at border posts. In the bigger towns confidence tricksters may operate highly skilled traps.

Remember that as an obvious visitor you will be a prime target. Distinct signs of a snare are over-friendly people and offers of a currency deal well above the going rate. If you don't want to risk the streets or falling foul of the law, use the secondary exchange markets (mercados secundários de câmbios), which offer a better exchange rate than the banks, but exist only in Maputo and Beira.

Taking the cumulative effect of various black-market rates, as well as official exchange rates, into account, in addition to United States dollars (U.S.$), Zimbabwe dollars (Z$) are the advisable currency to have with you in central Mozambique (or Malawi Kwacha when you are close to the Malawian border). In the southern parts of the country, South African rands and United States dollars are useful, with rands being especially cost-effective if you extend your visa or have to pay any government levies or fees.

Even though the country has not yet been frequented much by tourists, Mozambique is not a particularly cheap place in which to stay. This is mainly due to the chronic shortage of accommodation, and the deterioration (and even closure) of some hotels during the civil war. The influence of relatively affluent South Africa becomes more evident the closer to Maputo one gets.

There are very cunning confidence tricksters operating wherever there are visitors to Mozambique. Do not encourage folk who approach you with illegal items or suspicious deals. Although cash is easiest to use, do carry at least half of your money as traveller's cheques. **WEAR A MONEY BELT UNDERNEATH YOUR CLOTHES.**

Opening hours

BANKS. Open on Monday to Friday from 7.45 a.m. to 11 a.m. Banks are closed on Saturdays and Sundays.

SHOPS. Open on Mondays from 2 p.m. to 6 p.m.; Tuesday to Saturday from 8.30 a.m. to 1 p.m. and 3 p.m. to 6.30 p.m. Shops are closed on Sundays.

MAPUTO POST OFFICE. Open on Monday to Friday 7.30 a.m to 12.30 p.m. and 2.30 p.m. to 4.30 p.m. Post offices are not open over the weekend.

Getting there and around

Visitors of all nationalities wishing to enter Mozambique require a valid passport and visa (see page 20). Motorists must purchase a temporary import permit and third party insurance on the Mozambican side of the frontier. They must be in possession of the original vehicle registration papers and their driver's licence (an international driver's licence is recommended but not obligatory).

Getting there

FROM SOUTH AFRICA AND SWAZILAND. Luxury buses are run by Panthera Azul between Johannesburg and Maputo, and between Durban and Maputo; tel. Johannesburg (011) 337 7409, Durban (031) 304 5104 and Maputo (01) 49 4238.

Minibus taxis leaving from Johannesburg station go to Maputo. Spoornet (formerly South African Railways) operates a regular passenger train service which leaves from Johannesburg on Tuesdays, Thursdays and Sundays at 4.45 p.m. and reaches Maputo at 10.16 a.m. the next day. One-way fares: first class (luxury sleeper) R151; second class (sleeper) R108 and third class (seats only) R60. Trains leave from Maputo on Mondays, Wednesdays and Fridays at 1 p.m. and arrive at 6.16 a.m. the next day in Johannesburg. Tel. Johannesburg (011) 820 2479/773 2944.

FROM TANZANIA: Get your visa in Dar es Salaam and then catch a bus (or boat if the Rufiji River is flooding, thus preventing the ferry from operating) down to Mtwara. Air Tanzania has scheduled flights weekly to Mtwara. Cross the Rovuma by dugout (there is no bridge or ferry) or catch a dhow from Msimbati, 12 kilometres south of Mtwara – look for the Mzaliwa Hakosila Wama, the owner of which

charges U.S.$5 per person to Mocímboa da Praia (the trip may take as long as four days) where you can have your passport stamped by the immigration authorities. The rate of exchange in Mocímboa da Praia is poor, so don't exchange much money before you get to Pemba, which is 358 kilometres by road to the south. Pemba is a tourist centre with reasonably priced hotels and pensões.

FROM MALAWI: After obtaining your visa in Lilongwe or Blantyre, an unusual option might be to find out about trains from Liwonde to Nayuchi and Cuamba, or cross overland into Mozambique at Mandimba and then make your way by road to Cuamba and catch the train (there is one a week) down to Nampula. Both the railway line and road along this route have been upgraded.

There are passenger trains operating at present, but people do still hitch a free ride on the cargo trains between Nacala and Malawi.

There is also the conventional route from Malawi into Mozambique through Zóbué to Tete. The escorted convoys have not been in operation (nor are they necessary) since the hostilities ceased in Mozambique in 1992. The border post at Mulanje/Milange is open, but this route via Mocuba to Quelimane is definitely an 'enquire locally first' type of road.

FROM ZAMBIA: Get your visa in Lusaka. From here the only routes by road into Mozambique are through Chanida/Cassacatiza and the Zumbo border post.

FROM ZIMBABWE: There are plenty of buses and lift opportunities from Harare (where you can get your visa) east to Nyamapanda, and, in addition to these, there is a good passenger train service from Harare to

Mutare. As with Malawi, passenger trains are operating at present between the border and Beira, but people also ride on the cargo trains. Contact the C.F.M. (Caminho de Ferro de Moçambique) offices in Maputo, tel. (01) 2 0400, 43 0020 or 42 5614, for the latest position. The road from the Mount Selinda/Espungabera border post to the junction with the E.N.1 is in a fair condition, but it may be impassable after rain.

BY CAR. The secret to success at the often frustrating and confusing border posts in Mozambique is to be friendly and relaxed. If you are asked to pay any unexplained fees, courteously ask to see the regulation and the supervisor (if you can muster up enough Portuguese). Adopting a completely stupid façade is often the most effective approach when faced with difficult officials. There will be a fee for third party insurance and a temporary import permit for your car, and motorists will also need a driver's licence and the original registration papers for their vehicle.

Enter Mozambique from South Africa at the Komatipoort/Ressano Garcia customs post, or enter from Swaziland through the Namaacha gate. The distance to Maputo from Komatipoort is 92 kilometres, from Namaacha 77 kilometres and from Beira 2 212 kilometres.

Travellers to or from Tanzania should note that the Rovuma River divides Mozambique and Tanzania. There is still no road link between the two countries. It may be possible to drive (or winch) your vehicle across the river during the dry season – tempo da seca – which is from May to November, at the Masunguru/Negomane frontier post.

The main entry points from Malawi are via Zóbué on the Tete/Blantyre road and via Mulanje/Milange on the Blantyre/ Quelimane route. There is also an entry point at the southern end of Lago Niassa (Lake Malawi) at Mandimba on the Mangochi/Nampula road. The distance to Beira from Blantyre via Tete is 888 kilometres and via Quelimane 892 kilometres (note that the vehicle ferry over the Zambezi River is operating intermittently; contact 'Mariners' in Beira, see page 121).

The main entry points from Zimbabwe are via the Mutare/Manica post and the Nyamapanda gate between Harare and Tete. There are good tarred roads on both of these routes.

BY SEA. The Mozambique Channel between the mainland and Madagascar in the Indian Ocean makes up the entire eastern border. The main ports (from south to north) are Maputo, Beira, Quelimane, Nacala and Pemba. You must apply for a visa on arrival.

BY AIR. L.A.M. (Linhas Aéreas de Moçambique), S.A.A. (South African Airways), Aeroflot and Air Portugal are among the carriers offering direct flights to Maputo. An airport departure tax of U.S.$20 on international flights and U.S.$10 on domestic flights is payable.

Transport
Car hire companies operate in Maputo and Beira (see pages 48–50); however, due to the rough roads and high incidence of vehicle theft, charges are high, particularly if you are intending to travel between Maputo and Beira. Buses and minibuses operate on a regular basis between large towns at present, while quieter roads may be served by only one overloaded truck per week.

The domestic service of L.A.M. does fly to all the provincial capitals except Chimoio and Inhambane but, as flights are usually full, it is essential to book well in advance.

Passenger ships are presently not operating between ports on the coastline of Mozambique. (*See also* page 36.)

Arrival

All international flights into Mozambique land at Maputo International Airport, 10 kilometres from the city. If you have made advance arrangements with a reputable company (*see* page 50), you may be met at the airport by your host or guide.

Alternatively take a taxi (pay no more than about U.S.$5 or the equivalent in meticais or South African rands) into Maputo and use a map and the guidance of the driver to locate your hotel. If you plan to arrive by car, always take note of the border hours and try to enter the country before midday to avoid having to drive after dark when it is more difficult to see pot-holes and pedestrians and easier to get lost.

Road conditions

E.N. stands for Estrada Nacional.

RESSANO GARCIA–BOANE (E.N.4 and E.N.251). The road has been resurfaced. This is the recommended route from South Africa to Maputo. A new toll road between Nelspruit and Maputo is due for completion at the end of 1997.

NAMAACHA–BOANE (E.N.2). A five-kilometre stretch is in a bad condition. The route from Goba Fronteira, 50 kilometres to the south of Namaacha, is being surfaced at present and was scheduled to open in mid-1996 but it is not yet ready.

BOANE–MAPUTO (E.N.2). Narrow but in good condition. Watch out for pedestrians, slow-moving and broken-down vehicles, as well as reckless drivers.

MAPUTO–MACIA (E.N.1). Well signposted; the tarmac surface is in a good condition.

MACIA–BILENE (SAN MARTINO) (E.N.408). The turn-off to Bilene is not signposted. There are some pot-holes but overall the road is in a fair condition. This road is likely to deteriorate due to overloaded trucks and the effect of the rains.

MACIA–XAI-XAI (E.N.1). The tarmac is in a good condition. The toll bridge over the Limpopo River has been rebuilt and was opened in November 1993.

XAI-XAI–INHAMBANE (E.N.1). The tarred surface is deteriorating, with pot-holes that are likely to worsen in the rainy season.

INHAMBANE–VILANKULO (E.N.1 and E.N.212). The surface is damaged in places. Low speeds are recommended to allow for pot-hole evasion. Upgrading is continuing, and this route is likely to become smoother in the future.

VILANKULO–RIO SAVE (E.N.1). The tarmac surface is in good condition.

RIO SAVE–INCHOPE (E.N.1). No fuel is available on this route. In places the tarmac has disappeared. There are some bad patches and extreme caution is needed to avoid damage to your vehicle. Expect to do an average speed of 80 km/h.

BEIRA–CHIMOIO–MUTARE (E.N.6). This is one of the busiest roads in Mozambique. Although it was resurfaced in 1990, heavy trucks have taken their toll and the surface is beginning to break up in places, making roadworks necessary. Livestock and pedestrians are an additional hazard on some stretches.

BEIRA–CAIA (ZAMBEZI RIVER) (E.N.213). The route via Inhaminga is gravel and clay on which 4x4 vehicles are essential. The ferry over the Zambezi operates erratically.

Contact 'Mariners' in Beira at (03) 32 9071 for the latest on the Caia ferry. Locals cross the river in dugouts from Inhaminga to Mopeia, which is seven kilometres away from the north bank. The Sena bridge 60 kilometres north of Caia has been repaired and converted for road traffic.

CAIA–QUELIMANE (E.N.213). Due to damaged bridges, you may not manage to get to Quelimane during heavy rain. Consult 'Mariners' (see above) before attempting this route. If you have a lift to the river, cross over by boat, and then you may be able to hitch a lift to Quelimane, either on trucks or a bus (which has a maximum speed of 20 km/h and leans over perilously, as if it's ready to lie down and die), as well as to places further north.

Beware of sections where trenches, dug across the road by rebels during the civil war, have been poorly filled in.

QUELIMANE–MILANGE (MALAWI BORDER) (E.N.7). Inquire locally before using this route; a 4x4 vehicle is essential during the rainy season (October to March).

QUELIMANE–CHINDE. Not negotiable by car due to inoperational pontoons (pontões) and ferries. Get to Chinde (on the Zambezi delta) on a cargo boat or charter a plane through T.T.A. in Quelimane.

QUELIMANE–CUAMBA AND NAMPULA (E.N.7 and E.N.104). On some stretches speeds of 100 km/h are possible, while a 4x4 vehicle is essential on other stretches during rains. Trenches remain a hazard and it is a good idea to get a local guide from Quelimane along to point them out for you.

Warning: Between Mocuba and Molócuè there are two unmarked deviations off the tarmac road to the old bridges. Where new bridges should be, there is a gaping hole.

Do not stop to pick up local hitchhikers as there have been isolated incidents involving 'Ninjas' or bandits in this area. Certain routes to Pebane and Angoche along the coast are regarded by the locals to be clear of land mines. The road to Pebane from Quelimane via Malei, Olinga and Mucubela is in regular use, as is the road from Nampula to Angoche via Liupo (which is the recommended route at present).

NACALA/MOZAMBIQUE ISLAND–MANDIMBA (E.N.8). There is a good tarred road (a few pot-holes) between Nacala and Nampula and a passable one from the island (see page 141).

Nampula to Cuamba has steep gradients and river drifts which may become impassable immediately after rain storms. A 4x4 vehicle is essential during the rainy season (October to March). From Cuamba to Mandimba (on the Malawi border) the gravel road is badly rutted but otherwise in a fair condition.

MANDIMBA–LICHINGA (E.N.249). Lichinga is Mozambique's gateway to Lago Niassa (Lake Malawi). The road is in a fair condition, since it has recently been graded and gravelled.

LICHINGA–MARRUPA/MONTEPUEZ/PEMBA (E.N.242). This is a very remote route which was being cleared of land mines during 1995. No fuel or repair facilities are available on the 768-kilometre stretch between Lichinga and Pemba. A 4x4 vehicle is essential during all seasons. The wet season in Cabo Delgado is from the beginning of December to the end of April, during which the road may become temporarily impassable due to the lack of bridges.

PEMBA–MOCIMBOA DA PRAIA (E.N.106). The tarmac surface is pot-holed but is overall in fair condition.

MOCIMBOA DA PRAIA–QUIONGA. The road is sandy but negotiable in two-wheel-drive vehicles with a high ground clearance. Crossings over the Rio Rovuma (which forms the border between Mozambique and Tanzania) are possible by dugout canoe only, as there is no bridge or ferry.

MANDIMBA–TETE (THROUGH MALAWI) (E.N.249 and E.N.103). The road is generally good and armed convoys are no longer operating (or necessary) between Zóbué and Tete or between Tete and Nyamapanda. Don't stop to pick up hitchhikers.

CHANGARA (ON THE TETE CORRIDOR)–CHIMOIO (ON THE BEIRA CORRIDOR) (E.N.102). A recently resurfaced tarmac road which (in places) is probably the finest road in Mozambique (there is beautiful scenery too).

When and where it is safe to drive

Never underestimate the deadly serious hazard which land mines and banditry may present to the foolhardy in parts of Mozambique. Although the clearance of the most important roads has been a priority since the October 1992 peace agreement, estimates of the number of mines which remain undiscovered reach many hundreds of thousands. A general rule is that if you only use roads that have obviously been driven by a large number of vehicles (in fact, the majority of the roads that you are likely to use), you should be safe. However, as soon as you give in to the urge to blaze your own trail, you run a very real risk of encountering a few mines. Quite apart from the fact that it is illegal to drive over dunes and along beaches in Mozambique, it may be useful to consider that even these were mined.

Roads in Mozambique are not the exclusive domain of the motor vehicle. In the bigger towns they are crowded with pedestrians, hawkers, beggars, street kids and the homeless. In the countryside human- and animal-drawn carts jostle for a sliver of the smoothest road surface. Belching trucks wheeze their laborious way around pot-holes and this, combined with a sometimes precipitous verge, makes for difficult and dangerous overtaking.

While domestic (as well as wild) animals were almost entirely wiped out during the period of upheaval, they are making a strong comeback and are already becoming an additional hazard. Since for many years walking was the only way to get around the country, pedestrians became the 'kings of the road' and are now understandably reluctant to give up their status to motorists. They should be given the benefit of the doubt (i.e. a wide berth). It is recommended (and quite acceptable) that you hoot when approaching people. The upshot of the above is simply:

DRIVE CAREFULLY AND DON'T DRIVE DURING THE NIGHT.

Length of stay

Consider that by road via Tete and through Malawi (the recommended route) it is over 2 500 kilometres from Maputo in southern Mozambique to Quelimane in central Mozambique or Pemba in the north. If you are planning a 'whistle-stop' tour of the entire country in your own 4x4 vehicle, you may anticipate an average speed of 80 km/h, which amounts to at least a six-week journey.

If you intend to hitch and use public transport across the country, allow for an average speed of 40 km/h between places and expect delays due to unreliable schedules and possible breakdowns. If your time is limited and you still want to see the best of Mozambique, the only way is to fly. Book your seats on the domestic airline (L.A.M.) well in advance and contact the charter companies if you intend to travel to destinations that are not served by L.A.M.

Getting around

ROAD (PUBLIC TRANSPORT): Since little maintenance was possible until recently and due to past sabotage, some roads in Mozambique are still severely pot-holed.

Nevertheless roads, bridges and ferries are being continually repaired and it is already possible to drive from Maputo to Malawi via Tete in a two-wheel-drive vehicle, even during the wet season. Resurfacing from Ressano Garcia on the South African border, and from Goba Fronteira on the

Swaziland border to Maputo, was completed during 1996. Public transport within the cities and larger towns is provided by minibuses, Land Rovers and trucks (covered and open). These are collectively referred to as chapacem (tin one-hundreds) as they originally charged Mt100 (now Mt2 000 or about R1). Chapas can also be hired by individuals at very reasonable, negotiable rates. Taxis are usually available at the airports, railway stations and the major hotels. Expect to pay about Mt15 000 per kilometre for a town taxi.

Between towns chapacem and buses operate with prices that are relative to their reliability and degree of overcrowding. Fares are around Mt20 000 per 100 kilometres for the chapas and around Mt40 000 per 100 kilometres for the buses (machimbombos – the local expression for a bus that looks as if it has on occasion fallen from a cliff). Find out from the locals which vehicles are to be recommended. Expect frequent breakdowns and if you need to get somewhere far away in a hurry, for instance to catch your plane home, rather go by air.

Getting around the country is hampered by an inadequate domestic airline, poor roads, lack of bridges and long distances. For example, it is nearly 3 000 kilometres by road from Maputo in the south to Quionga in the north, assuming that the ferry over the Zambezi is operating. In the southernmost half of Mozambique reliable bus services operate, while in other areas along the coast rides in dhows may be more comfortable and easier to get than lifts on the rare, uncomfortable trucks. The point where buses and taxis leave from is called the Terminus and these are often adjacent to the Central Market (mercado).

CYCLING: Bear in mind that, unless you purchased your bicycle in Mozambique, you will not be able to find any spares.

TRAIN: A train trip from Maputo to Ressano Garcia will cost Mt45 000. If you ride on the goods train from Cuamba to Nampula, the trip will cost you nothing at all.

AIR: Inside Mozambique, L.A.M. operates domestic flights between Maputo and the following towns: Beira (Sofala province), Tete (Tete province), Quelimane (Zambezia province), Nampula (Nampula province), Pemba (Cabo Delgado province) and Lichinga (Niassa province). At the time of writing the flight from Maputo to Pemba (single) cost U.S.$250.

Air charter companies such as Natair, T.T.A., S.T.A., Metavia and Air-Serve operate from airports in Maputo, Beira, Quelimane, Tete, Nampula, Lichinga and Pemba. Rates are competitive. (*See* also pages 49 and 50 for more information.) On domestic flights you will have to pay an airport departure tax of U.S.$10.

BOATS: Apart from short trips in chartered speedboats from the mainland to the islands off Maputo, Inhambane, Vilankulo and Pemba, there are no regular passenger boats in operation between ports on the Mozambican coastline. Transmaritima in Maputo, tel. 42 6146, as well as Navique in Maputo, tel. 42 3118 or 42 5634, may be able to help you get onto a boat going along the coast.

A luxury ocean passenger cruiser does anchor off Bazaruto Island irregularly. Contact Starlight Cruises, tel. Johannesburg (011) 884 7680, second floor Norwich Life Towers, 13 Fredman Drive, Sandton.

Travelling

Until a reliable passenger ship service is re-implemented along the coast of Mozambique, you will have to settle for buses, minibus taxis, the domestic airline (L.A.M.), private air charter companies or your own vehicle (be it a bicycle, car, four-wheel-drive pick-up [bakkie] or overland 'muscle' truck) to get around Mozambique.

The security situation is likely to remain fluid, with some continuing risk to overland travellers who ignore the advice of the local police and population. If you hear rumours of unofficial roadblocks or are concerned that a particular route may have become unsafe (whether due to bandits or land mine incidents), consult with bus and taxi drivers as well as with aid workers who use the road regularly before you use it. If you are in Maputo, contact your consulate. (*See* page 48.)

A general rule, which will remain valid even under the most benign of scenarios, is don't drive after dark. Mozambican cars and trucks often have no lights, while the drivers are not the world's most predictable. Livestock also wander about unsupervised along the roads and pot-holes are difficult to negotiate at night. Even official police checkpoints often have no warning signs and are difficult to spot, even during the day, let alone under conditions of poor visibility.

There is a 30 km/h speed limit in all urban areas, which is apparently being strictly enforced by means of radar. A fine of Mt100 000 is standard throughout the country.

MOTORING: A carnet de passage is not presently required, no matter what the registration of your car. What is essential is the vehicle registration papers, while third party insurance and temporary import permits are sold at the border. The price varies from frontier to frontier.

The southern half of Mozambique (including Tete Province) is easily accessible by road from South Africa, Swaziland and Zimbabwe. Most main routes through the provinces of Maputo, Gaza, Inhambane,

Sofala, Manica, and Tete have either been upgraded or are presently undergoing improvement. Petrol and diesel are readily available and the longest distance you can anticipate between pumps is 500 kilometres. Note however that disruptions of fuel supplies do occur periodically due to unforeseen circumstances, and some towns away from Maputo and Beira may on occasion run out of petrol and diesel unexpectedly.

If you are driving your own vehicle, a diesel engine is an advantage as, not only is this type of fuel around 40% cheaper than petrol, it is also more likely to be available from construction companies and mining operations (if you ask nicely) in outlying areas where there are no formal sources of supply.

Petrol is sold at markets in most towns. It will probably cost more than you would pay at a petrol station, so buy just enough to get you to the next station.

The northern half of Mozambique, that is north of the Zambezi River (Rio Zambeze), has always been less developed and this is reflected by a lack of good roads and a scarcity of opportunities to fill up your fuel tank. The inaccessibility of the provinces of Zambezia and Nampula is presently aggravated by the lack of all-weather roads.

The Caia ferry and the bridge between Vila de Sena (Tchena) and Mutarara have been repaired; the only other overland route from the southern to the northern half of Mozambique remains via Liwonde or Mulanje in Malawi. Niassa province is served by two access roads, one from Mandimba on the Malawi border and one from Pemba via Montepuez in Cabo Delgado province. If you are driving in northern Mozambique, haul sufficient fuel with you to last you for at least 800 kilometres.

DOMESTIC FLIGHTS: L.A.M. (*see* page 32) serves all the provincial capitals (except Inhambane) with excursion fares for periods of 7 to 30 days at a 10% discount. Flights are usually fully booked, with Pemba and Nampula being especially popular destinations during December and January. If you want to be assured of a flight on a particular date, it is essential that you book at least three months in advance.

Unfortunately L.A.M. flights have in the past been dogged by robberies during loading and off-loading from the baggage hold, and it is advisable to carry all your valuables and important documents with you in the cabin. If you would like to be met at the airport, make this clear when you are booking accommodation, failing which private taxis do meet most scheduled domestic flights as they arrive. Airports are usually less than 10 kilometres from town centres and a taxi ride should cost you no more than U.S.$ 5 or the equivalent in meticais.

LONG-DISTANCE BUSES AND TAXIS: In Mozambique long-distance buses are called machimbombos (pronounced 'mashinbonbos'), long-distance taxis are called chapas (pronounced 'shappas'), while taxis that operate in town are simply called taxis. New bus services are operating along the main routes in southern Mozambique and, while they are fairly comfortable, journeys are slow, due to frequent stops to drop off and pick up passengers. Chapas range from minibuses and pick-ups (bakkies) to tired-out trucks and even tractors. While much cheaper on the long haul than machimbombos, chapas are often overcrowded and generally an unsafe mode of transport.

Bus termini are located either adjacent to the main municipal markets or on the outskirts of town on the main road to the next large village.

If you are planning to make use of machimbombos and chapas, don't allow your luggage to be packed on the roof, as this lays it open to theft and damage. Arrive well before the departure time to ensure that your gear is packed safely in the lockers underneath the bus, or in the back of the chapa. Place all your valuables in a small bag and keep this with you at all times – travel with it on your lap.

Take a towel or sarong along with you to hang up against the window to provide shade; a bottle of water is a good idea and make sure you have small change (in meticais) handy with which to purchase the food and curios that will be on offer wherever the bus stops. Remember, especially on less-travelled routes or on the poorer roads, the rickety truck or trembling tractor you've managed to hitch a ride on may just break down in the middle of nowhere. So be prepared to be self-sufficient for a few days when using public transport in Mozambique.

Before you leave

Things to see

Since Mozambique is blessed with what may just be the longest stretch of coral-fringed beach in Africa, scuba divers, game and fly fishermen, snorkellers and nature lovers can spend months exploring the coastal resorts and camp sites without boredom setting in.

Historical sites, dating back to the daring days when voyagers risked being swallowed by a gigantic seamonster or sailing off the edge of the world, are found throughout the country.

Absorb an atmosphere that has been unaltered through the ages, while standing atop the haunted ramparts of the fortress on Mozambique Island, or visit a house in Maputo (made from steel plates shipped from Portugal a century ago) designed by the creator of the Eiffel Tower in Paris.

Mozambique's inhabitants display a interesting and rewarding blend of traditional African ways and assimilated Muslim, Indian and Portuguese culture.

From the proud and isolated Makonde tribe in the north, with their bizarre and intricate sculptures in ebony, to the Makua, Chuabo and Chope tribes along the coast with their dances, dhows and dugouts, Mozambique's real treasure is its friendly and fascinating people.

Things to do

FISHING. Fishing, whether from the rocks on the shoreline or from ski-boats on the deep sea, has reached legendary proportions off Mozambique, especially in the areas around the Bazaruto Archipelago, Nacala, Pemba and the northern Ilhas das Querimbas.

Mozambique is world-renowned for its game fishing. Travel agents (see page 50) can refer you to sport fishing companies which operate from Maputo, Ponta do Ouro, Inhaca, Bilene (San Martino), Xai-Xai, Benguerra, Magaruque, Bazaruto, Beira and Pemba. Enquire about 'Gone Fishin' on Inhaca Island. Contact Polana Tours in Maputo tel. (01) 49 3533, or Charles Norman Fishing Safaris, tel. Johannesburg (011) 888 3168.

Boats are sometimes available for charter at the following places: Ponta do Ouro, telephone (0323) 73 2503/5, Bilene, telephone South Africa (01351) 5 3996, Xai-Xai, telephone Johan Erasmus, Xai-Xai (022) 2 2942, fax 2 2804, and at the islands of Bazaruto, Benguerra and Magaruque, telephone Johannesburg (011) 339 7275.

SCUBA DIVING AND SNORKELLING. Wherever there are ski-boats for hire, you can assume that there should be scuba gear available as well. If you are a novice, enquire whether resort diving courses are on offer at the hotel or lodge you intend to visit – Bazaruto Lodge, for example, runs outstanding diving courses; contact Pestana Hotels and Resorts, tel. Johannesburg (011) 368 1947.

There are excellent scuba reefs situated off the following locations: Ponta do Ouro, Ponta Mamóli, Inhaca Island (see map on page 91), Praia da Xai-Xai (see map on page 97), Praia de Závora, Praia da Barra (see map on page 105) near Inhambane, Morrungulo, Bazaruto, Magaruque, and Santa Carolina Islands, Vilankulo, Inhassoro, Pebane, Fogo (fire) Island, which is 150 kilometres north of Quelimane, Angoche town, Mozambique Island, Pemba and amongst

the Querimba Archipelago between Pemba and the border with Tanzania, particularly opposite the village of Pangane.

For snorkellers there are numerous shallow reefs along the entire Mozambican coastline (which is more than 2 500 kilometres long). Favoured places are the reefs around Inhaca island at Santa Maria and off the lighthouse, while Praia do Xai-Xai boasts reefs near the Complexo Halley and a tidal pool at Wenela.

In the Inhambane area ask for Praia do Tofo, Pandane and Coconut Bay, while up at Pemba the reefs off Praia da Wimbe are shallow and spectacular. Snorkelling is also superb around any of the coral islands of the Querimba Archipelago.

Scuba diving and snorkelling facilities are available at some resorts to the south of Beira (Inhaca Island, Xai-Xai, Morrungula, Vilankulo and the islands of Magaruque, Benguerra, Bazaruto and Santa Carolina). Mozambique's kaleidoscope of corals and exotic tropical fish offers some of the finest diving and snorkelling in the world.

BIRD-WATCHING. The opportunities for bird-watching are excellent amongst the foothills of Mozambique's mountainous regions, for example mounts Gorongosa and Vumba in Manica province and Namuli and Chiperone in Zambezia province.

SURFING. Surfing spots along the seemingly endless coastline include Ponta do Ouro in the far south and Tofinho, a few hundred metres south of Tofo, close to the fascinating town of Inhambane.

DHOW TRIPS. Although not offered on an organized basis and dangerous offshore during the cyclone season, which lasts from November to April, dhow trips are a memorable experience, as well as being the only available means of transport along some sections of the coast. These graceful craft are still built according to the same design and manner as the vessels which first plied the trading routes between India and Africa centuries ago. To watch the crew as they effortlessly manoeuvre their boat through shallow channels that weave between coral islands is a privilege and experience which you will cherish forever.

PRAWNS. Eating prawns has become more expensive since the glory days of vinho verde and chamuças, partly due to over-exploitation of this resource by Russian trawlers during the 1970s and 1980s, and partly because the local population was forced to strip the coastline to survive during the past conflict, after their cattle were rustled or shot by bandits. And yet it is still possible for example to buy prawns weighing up to 300 g each for Mt3 000 (about R1,50) at small beach restaurants in the vicinity of Inhambane, Vilankulo, Inhassoro, Beira, Quelimane and Angoche.

Eating, sleeping and spending

Useful prices
The prices below were obtained during 1996 at open-air and municipal markets (mercados), as well as on the streets. Supermarkets, e.g. Interfranca in Maputo, can be up to 100% more expensive. The official exchange rate in October 1996 was about Mt12 000 to the U.S.$.

Minimum (legal) wage of an unskilled labourer: Mt120 000 per month (but in practice about half of this amount)

Fuel
Petrol (gasolina) (per litre): Mt7 500/U.S.$0.63
Diesel (gasóleo) (per litre) : Mt5 000/U.S.$0.42

Airport departure tax
U.S. $10 (Domestic)
U.S. $20 (International)

Sundries
• Daily newspaper (Notícias): Mt1 500
• Weekly newspaper (Savana): Mt4 000
• Torch batteries: Mt4 000 each
• Detergent powder: Mt20 000 (500 g Omo)
• 135 Film (36 exposures): Mt80 000 (Fuji)
• Toothpaste: Mt7 000 (50 ml Colgate)
• Local beer (often difficult to get): Mt10 000 per 500 ml (2M/Dois Em)
• Imported beer (available everywhere): Mt10 000 per 340 ml (Castle)
• Wine 750 ml bottle (imported): Mt100 000
• Local cigarettes (Habanas): Mt4 000 per 20
• Coke (imported): Mt8 000 (340 ml)
• Coke (local) Mt3 500
• Loaf of bread: Mt2 000
• Rice per kg: Mt4 000
• Maize meal per kg: Mt3 000
• One egg: Mt1 500
• Bananas: Mt3 000 per kg (seasonal)
• Tomatoes: Mt1 000 per kg (seasonal)
• Litre of milk (imported): Mt10 000
• Cheese (imported) per kg: Mt120 000
• Chicken (live): Mt25 000
• Chicken (frozen): Mt60 000 per kg
• Beef (very scarce): Mt100 000 per kg
• Fresh fish (from the beach): Mt25 000 per kg (cheaper away from Maputo)
• Fresh prawns (from the beach): Mt60 000 per kg (cheaper away from Maputo)
• Processed cashew nuts: Mt70 000 per kg (cheaper away from Maputo)

Eating out
• Basic meal (fish and rice): Mt5 000
• Fried potato chips: Mt8 000 per plate
• Take-away (in Maputo, Beira or Pemba): roughly Mt15 000
• Cup of black coffee: Mt1 500
• Pot of black tea: Mt2 000
• Hamburger: Mt10 000

- Ice cream cone: Mt8 000
- English breakfast (reasonable hotel, e.g. Hotel Central, Maputo): Mt25 000
- Table d'hôte (at a good hotel, for example the Nautilus, Wimbe Beach at Pemba): Mt65 000
- Meal at modest restaurant: Mt30 000
- Meal at average restaurant: Mt80 000
- Meal at upmarket restaurant (e.g. Hotel Polana, Maputo): U.S.$40

Accommodation

- Average pensão per night (e.g. Pensão Central, Maputo): Mt120 000 (double)
- One night camping: Mt20 000–Mt60 000 per person

Transport

- Chapa trip (minibus or truck): Mt10 000 per 100 kilometre
- Machimbombo (decent long-distance bus): Mt20 000 per 100 km
- Taxi (sedan car around town): Mt25 000 per kilometre (in Maputo and Beira only)
- Train trip: Mt25 000 (from Maputo to Ressano Garcia
- Cuamba to Nampula: hitch a ride free on the goods train
- Domestic Flight (L.A.M.): Mt1 000 000 from Beira to Quelimane

Activities

- Diving course (open-water I): U.S. $232 (8-dive package, Bazaruto Lodge)
- Charter dive (for qualified divers): R90–R140 (Morrungulo Dive Centre)
- Fishing charter (ski-boat): R800 per day, equipment extra ('Hutnic', Inhassoro)
- Sailing charter: R800 per day (catamaran off Benguerra Island)
- Dhow hire: Mt75 000 per day at Inhambane Bay. U.S.$20 Ibo Island to Tanzania (3–7 days)
- Dugout canoe hire: A T-shirt or sandals for 3 days on Rovuma or Zambezi rivers.

What to take home

While parts of Mozambique are still the best in the world to buy prawns, a limited shelf life makes old prawns good for nothing but attracting flies. Cashew nuts are a far better bet if you want a nibble to sustain you during the homeward journey or as a present to impress your family and friends. Although available throughout Mozambique, best value for money is obtainable at the cashew processing factory at Monapo between Nampula and Mozambique Island.

Arts and crafts have certainly attracted increasing attention in Mozambique since the return of tourists to this country in 1993. Coming to Mozambique and leaving without a Makonde statuette or a Malangatane painting (if you can afford it) would be like visiting Italy and not eating pasta. Although the Makonde tribe originates from a very limited area straddling the Rovuma River in Cabo Delgado Province and Tanzania, Makonde co-operatives have been set up in Maputo, Beira, Nampula and Pemba. Prices depend on the fame of the artist, the quality and size of the piece of wood used and the degree of intricacy inherent in the sculpture.

Mozambican painters are producing works which are presently highly coveted by some of the world's art collectors. Although brightly coloured fantastic examples of local scenery are enthusiastically produced by amateur artists even in the most unlikely corners of the country, watch out for names like Malangatana, Fatima (on Ibo Island), the Fundação Chissano Gallery at Matola near Maputo, Jorge Almeida and Luis Souto at the Co-operativa Alpha in Maputo, Conde and Paulo Soares at the Museu Nacional de Arte, Maputo.

Beautiful, intricately woven baskets, bags, hats and furniture are sold along many of the main national routes and in the parts of towns most frequented by visitors (e.g. next to the Café Continental and close to the Hotel Polana on Av. Julius Nyerere in Maputo).

Silver jewellery is crafted by traditional smiths on the islands of Mozambique (in the crowded bairros) and on Ibo (in a dilapidated warehouse across the square from the cathedral). The genuine article (much is in fact made from nickel and tin) is made from melted-down old Portuguese coins.

Public holidays

1 JANUARY: New Year's Day
3 FEBRUARY: Heroes' Day (the date of the death of the first Mozambican president, Eduardo Mondlane)
7 APRIL: Women's Day (the date Josina Machel died)
1 MAY: Workers' Day
25 JUNE: Independence Day
7 SEPTEMBER: Victory Day (the date of the Lusaka Accord, when the Portuguese agreed to independence)
25 SEPTEMBER: Armed Forces Day
19 OCTOBER: Samora Machel Day
10 NOVEMBER: Maputo Day (in Maputo only)
25 DECEMBER: Family Day (Christmas Day)

Easter and Boxing Day (26 December) are at present not official public holidays, but this may change. Islamic holidays, although not officially recognized, are observed by Muslim communities, which increase in size the further north one travels.

Translation guide

The most important phrase to know in Mozambique is 'Dá licença?' (May I?) Other than at tourist lodges, English is not widely spoken or understood anywhere in Mozambique, so be patient as misunderstandings

can occur. Portuguese is widely used in the urban areas, while, in the rural areas 'Funakalo', the discredited language of South Africa's mines, will be of more use to you than English. A simple 'bom dia' (good morning), 'boa tarde' (good afternoon) or 'boa noite' (good evening) will smooth your dealings with officials. Please is 'faz (pronounced 'fash') favor', thank you 'obrigado', how much? is 'quanto custa?' and write it down 'escrever' (pronounced 'ishkrayva').

Pronunciation

The following tips on how to pronounce commonly used words apply to Portuguese as spoken in Mozambique, as distinct from that which echoes around the hallowed halls of Lisbon universities.

Moçambique: 'ç' is usually translated as 'z', but sounds like 'zsh'.
Como: this 'c' is the same as the English 'c', as in cat.
Bom: 'm' usually sounds like 'n'.
Café: 'é' is 'eh'.
Chá: 'ch' becomes 'sh'.
Leite: this 'e' is an 'ay' sound.
Jantar: the 'j' is like the 'g' in giant.
Água: 'á' sounds like an emphasized 'ah!'.
Como está: for 's' read 'sh'.
Escrever, thus becomes 'ishkrayvar'.
Amanhã: 'hã' together form 'yaan' (say the 'n' through the nose).
Bilhete: 'he' is the same as the 'ye' as in yes.
Banho: the 'ho' becomes 'yo' as in yo-yo.
Camarão: 'ão' is similar to 'ow' as in now. Thus *pensão* becomes 'penshow'.
Quanto: 'qu', as in queen, is 'kw'.
Quiosque: 'qu', as in quay, is 'k'.
Muito: here the 'ui' should be 'oo-een'.
Faz favor: 'z' here sounds like 'zjh'.
Até logo: 'é' comes out as 'ay'.

Speaking Portuguese

Outside of the cities, very few Mozambicans speak any English, so it is important to know a few useful words and phrases (the endings -o and -e are applied to males, and -a to females).

Practicalities
Aeroplane : *Avião*
Banknotes : *Bilhete (notas)*
Bed : *Cama*
Customs : *Alfandega*
Danger/dangerous : *Perigo/perigoso*
Day : *Dia*
Excuse me! (Calling a waiter) : *Faz favor!*
Friend : *Amigo*
Good afternoon! : *Boa tarde!*
Good evening! : *Boa noite!*
Good morning! : *Bom dia!*
Goodbye! : *Adeus!* (not used much in Mozambique)
Goodbye! : *Ciao!* (used in Maputo and Beira)
Have you got ... ? : *Tem ... ?*
Here : *Aqui*
Hotel room/single/double : *Quarto/simples/duplo*
House : *Casa*
How are you (is it)? : *Como está?*
How much (does this cost)? : *Quanto custa?*
I am a poor traveller : *Eu sou viajante pobre*
I am fine, thank you : *Muito bem obrigado/a*

I am from ... : *(Eu) sou de ...*
I am tired : *Cansado estou*
I do not understand : *Não compreendo*
I don't speak Portuguese : *Não falo Português*
I have lost my passport : *Perdi o meu passaporte*

I would like that thing : *(Eu) gostaria desta coisa*
Journey : *Viagem*
Kiosk : *Quiosque*
Ladies' (toilet) : *Senhoras*
Late : *Tarde*
Left : *A esquerda*
Letter : *Carta*
May I? (Used before entering private property, or taking photos, etc): *Dá licença?*
Men's (toilet) : *Senhors*
Money : *Dinheiro*
Month : *Mês*
My name is ... : *(Eu) sou ...*
Near to ... : *Perto de ...*
No : *Não*
No problem! (Never mind!) : *Não faz mal!*
No way (never)! : *Nada!*
Now (these days) : *Agora*
OK! : *Tudo bem!*
Perhaps : *Talvez*
Please : *Por/faz favor*
Post-office box (P.O. Box) : *Caixa Postal (C.P.)*
Rate of exchange? : *Qual é o cambio?*
Rest well : *Bom descanso*
Right : *A direita*
Right now! : *Agora mesmo!*
Road : *Rua*
Room for married couples (often cheaper) : *Casal*
See you later : *Até logo*
Sorry : *Desculpe*
Stay well : *Fique bem*
Thank you : *Obrigado*
The bill : *Conta*
There : *Ali; lá*
Ticket : *Bilhete*
To clean clothes : *Limpar roupa*
To write (e.g. for prices) : *De o escrever*
Today : *Hoje*
Toilet/paper : *Casa de banho/papel*
Toilets : *Casa da banho*
Tomorrow : *Amanhã*
Train : *Comboio*

Traveller : *Viajante*
Until next time : *Até à proxima*
Until tomorrow : *Até amanhã*
Visa : *Um visto*
Wash : *Lavar*
We want to go to ... : *Queremos ir a ...*
Week : *Semana*
What is this thing? : *O que é esta coisa?*
What's your name? : *Como se chama?*
When? : *Quando?*
Where? : *Onde?*
Write it down : *Escrever por favor*
Year : *Ano*
Yes : *Sim*
Yesterday : *Ontem*

At the market *(mercado, bazar)*
All that : *Todos*
Beer : *Cerveja*
Beer/local/imported : *Cerveja/nacional/ importada*
Beverage : *Bebida*
Boiled water : *Água fervida*
Bread : *Pão*
Butter : *Manteiga*
Butterbean : *Fava*
Cashew nuts : *Castanha de caju*
Cheap : *Barato*
Cheese : *Queijo*
Chicken : *Frango, galinha*
Cooking oil : *Azeite*
Corn on the cob : *Espiga de milho*
Crab : *Caranguejo*
Crayfish : *Lagostim*
Dirty : *Sujo*
Eggs : *Ovos*
Fair price! : *Bom preço!*
Fish : *Peixe*
For sale? : *Vende-se?*
Fresh : *Fresco*
Fresh water : *Água fresca*
Fruit : *Fruta*
Garlic : *Alho*
Hot chips : *Batata frita*
Hot water : *Água quente*

How much? : *Quanto custa?*
I am hungry : *Tenho fome*
I like ... : *Gosto ...*
I want to buy ... : *Quero comprar ...*
Is this good to eat?/edible : *É bom para comer?/comestível?*
Jam : *Compota*
Less : *Menos*
Lobster : *Lagosta*
Maize meal : *Farinha de milho*
Meat : *Carne*
Milk : *Leite*
Mineral water : *Água mineral (água Vumba)*
More : *Mais*
Olive oil : *Azeite*
Onions : *Cebola*
Peanut butter : *Manteiga de amendoim*
Peanuts : *Amendoim*
Pepper : *Pimento*
Pineapple : *Ananás*
Potato : *Batata*
Prawn : *Camarão*
Rice : *Arroz*
Running water : *Água corrente*
Salt : *Sal*
Sauce : *Molho*
Snacks : *Petiscos*
Spices : *Especiaria*
Spring water : *Água doce*
Sugar : *Açúcar*
That's enough! : *Chega!*
The other : *Outro*
This is stale! : *Isto está passado!*
Tomatoes : *Tomate*
Too expensive! : *Muito caro!*

Vegetables : *Legumes*
When was this caught? : *Quando foi capturado isto?*

Eating out
Breakfast : *Pequeno almoço*
Coffee : *Um café*
Fresh fruit : *Fruta fresca*
Glass/beer mug/cup : *Copo/caneco/chávena*
Hand-written menu : *Ementa*
I like my food really hot : *Quero a minha comida muito quente*
I would like this ... : *Quero isto ...*
I would like to order now : *Quero pedir agora*
Ice cream : *Gelado*
Lunch : *Almoço*
Plate/knife/fork/spoon : *Prato/faca/garfo/colher*
Printed menu : *Cardápio*
Restaurant : *Restaurante*

Roadside restaurant : *Quiosque*
Set menu : *Menu*
Steak/well done/medium/rare : *Filé bife/bem passado/médio/mal passado*
Supper : *Jantar*
Take-away food : *Comida para levar/Pronto-a-comer*
Tea : *Chá*
The bill : *Quanto*
The receipt : *Recibo*
Water : *Água*

Famous Portuguese dishes
Calamari (squid) : *Lulas*
Cheese : *Queijo*
Dried cod : *Bacalhau*
Fillet of fish : *Filete de peixe*
Fried eggs : *Ovos estrelados*
Grilled pork chops : *Febras de porco na brasa*
Ice cream sorbet : *Gelado sorvete*

Kebab (sosatie) : *Espetada*
Mixed salad : *Salada mista*
Mixed vegetables : *Vegetais misturados*
Peri-peri fried chicken : *Galinha frita com peri-peri*
Potato chips : *Batata frita*
Prawn crumbed rissoles : *Rissois de camarão*
Pudding : *Pudim*
Samoosas : *Chamuças*
Scrambled eggs : *Ovos mexidos*
Shellfish soup : *Sopa de mariscos*
Spicy sausage (black pudding) : *Chouriço*
Steak roll : *Prego*
Stewed fish with 'the works' : *Peixe cozido 'com todos'*
Stuffed crab : *Caranguejo recheado*

Getting around
Avenue : *Avenida*
Beach : *Praia*
Bus : *Ônibus (machimbombo)*
Car : *Carro*
Corner : *Esquina*
Do you have a room? : *Tem um quarto?*
How far to ... by car? : *Quantos kilometros até ... com carro?*
How far to ... on foot? : *Quantos kilometros até ... a pé?*
I want to go to ... : *Quero viajar parñ ...*
Main road : *Estrada Nacional (E.N.)*
May I camp here? : *É permitido acampar aqui?*
Name of next village? : *Nome da proxima aldeia?*
Name of this town? : *Nome desta vila?*
Square (traffic circle) : *Praça*
Street : *Rua*
Taxi (individual) : *Taxi*
Taxi (mass transport) : *Chapacem*
To hike : *Excursão*
To the left : *Á esquerda*
To the right : *Á direita*
To walk : *Andar*
When does that bus leave? : *Quando sai este machimbombo?*

When does the bus arrive? : *Quando chega este machimbombo?*
Where is ... ? : *Onde ... ?*

Trouble-shooting
I (or point to someone else) feel sick : *Estou enjoado*
I am lost : *(Eu) estou perdido*
I need a mechanic/spares : *Quero um mecânico/peça sobressalente*
My car is broken down : *Meu carro está quebrado*
Take me to the hospital please! : *Levar-me para hospital, faz favor!*
Where is a doctor? : *Onde está um médico?*
Where is the nearest village? : *Onde é próxima vila?*

Useful contacts and information

International calls from outside of Mozambique are possible to the following locations inside the country: Maputo, Beira, Namaacha, Xai-Xai, Maxixe, Nampula, Nacala, Mozambique Island, Quelimane, Pemba, Inhambane, Chimoio, Tete and Lichinga. For updated information on connecting with Mozambique contact International Directory Enquiries in South Africa at 0903. Although once you get through the line is usually very clear, there are too few international connections available to cope with the load and you may have to persevere for hours if you try to call during business hours. If at all possible, send a fax to Mozambique after hours.
The dialling code from South Africa to Mozambique is 09258.

Diplomatic missions abroad
• Belgium and the E.U. (Brussels). Tel. (0932 2) 736 0096/7.
• Ethiopia and the O.A.U. (Adis Ababa). Tel. (09251) 71 2905 or 71 0021.

- France (Paris). Tel. (0933 1) 4764 9132.
- Germany (Bonn). Tel. (0949 228) 22 4024/5.
- Italy (Rome). Tel. (0939 6) 59 2145.
- Malawi (Lilongwe). Tel. (09265) 73 3144 or 73 3803.
- Portugal (Lisbon). Tel. (09351 1) 797 1747 or 797 1994.
- Russian Federation (Moscow). Tel. (097 095) 284 4007.
- South Africa (Johannesburg). 13th floor, Bosman Building, 99 Eloff Street, Johannesburg, tel. (011) 337 7721 and Nelspruit, tel. (01311) 2 7396.
- Swaziland (Mbabane). Tel. (09268) 4 3700.
- Sweden (Stockholm). Tel. (0946 8) 666 0350.
- Switzerland (Geneva). Tel. (0941 22) 47 9046.
- Tanzania (Dar es Salaam). Tel. (09255 51) 3 3062/8.

- U.K. and Northern Ireland (London). Tel. (0944 71) 383 3800.
- United Nations Organization (New York). Tel. (091 212) 51 7450/30.
- U.S.A. (Washington). Tel. (091 202) 293 7146.
- Zambia (Lusaka). Tel. (09260 1) 25 335.
- Zimbabwe (Harare). Tel. (09263 4) 79 0837/8/9.

Consulates in Maputo

British : (01) 42 0111
Canadian : (01) 43 0217
French : (01) 49 1693
German : (01) 49 2714
Italian : (01) 49 2229
Norwegian : (01) 49 0514
Portuguese : (01) 49 0316
South African : (01) 49 1614
Swazi : (01) 49 2451
Tanzanian : (01) 49 0110
American : (01) 49 1215

Other addresses & telephone numbers

AEROCLUBE DE MOÇAMBIQUE. 1697 Av. Martires Machava. Tel. (01) 49 1464.

APIE. (State Estate Agent). 2185 Av. Eduardo Mondlane. Director Mr Joaquim Manuel Mauricio. Tel. (01) 40 0454/458/770, fax 40 0342.

AVIS. Maputo Office, Maputo Airport. Tel (01) 46 5140, 46 5497, fax 46 5493.

AVIS. Beira Office, Beira Airport. Tel. (03) 30 1263, 30 1265, fax 30 1265.

BANCO STANDARD TOTTA (for exchange rates and forex). Tel. Carlos Carvalho at Maputo (01) 42 9082, fax 42 6967.

BAZARUTO ISLAND LODGE. P.O. Box 2479, Maputo, telex 6702 FOGA MO. Tel. Johannesburg (011) 447 3528.

BEIRA AIRPORT. Tel. (03) 30 1071.

BEIRA CITY COUNCIL (João Zandamela speaks English). Tel. (03) 32 2125/32 4123 (w) or 32 2422 (h).

BENGUERRA ISLAND. Tel. Johannesburg (011) 483 2734, fax 728 3767.

BUREAU DE INFORMAÇÃO PUBLICA (B.I.P.) Corner Av. Eduardo Mondlane and Av. Francisco Magumbwe. Tel. Maputo (01) 49 0200.

CANON COPYING SERVICE. 484 Av. Karl Marx. Tel. (01) 42 4812.

C.P.I. Centre for the Promotion of Investments (formerly GPIE). 2049 Av. 25 de Setembro, Maputo. Director Dr Augusto Sumburane. Tel. (01) 42 2454/7, fax 42 2459.

CHAVEIRO ECONOMICO (locksmith). 205 Av. Zambia, Maputo. Tel. (01) 73 3218.
CLUBE NAVAL (Yacht Club). Av. Marginal, Maputo. Tel. (01) 41 2690, Comodoro 49 7674, 74 4484, Secretary 34098.
DHL INTERNATIONAL (courier service). Av. 25 de Setembro, Maputo. Tel. (01) 42 1266/ 42 0897.
DINAGECA (Maps and Land Attribution). 537 Av. Josina Machel, Maputo. Tel. (01) 42 3217, 42 3376, fax 42 1460.
DIREÇAO NACIONAL ESTRADAS E PONTES (National Directorate for Roads and Bridges). 1225 Av. de Moçambique, Maputo. Tel. (01) 47 5145, fax 47 5290.
UNIVERSITY OF EDUARDO MONDLANE. Department of International Studies. Tel. Maputo (01) 42 0354.
ENDANGERED WILDLIFE TRUST. Tel. Johannesburg (011) 486 1102. In Maputo, Fundação Natureza em Perigo (F.N.P.) tel. (01) 42 4832.
FIRE BRIGADE. Telephone (Maputo only) 197.
GELO EM BARRAS/CUBOS (if you want ice in Maputo). Tel. (01) 40 0906, fax 40 1317.
HERTZ (FREXPO Automóveis de Aluguer Lda). Maputo Office, 2006 Av. 24 de Julho. Tel. (01) 33172/3, fax 42 6077.
HERTZ. Beira Office. Av Armando Tivane. Tel. (03) 32 2315, fax 32 2415.
HOSPITAL SPECIAL CLINIC. Tel. (Maputo) (01) 42 4663.
ILHA DE MAGARUQUE. P.O. Box 2705, Harare, Zimbabwe. Tel. Harare, Zimbabwe (09263 4) 79 6411, fax 70 6148.
IMPAR INSURANCE. 625 Rua da Imprensa, Maputo. Tel. Arlindo Ubisse (01) 42 9696, fax 43 0620.
INTERNATIONAL COMMITTEE OF THE RED CROSS. Mr Dominique Buff. Tel. Maputo (01) 49 0152/0545, 49 2475, 49 1994, fax 49 1652.
L.A.M. (Domestic Airline). Tel. Maputo (01) 42 6001.
JARDIM ZOOLOGICO (Maputo). Zoo Fund. P.O. Box 122, Skukuza, 1350, South Africa.

The zoo is in dire need of financial support.
LINHAS AÉREAS FRANCESAS (Air France). Tel. Maputo (01) 42 0337/8.
LOMACO (Lonrho Moçambique Agro Industrial Company). 1509 Av. 25 de Setembro, Maputo. Mark Lucas (Commercial Manager). Tel. (01) 42 2126/9, 21831/4, fax 42 2634.
LUNAT CAMBIOS LDA, Secondary Foreign Exchange Market. 65 Rua Consiglier Pedroso, Maputo. Tel. (01) 3 1900, fax 42 8333.

MADAL (Cattle and Game Ranching). Tel. Rudolf Müller at Maputo (01) 42 1495, fax 42 1497.
MAPUTO AIRPORT. Tel. 46 5074/79, (01) 46 5834/39, 46 5029/30.
MAPUTO PORT AUTHORITIES DIRECTOR (for ship and rail enquiries). Carlos Bambo. Tel. (01) 42 5368, fax 42 1740.
MEDICAL AIR RESCUE SERVICE (M.A.R.S.). Tel. Harare (092634) 73 4513, fax 73 4517, Telex 33114 MARS ZW.
METAVIA. Tel. Maputo (01) 46 5487.
MIDAS (vehicle spares). 95 Av. Olaf Palme. Tel. (01) 42 1989.
MOZAMBIQUE TOURIST BOARD. Mr Arlindo Langa. Tel. Maputo (01) 42 5011/3, 42 1097.
MOZAMBIQUE OPPORTUNITIES (Management Consultant Bulletin). Tel. Maputo (01) 3 3445, 3 3456, fax 42 3414.
NATAIR CHARTERS. 1350 Av. Armando Tivane, Maputo. Tel. (01) 74 1902.
NATIONAL DIRECTORATE OF FLORA AND FAUNA (Direção Nacional de Flora e Fauna Bravia).

333 Av. Zedequias Manganhela, Maputo. Contact Dr Milagre Cezerilo, tel. (01) 43 1789.
NATIONAL DIRECTOR OF TOURISM. Mr Victor Zacarius. Tel. Maputo (01) 42 5011.
P.G. AUTOGLASS. 2696 Av. Angola. Tel. (01) 46 5683/46 5730.
POLANACOLOR PHOTOGRAPHIC STUDIO (processing and passport photos). 726 Av. 24 de Julho, Maputo. Tel. (01) 42 7106, fax 42 2182.

POLICE. Tel. 199 (Maputo only).
SOUTH AFRICAN AIRWAYS (SAA). Tel. Maputo (01) 42 0740, fax 42 2481.
S.A. RESIDENT DIPLOMATIC REPRESENTATIVE (John Sunde). Tel. Maputo (01) 49 2096, 49 1614.
SYSCOM (IBM Authorized Computer sales and service). 1111 Av. 25 de Setembro, Maputo. Tel. (01) 42 4036.
TOYOTA DE MOÇAMBIQUE. 141 Rua Lago Amaramba. Tel. (01) 40 0405/6.

Travel agencies
BUDGET OVERLAND TOURS. Africa Travel Centre. Tel. Cape Town (021) 23 4530, fax 230065.
EURO TRAVEL. Tel. Maputo (01) 74 2657.
GO AFRICA TOURS. (Mozambique Flight Packages to Maputo, Inhaca, Bazaruto and Benguerra.) Tel. Johannesburg (011) 487 1254, fax 487 2789.

KWEZI TRAVEL. (Mozambique visa service.) Telephone Liz, Paul or Nigel at Maputo (01) 40 0628 or 40 1198.
MARINE SAFARIS. Game fishing and scuba diving at Morrungulo and Benguerra. Telephone Jacques or Heidi at Pretoria (012) 998 9989.
MEXTUR. 1233 Av. 25 de Setembro, Maputo. Tel. (01) 42 8427/8/9, fax 42 8430.
MOZAMBIQUE CONNECTION. Tel. Johannesburg (011) 394 8727, fax 975 2595.
MOZAMBIQUE HOLIDAY SERVICES. 758 Av. Mao Tsé Tung, Maputo. Tel. (01) 49 3025/6/7, fax 49 3025.
MOZAMBIQUE TRAVEL AND TOURS. Tel. Maputo (01) 42 4002, fax 42 4006.
MOZINFO. Tel. Johannesburg (011) 726 6467.
NATAIR. Av. Armando Tivane, Maputo. Tel. (01) 49 1811, 46 5477/8/9, fax 49 1872.
NKOMATI SAFARIS. Tel. Maputo (01) 49 2612, fax/voice 74 3139.
PESTANA. Tel. Maputo (01) 42 9277.
POLANA TOURS. Hotel Polana, 1380 Av. Julius Nyerere, Maputo. Tel. (01) 49 3533/4, fax 49 3538.
PROSOL VIAGENS E TURISMO. 809 Av. Filipe Samuel Magaia, Maputo. Tel. (01) 3 4098, 2 9506, fax 42 1908.
S.E.T. Hotel Turismo, Av. 25 de Setembro, Telephone Prédio Carvalhoin Maputo, (01) 74 1035.
STA AIR CHARTERS. 161 Rua de Gorongosa, Maputo. Tel. (01) 49 1765.
STARLIGHT CRUISES. (Luxury passenger liner cruises between Durban and Inhaca and Bazaruto islands.) Second floor, Norwich Life Towers, 13 Fredman Drive, Johannesburg , South Africa. Tel. (011) 884 7680.
SUNDOWN TRAVEL. Tel. Maputo (01) 42 5842.
TAP (Air Portugal). Tel. Maputo (01) 42 0635.
TRANSMARITIMA DA SOFALA. 153 Av. Karl Marx. Telephone Mr. Elliot at Maputo (01) 32 6724, 32 2147 or 42 2602.
TRAVELLER'S DREAM. (Custom tours.) Tel. Johannesburg (011) 888 6570.

TROPICAL TRAVEL INTERFRANCA SUPERMARKET. Av. 24 de Julho, Maputo. Tel. (01) 42 5078, fax 42 5082.

TTA AIR CHARTERS. Maputo Airport. Tel. 46 5292. **TURMOL.** 472 Av. Karl Marx, Maputo. Tel. (01) 42 0734 or 42 8975, fax 3 3788.

Southern Mozambique

The Mozambican Plain (Planície Moçambicana) with its endless sweeping savannas, meandering rivers and a string of coastal lakes and high sand dunes, dominates the landscape of the southern region. Although most of the land lies below 100 metres, the eastern border with Swaziland and South Africa is marked by the Lebombo Mountains which do reach over 500 metres occasionally. At its mouth the Limpopo River drains more than 60% of this sector, while the Incomati, Inharrime and Nhavarre rivers have drainage basins covering the rest of the area.

The low altitude and the fact that much of the southern region falls within the driest parts of Mozambique results in the characteristic grasslands dotted with mopane and acacia trees. The coastal dune belt is covered by dense scrub and forest, which gives way to deciduous miombo woodland a little further inland. The flood plains of the rivers are populated by herbaceous meadows and savanna well suited to the saline alluvial soils. The higher margin in the south-west is characterized by distinctive Lebombo savannas. While the once extensive mangrove swamps have been almost completely drained in the vicinity of Maputo city, those in the Maputo Elephant Reserve and around the edge of Inhambane Bay are still thriving.

From Piti and Chinguti in the south to Poelela and Manhali in the north, this region of Mozambique is dotted by 24 fair-sized freshwater lakes. This is a feature unique to this area of the country, as there are no natural coastal lakes anywhere else in Mozambique.

People of the Shangaan tribe make up 70% of the population of the southern region, with the Ronga nation comprising most of the balance. This is also the part of Mozambique where the influence of the Portuguese colonial period is most evident. Catholicism is the dominant religion, while 50% of the inhabitants of Gaza, Inhambane and Maputo provinces speak Portuguese, with the percentage rising to 70 in Maputo city itself.

South of the Sabi River (Rio Save) lies Mozambique's southern region which is made up of the provinces of Inhambane, Gaza and Maputo. The northernmost point of this region is Nova Mambone at the mouth of the Sabi River and the southernmost location is Ponta do Ouro. Pafúri and Cabo Inhambane are the western- and easternmost reaches respectively. The southern region's highest point is Mount M'Ponduíne (801 metres) in the Lebombo range on the border with Swaziland. Otherwise the rest of the land rarely rises more than 100 metres above sea level.

All three provinces comprising the southern region have boundaries with the Indian Ocean's Mozambique Channel, with Inhambane's coastline, at over 600 kilometres, being the longest. The powerful Mozambique Channel, with its inshore counter-currents, has created significant coastal features such as spits, dunes, lagoons, sand bars and islands. The best known of these are Uembje lagoon at Bilene, Pontas do Ouro and Pomene, and the Bazaruto Archipelago. Long, white, sandy beaches, protected in the main by offshore coral and rock reefs, border almost the entire length of this quarter of Mozambique. Three main rivers drain southern Mozambique. In order of size these are the Komati (Incomati), Limpopo and Sabi (Save) rivers. The lack of elevation in this very flat area called the Mozambican Plain (Planície Moçambicana) prevents the formation of spectacular features such as waterfalls and rapids, with wide meanders, marshes and mangrove swamps being dominant geomorphological features. Suitable dam sites are consequently few and far between. Inhambane Province has no major dams and Maputo and Gaza provinces only one each (Umbuluzi and Massingir, respectively). Much use is made of ground water and natural lakes to supply the southern region's towns and cities with water for domestic and industrial usage.

The surface geology of this area is characterized by the sedimentary lavas of the Lebombo Mountains and the depositional sand flats of the Limpopo and Changane rivers. The limits of the continental shelf extend over 100 kilometres out to sea off Beira, accounting for the formation of the islands and sand bars in the mouth of the Rio Púngoè, as well as for the immense delta of the Rio Zambeze, which extends for 50 kilometres beyond the coast and is over 150 kilometres wide during flood season (April to July at the mouth).

2

Maputo

When in 1975 most of the Portuguese settlers switched off the lights and left Mozambique under protest, Lourenço Marques was considered to be one of the most beautiful cities of the world. Since then, suffocating socialism, civil strife and cynical interference from outside its borders have held the Mozambican economy in limbo. Visitors to Mozambique over the past few years may concur that in Maputo the fabled phoenix has struggled towards the light from the bottom of a deep pile of the ashes of neglect and banditry.

Only two years ago Mozambique was the poorest country in the world and visitors returned with tales of abject poverty and consummate devastation. Maputo's pot-holed streets ran with sewage and rusted street lamps had last glowed 15 years previously. Electricity was available only intermittently and running water had become an unheard-of luxury. Only the celebrated Hotel Polana, rebuilt in 1990 at a cost of millions of dollars, offered amenities of an acceptable standard. Gunfire often rattled out from the bairros and teenagers with AK47 assault rifles ruled the streets at night. The October 1992 Peace Accord between the rebels and the rulers has had a remarkable impact. Today Maputo is being transformed with results both swift and stunning. Streets in the city have been resurfaced and the guns have disappeared.

The notorious bureaucratic hurdles in visitors' way have been largely removed, and the roads from Komatipoort and Namaacha resurfaced. Visitors are sneaking back to

'L.M.' (as many folk prefer to remember Maputo) to take what might at first be a tentative peek at what's happening, only to be carried along by the unexpected enthusiasm and resourcefulness. Maputo today is vibrant, confident and cosmopolitan, with an atmosphere that has more in common with Rio de Janeiro than with any city in Africa. Nightclubs swing to the samba and the salsa, while a challenging array of restaurants serve prawns, peri-peri chicken

and the finest fried potato chips in the world. And, if you are not accustomed to compromising in matters of quality and style, there are at least two eating establishments which rub shoulders with the best anywhere. Literally hundreds of sidewalk cafés (salões) have opened recently, bringing back that relaxed, friendly atmosphere so reminiscent of the city's past glory.

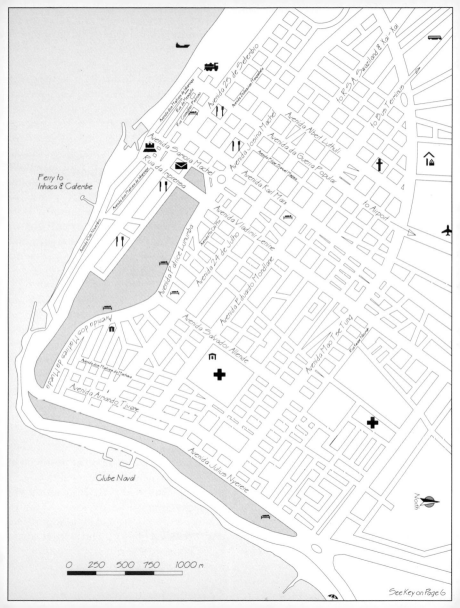

Ferry to
Inhaca & Catembe

Avenida dos Mártires da Machava
Rua Consiglieri Pedroso
Avenida Samora Machel
Rua da Imprensa
Avenida 25 de Setembro
Avenida dos Mártires de Mueda
Avenida Filipe Samuel Magaia
Avenida Albert Luthuli
Avenida Josina Machel
Avenida da Guerra Popular
Avenida Karl Marx
Avenida Vladimir Lenine
Avenida Patrice Lumumba
Avenida 24 de Julho
Avenida Eduardo Mondlane
Avenida Salvador Allende
Avenida Mao Tse Tung
Avenida Marginal do Maputo
Avenida dos Mártires da Machava
Avenida Armando Tivane
Avenida Julius Nyerere
Avenida Olof Palme
Avenida Ho Chi Minh
Avenida Olof Palme
Rua Licenciado Coutinho

Clube Naval

to R S A Swaziland & Xai-Xai
to Bus Terminus
to Airport

North

0   250   500   750   1000 m

See Key on Page 6

Although it can be bewildering to the unsuspecting newcomer, Maputo holds hidden rewards for visitors who take the trouble to absorb the rich cultural mix and socialize with the residents. As the country of Mozambique is a very recent addition to the list of African destinations which are accessible to travellers, facilities aimed at the budget-conscious may be difficult to find. However, the hotels, restaurants, nightspots and other interesting places that are listed in this chapter have elicited favourable reviews.

In Maputo there are traffic lights only at the beginning of intersections, making them difficult for the uninitiated to see. Street names have been repainted and pedestrians will notice that they are often also marked on marble plaques fixed to the corners of buildings.

Road conditions and borders

When you are on the Mozambican side of the **Komatipoort/Ressano Garcia** and **Lomahasha/Namaacha** frontiers, there are no signs to guide you, officials often do not speak English, and queuing is not practised. Parking is a random affair, and there may be a car or a truck or two blocking the way. The Komatipoort/Ressano Garcia border post is much less busy than Lomahasha/Namaacha (except during South African school holidays) and so, should you be hitchhiking, there are fewer opportunities for lifts.

You may be offered assistance by a tout expecting a tip in return. Accept his help if you wish, but do not hand over your documents to him. The only way to win is to relax and be polite. Although you will be approached by folks selling meticais, ignore them as they may con you, and the banks offer better rates anyway.

The best route (and the shortest) from the Witwatersrand area in South Africa to Maputo is presently via the Komatipoort/Ressano Garcia border post (open from 6 a.m. to 8 p.m.).

The road from Ressano Garcia to Maputo was resurfaced in 1995, and is in good condition. The road via Swaziland through the Lomahasha/Namaacha frontier has also been repaired. A new, much shorter toll-road between Nelspruit and Maputo is due for completion by 1998.

If you intend to approach Mozambique via Swaziland, an alternative and very scenic route which avoids the busy trans-Swaziland highway (via Mbabane and Manzini) is to travel via Komatipoort, using the wide new road entering Swaziland at the Mananga border gate (which is open from 8 a.m. to 6 p.m.) and leaving at Lomahasha/Namaacha into Mozambique. The rehabilitation of the road from Namaacha to Boane has been completed.

Manguzi/Farazella (Ponta do Ouro) Gate (open seven days a week from 8 a.m. to 4 p.m.). On the South African side, the road to KwaNgwanase (Manguzi) is tarred. KwaNgwanase has fuel, a supermarket, butchery, bakery and ice for sale. It is 20 kilometres on a sandy track (which splits occasionally), suitable for 4x4 vehicles only, to Farazella where the border post is an old caravan. The junction of the Ponta do Ouro to Bella Vista road is 5,8 kilometres from Farazella. Don't drive off the road, as this area was extensively mined during the conflict in Mozambique. The border post is open between 8 a.m. and 4 p.m.

Getting through the border

You will need
• Passport, visa (this may be dropped), original car registration papers (and pen). Police

clearance for your vehicle may be requested (on the South African side). International Health Certificates are not usually requested. Officially, yellow fever, smallpox and cholera vaccinations are not obligatory (but recommended if you have come from an endemic area). This may change in the near future, so check.

• The driver will need to present a driver's licence. An international type is recommended though not required. Licences must be shown at roadblocks.

• The customs declaration you filled in on the South African or Swaziland side of the border. The Mozambicans do not print their own forms.

• R85 (it may be higher) to pay for Mozambican third party vehicle insurance (seguros, pronounced 'sigooroosh'). This insurance is compulsory, and police may want to see the policy at roadblocks. Ensure that you are actually issued with a seguros, as many is the tale of the hapless motorist who paid at the border, only to be fined at the first roadblock having failed to obtain the required insurance papers.

• Mt50 000 (meticais) or R40 (a poor exchange rate) for your vehicle's temporary import permit (importado).

You may find it expedient to change rands into meticais at the Lomahasha Service Station in Swaziland on the left-hand side just before the border. The going rate of exchange in October 1996 was approximately Mt2 500 to the rand.

• R10 'administration fee' per person to have your passport stamped. You may (or you may not) then be handed a gate-pass, your car may be searched, and you may be charged duty on any items you intend to sell or leave in Mozambique. After showing your pass at the gate you will be allowed to proceed. The guard may send you back if you do not have third party vehicle insurance.

After the border

Apart from a few dangerous potholes and rubble, there may be animals, people and broken-down trucks on the roads, so don't drive after dark. There are official police roadblocks. If you are waved down, pull off the road to the left and have your passport, licence and insurance papers handy should you be asked for them. Only stop for people wearing the white shirt and black trousers of the traffic police.

Overnight stops

Due to possible delays at border posts on the way to Maputo from Johannesburg and the poor road conditions which make driving at night hazardous, it is best to enter Mozambique during the morning. Quite apart from this, Mpumalanga and Swaziland are areas of great scenic beauty, making it a pity to rush through.

Middelburg/Nelspruit – Komatipoort/Ressano Garcia

Nelspruit has comfortable hotels and lodges for every pocket. Catering for everyone from motorists to backpackers is the Nelspruit Holiday Resort on the banks of the Crocodile River, tel. (01311) 4 3253. Look for the signposted turn-off to the right just before you enter the town. Accommodation ranges from R30 per person for camping, to R160 for a luxurious fully-equipped six-bed chalet. If you include a slight detour, take the breathtaking pass into Swaziland via the Bulemba/Josefsdal frontier (open from 8 a.m. to 4 p.m.) to Pigg's Peak. Barberton is a perfect historic town for a stopover. Try the Impala Hotel, tel. (01314) 2 2108, on De Villiers Street, Barberton, or head for the municipal caravan park, which is on the left as you enter the town from Nelspruit.

Middelburg – Carolina – Oshoek

Swaziland has good roads and numerous places to spend a night before entering Mozambique in the morning. The Tavern Hotel on your right as you enter Mbabane from Oshoek has an 'Olde Worlde' atmosphere and is reasonably priced. Tel. (09268) 4 2361/2, 4 2568/9 or 4 2454. Campers and backpackers would do well to stop at one of Swaziland's delightful game parks. Both Mlilwane and Hlane game parks are situated only a few hundred metres from the route to the Lomahasha/Namaacha border post. Camping facilities and cabins are excellent. Contact Central Reservations in Mbabane, Swaziland, tel. (09268) 4 4541 or 4 5006, fax 4 4246, or use the after-hours numbers – tel. 6 1591, fax 6 1594.

Orientating yourself

While the vegetation and climate of Maputo may be typically tropical, in fact the city lies just south of the Tropic of Capricorn. Winter nights are cool enough to warrant wearing a sweater or a light coat. Even during summer the cooling sea breeze can at times cause you to put on a little more than simply a summer dress or shorts and T-shirt.

Maputo can sometimes be intimidating, frustrating and bewildering to visitors who do not speak Portuguese, but, with just a little advice and guidance, your visit will be stimulating and fascinating.

To help those who have not visited the country since the pre-independence days of 'Lourenço Marques', I have endeavoured wherever possible to include the old name in brackets after the current street names and other features.

The city has changed quite significantly since Mozambique's independence in 1975, but it is still filled with charm and passion –

its heart beating to the rhythm of the lambada and salsa dances of Latin America.

To orientate yourself in Maputo, take note of its layout relative to the bay and docks as well as to Avenida Marginal (marine drive) along which the Yacht Club (Clube Naval), bathing beaches (praias) and Costa do Sol are located.

The city's streets and avenues run almost parallel to either the bayfront and docks, or to the beachfront and marine drive (Marginal), intersecting at right angles to one another.

Thus the 'long' avenues (Avenidas), beginning closest or parallel to the docks, are 25 de Setembro (Republica), Josina Machel (5 de Outubro), Patrice Lumumba (Dr Brito Camacho), Ho Chi Min, 24 de Julho, Eduardo Mondlane (Pinheiro Chagas) and Mao Tsé Tung (Massano de Amorim), all of which run at right angles to (or away from) the beachfront (Marginal).

The 'short' avenues (Avenidas), starting closest to the beachfront, are Julius Nyerere (Antonio Enes), Vladimir Lenine (Augusto de Castilho), Karl Marx, Filipe Samuel Magaia (Paiva Manso), Guerra Popular and Albert Luthuli (Paiva de Andrade).

Money matters

Mozambican regulations require that all visitors change foreign currency into meticais on arrival, but this has not been enforced in recent times. You may find, however, that you will receive a poor rate of exchange if you pay your bills in South African rands. Many hotels, such as the Polana, cater largely for international tourists, and their rates are quoted in dollars. It is possible to pay in meticais, but again you will receive a poor exchange rate. Others, catering largely for South African tourists, quote their prices in rands.

Rands are in demand from Ponta do Ouro in the south as far north as Vilankulo, after which U.S. dollars as well as Zimbabwe dollars may be more acceptable to money changers and banks.

In Maputo during October 1996, one rand would get you roughly Mt (meticais, pronounced 'metticaysh') 2 500 at Banco Standard Totta, Av. 25 de Setembro, and about the same at the Mercado Municipal (the unofficial 'black' market), also on Av. 25 de Setembro. One U.S. dollar exchanged at the same bank (Banco Standard Totta) for Mt11 500, while the 'secondary' rate was slightly better at Mt12 000. Anticipate an inflation rate of about 5% per month and a corresponding change in prices and the exchange rates. Most banks and some black market dealers regard American Express traveller's cheques as cash but you might have to pay a high handling fee per cheque. Note that, due to a proliferation of forgeries, U.S.$50 and U.S.$100 bills are becoming difficult to change, even at banks. Transactions in pound sterling attract an automatic £20 levy.

In Maputo credit cards (both Visa and Mastercard) are accepted at the more upmarket hotels and restaurants, while it is possible to arrange to obtain local currency (U.S.$100 per day) via your credit card by phoning the Banco Standard Totta in Maputo at 42 9082 and asking for Mr Carlos F. Carvalho, or by visiting a branch of the Banco Comercial de Moçambique. Note that credit cards are not accepted anywhere else in Mozambique.

Accommodation

Accommodation that is reasonably priced, has clean toilets and is reasonably close to the city centre is not easy to come by in Maputo. A caravan park (Campismo Municipal) is marked on some maps, but it is now defunct (see below). You may come across a quaint, antiquated ruling in some hotels that have rooms called casal reserved for use by married couples only! These sometimes have a double bed and may be cheaper than normal double rooms.

Find a safe place to dump your gear (for instance at a travel agency), and get a map from B.I.P. (Public Information Bureau) on the corner of Av. Eduardo Mondlane and Av. Francisco Orlando Magumbwe. Alternatively photocopy the map in the telephone directory, and then check out the following options, which range from camping to five star hotels:

FATIMAS. Closest thing to a 'Backpackers' in Maputo. Camping, dorms and rooms. 1317 Av. Mao Tsé Tung.

CAMPISMO MUNICIPAL. On the beach road. Closed at present but due to be revamped. Do not rely on its continued existence.

PENSÃO CENTRAL. Located at 1957 Av. 24 de Julho, just up the road from the Conselho Executivo (City Hall). A meticulously maintained building, which has a flat roof which is deal for braais (barbecues), sundowners and tanning. Great view of Maputo from the roof. The toilets are not always clean. Within a 20-minute walk of the jetty, Central Market, station, post office, public phones and B.I.P. Single Mt20 000. Double Mt60 000. Contact Senhora Alice (Alisy) for bookings. Tel. 42 4476.

HOTEL SANTA CRUZ. Located at 1417 Av. 24 de Julho near to the Pensão Central. Friendly, helpful staff. Double room, shared bath, for Mt90 000. Tel. 42 7161.

HOTEL UNIVERSO. Corner Av. Karl Marx and Av. Eduardo Mondlane. Clean rooms and toilets, running cold water. Double with shared bath Mt39 000. Casal (for married couples only) U.S.$20. Tel. 42 7003.

HOTEL GIRASSOL (SUNFLOWER). Situated at 699 Av. Patrice Lumumba. Just up that road

from the British Embassy. Bizarre medieval decorations, rooftop sundowners – bring your own. Very primitive, unlikely to be full. Some rooms have great views over the bay. No lifts or running water. Prices negotiable. Tel. 42 1644.

RESIDENCIAL TAJ MAHAL. On the downtown or baixa (i.e. away from Av. Julius Nyerere) end of Av. Ho Chi Min. Well run, very clean but usually full. The manager speaks a little English. Price Mt85 000 per double room with a shared bath. Full breakfast is available for Mt5 000. Tel. 73 2122 – prior booking is essential as this is a very popular place.

HOTEL MOÇAMBICANO. 961 Av. Filipe Samuel Magaia. Single U.S.$60. Double U.S.$80, shared bath. Tel. 42 9252.

ACIJOL GUEST HOUSE. Xai-Xai road. Comfortable rooms, TV, pool, ample parking for cars and boats. Tel. 40 1476/40 1583. Business hours only; ask for Wyona.

HOTEL TIVOLI. Av. 25 de Setembro. Mt150 000 double with bath, Mt105 000 double, shared bath. Tel. 42 2006/7.

HOTEL CENTRAL. One the corner of Rua do Bagamoio and Rua da Mesquita. Good place to get the real feel of Maputo over a few Laurentina beers. Recently renovated. R75 single. R125 double room and breakfast, with shared bath. Tel. 42 7059.

THE BURGER INN. Bairro de Triunfo. Single R92, double R165 (including breakfast). Tel. 45 5211.

COSTA DO SOL. Av. Marginal. Comfortable rooms above the restaurant at a price of R120 per person per day. Tel. 45 5115.

PENSÃO MARTINS. 1098 Av. 24 de Julho. Intimate, good service. A double room costs U.S.$80. Tel. 42 4930.

TERMINUS. 'Five-star comfort at a three-star price.' can be had at 587 Av. Francisco Orlando Magumbwé. A single will cost U.S.$70, a double U.S.$112. Tel. 49 1333.

HOTEL CARDOSO. The best view in Maputo. Situated at 707 Av. Mártires de Moeda. Upmarket with good food. There is TV and air conditioning in the rooms. Average rates U.S.$150 single, U.S.$250 double. Full breakfast included. Tel. 49 1071.

HOTEL POLANA. 1380 Av. Julius Nyerere. Built in the 1920s, this is a five-star hotel with a history. Great pool, complete conference facilities, tennis courts and sauna. By far the best accommodation available at present in Maputo. At U.S.$185 single with breakfast, U.S.$250 double with breakfast, this may be an expensive way to get the Polana's useful complimentary bottles of shampoo, conditioner, bubble bath, aftershave and hand lotion, not to mention the cashew nuts and fruit. Tel. 49 1001.

Eating and drinking

EAGLES BAR AND CLUBE DESPORTIVO. Av. Zedequias Manganhela. Eagles is where the local movers meet. Outdoor setting, serious partying on weekends. Behind Eagles, Clube Desportivo has weekend live music.

Other good pubs in Maputo are **NAUTILUS** (upmarket) at Ungumi Restaurant, situated diagonally across the road from the Hotel Polana, **ZAMBI** on Av. 10 de Novembro (near the Catembe ferry jetty) and **CLUBE NAVAL** on the Marginal, if you are prepared to pay a temporary membership fee. **LUSO NIGHTCLUB AND STRIPTEASE** is putting the trouble back in the old 'street of sin' (which is Bagamoio's former nickname).

FEIRA POPULAR. If you want to mix with the locals, head for Feira Popular (funfair) on Av. 25 de Setembro, where there are dozens of quaint pubs and eating places.

KOWHANA. Leave your valuables behind at your hotel or pensão and make your way to Kowhana near the infamous Mercado Xipamanine in notorious Mafalala district.

Other places worth exploring are:

MERCADO JANET. Av. Mao Tsé Tung. Chicken and rice Mt7 000. Fish and rice Mt3 000.

CAMPISMO MUNICIPAL (caravan park). Av. da Marginal. Not operating as a caravan park at present, but ask for Olga who speaks English. She runs a pub and shop and will prepare a square meal for Mt15 000. She prepares fish, prawns, chicken and crab if you buy these at the market near the Clube Maritimo and bring them to her.

CAFÉ CONTINENTAL. Situated on the corner of Av. Samora Machel and Av. 25 de Setembro. Prégo Mt10 000, hamburger (large) Mt10 000, sandwiches Mt4 000 to Mt10 000. Great cakes!

CAFÉ DJUMBU. Av. 25 de Setembro. Serves excellent breakfasts.

CAFÉ LILY. Av. Ho Chi Min. Ethiopian – no cutlery. Tel. 42 6831.

Also try **O COQUINA, MBANGO FENIX** and any other of the Feira's many quaint restaurants, which cater for both halal and vegetarian tastes.

RESTAURANTE DIOGO (the owner hails from Goa Island near Bombay). In Catembe and five minutes' walk from the ferry terminal. It's well worth your while to make the trip – they serve good, cheap prawns.

HOTEL CENTRAL. Corner Rua do Bagamoio and Rua da Mesquita (mosque). Daily specials for around Mt50 000. Reasonable beer prices. Tip the security guard to ensure that he watches your car.

CLUBE DOS EMPRESARIOS RESTAURANTE/PISCINA (swimming pool). The club is famous for its Sunday buffet. Located on Rua de Mateus Sansão Muthembe, behind the Museum of Natural History.

GAIVOTA. At the Clube Marítimo on the Marginal. Seafood to leave home for. Tel. 49 1373.

CENTRO SOCIAL DE RADIO MAPUTO. Situated at the top of Parque Tunduru (Botanical Gardens), behind the studios. Beef dishes which range from Mt20 000 to Mt60 000. There are pleasant views of the gardens.

COSTA DO SOL. Situated right at the end of Av. Marginal just before it becomes a dirt track. A good spot for sundowners, jazz on Saturday afternoons and the beach is popular over weekends. Meals from Mt30 000 to Mt100 000. Try their prawns. Tel. 45 5115.

MINI-GOLFE. Situated on the Marginal or Marine Drive, 500 metres past the former Campismo Municipal.

Putt-putt course and braai (barbecue) area around a swimming pool. Try their shellfish special for two, which could easily feed four. Tel. 49 0382.

SNACK-BAR ROSSIO. Located opposite the Central Hotel on Rua da Mesquita. Large lobster Mt80 000. Gigantic prawns Mt100 000. Rossio boasts the best camarão chamuças (prawn samoosas) to be had in Maputo. Tel. 3 2840.

PEQUIM. 497 Av. Julius Nyerere. Across the road from the South African Embassy. There is good spaghetti bolognaise and steak on the menu. Tel. 49 0497.

IVANA. Off Av. dos Presidentes in the Co-op area. Food from Zambezia province. Try Mocoana and Mocopata. Tel. 41 8554.

TAI PAN. Located at 343 Rua Consiglieri Pedroso, near the railway station. Look for the private lift at the end of an alley. Best view after dark of Maputo. Great Chinese food. U.S.$30 per person.

HOTEL POLANA (restaurant), 1380 Av. Julius Nyerere. Good service, traditional Portuguese and Mozambican dishes. Upwards of U.S.$40 per person.

Dining in style

RESTAURANTE UNGUMI. Situated on Av. Julius Nyerere. Tel. 49 0951 for reservations.

The Ungumi Restaurant, close to the Hotel Polana on Maputo's millionaire mile, occupies a magnificent Portuguese colonial home. Built during the early part of the twentieth century, the house was originally the residence of a wealthy land-owning Portuguese/Italian family.

At independence the house was seized by the Frelimo government and became the Vietnamese Embassy for 15 years, during which time it was neglected and became severely dilapidated.

In 1989 the owners of a major Dutch company entered into a protocol with the Mozambican government, in terms of which the house would be refurbished and used as an exclusive restaurant.

The agreement further dictated that all profits would be donated to a charity administered by Mozambique's First Lady, who was then Josina Machel.

Over a million dollars have been spent to bring it into existence and justifiably so. The Ungumi is without doubt the finest,

most exclusive and most expensive restaurant in Maputo. Period furniture, luxurious carpets and exclusive fabrics were imported from Europe, and the crockery is Italy's finest. There are three separate main dining rooms, with four to six tables in each room; private groups are catered for in smaller, more intimate areas. The Nautilus, an English pub on the ground floor, has become the place to meet the movers and shakers of Maputo.

The group which are responsible for this transformation evidently view their investment as a philanthropic contribution to the rebuilding of Mozambique. They continue to pay for the maintenance and upgrading of Ungumi and are, for instance, continually purchasing new works of Mozambican modern art which then adorn the walls. This unique arrangement leaves the management and staff free to pursue their main objective of presenting the finest cuisine along with the highest standards of service and presentation, regardless of cost.

The Mozambican artist, Malangatana, is to African modern art what Salvador Dali was to Surrealism. Outside of the Museum of Modern Art in Maputo, the Ungumi is the only place in the country where works by the contemporary Mozambican masters are on display.

The startling, unique and bizarre creations by Malangatana and Naguib, as well as by other celebrated local painters, are reason enough in themselves to pay a visit to the Ungumi.

The staff and clientele rank the Ungumi amongst the best in the world, and the prices certainly reflect this status. Without drinks the average meal is priced around U.S.$100 per person, and if you include champagne and wine (for example Mouton Rothschild at U.S.$365 per bottle) your bill for two could easily approach U.S.$1 000.

This may appear a little excessive, but when one considers that the ingredients for meals are specially selected and imported fresh from all over the world, and that multi-million dollar deals are often clinched at the Ungumi, price becomes a secondary consideration to taste, style and ambience.

Dress at the Ungumi is smart-casual, and the menu varies according to the creative mood of the chef as well as the availability of the best ingredients. A special dish available during our visit was Surf and Turf, a scrumptious creation which involves lobster and steak.

RESTAURANT 1908. Situated at 560 Av. Salvador Alende (on the corner of Av. Eduardo Mondlane). Tel. 42 4834.

Situated in a building with its origins in the gracious post-Victorian era, Restaurant 1908 offers Mozambican, Indian and Italian food. Don't leave without tackling the 'Cherry Jubilee' dessert.

Restaurant 1908 boasts an indoor bar and an outdoor pizza oven which is adjacent to a shady patio – blissfully cool during the balmy tropical evenings.

The house was the original hospital in Lourenço Marques and the pressed steel pillars supporting the veranda bear the stamp of a Glasgow forge. The structure and fittings were ferried by boat from Britain and erected in 1908 on a breezy hill above the steamy tropical forest covering the site of what is today downtown Maputo. Since then the Maputo hospital has moved into much larger premises next door and the original building has been restored to its former grandeur.

Dress is casual and the quality of service is in keeping with Restaurant 1908's southern European ambience. For a reasonably priced, well-prepared, typically Italian meal served in a bright, airy, easy atmosphere, Restaurant 1908 is in a class of its own.

A selection of salads and entradas (entrées) range in price from Mt10 000 to Mt40 000, while main courses will slim down your wallet to the tune of between Mt30 000 and Mt100 000. Pizzas cost around Mt40 000. Do allow yourself to be tempted by one of the range of coffees and enticing puddings to end off your meal. The main menu and pizzeria are only available during the evenings, while bar snacks ranging in price from Mt10 000 to Mt25 000 are served from midday onwards.

Buying food on the street

Prawns are available for Mt40 000 per kilogram (size S.S. or small) at the Mercado Municipal (Central Market). Don't buy them if they are limp, or have been frozen. Fresh fish can also be bought at the Mercado Municipal or directly from the fishermen at midday from the beach, next to the Clube Marítimo on the Marginal. This is to be strongly recommended, as the seafood available at the Mercado Municipal is often not particularly fresh.

Cashew nuts cost up to Mt60 000 per kilo at the market, but crumbled cashews can be bought by the cupful for Mt2 000 at **Nelson Mandela Market**, situated on Av. Guerra Popular. Because only a fraction of the cashew crop is being harvested, and prawns are sold in bulk to South African firms, Maputo is not at present a very cheap place to buy them. Prawns are cheaper the further away from Maputo one travels and cost, for example, Mt20 000 per kilogram for the medium size in Quelimane, Zambezia Province (where giant prawns weighing up to 500 grams each occur).

Maputo's markets are the cheapest places to find a hot meal. Try **Nelson Mandela Market**, **Mercado Janet**, Av. Ho Chi Min and **Mercado Central**, Av. 25 de Setembro. Fish and rice costs Mt4 000, chicken and rice Mt6 000 and coffee Mt1 000.

Coffee breaks

The following restaurants and tea rooms (Salões de chá – a misleading name, as the last thing some of them serve is tea) have proved to be quite popular with budget-conscious travellers. Down Av. 25 de Setembro (walking away from the station), the following places are within a 15-minute walk of each other:

CAFÉ CONTINENTAL is an ideal meeting place which actually serves a good pot of tea and great coffee. Sit outside next to Maputo's busiest intersection and absorb the chaotic activity of the city's streets and sidewalks. The Continental offers a snack menu and fresh cakes, as well as a more comprehensive selection in the adjacent restaurant. SCALA, opposite the Continental, has been renovated and is worth a visit.

CAFÉ DJAMBU has friendly staff and is less noisy than the Continental. Try their tasty omelettes and breakfasts.

CAFÉ ESTORIAL. Av. Mao Tsé Tung next to the American Information Centre.

CAFÉ MA STOP. Rua da Imprensa, ground floor of the 33-storey building, corner of Rua da Imprensa and Av. 25 de Setembro.

Other cheap options

Many, varied value-for-money restaurants can be found elsewhere in Maputo, ranging in atmosphere from a taste of authentic, smoky, noisy, Mozambique in the open air, to air-conditioned sophistication that is sealed off from the outside.

PERI-PERI on the corner of Av. 24 de Julho and Av. Julius Nyerere serves American style fast food and Mozambican style snacks (petiscos). See a movie for a mere Mt1 000 at the spacious Cinema Xenon on Av Julius Nyerere before your meal (see page 81).

KOWHANA (not to be missed; open from Friday to Sunday) near the Mercado Xipamanine (pronounced 'zipamaneeneh'). Offers a slice of genuine Mozambique with huge servings, loud music and Latin American-style dancing. Get a local to show you the way and bring only enough money for the evening.

RESTAURANTE O'BAU (named after the Arab board game) on Av. Vladimir Lenine one block up from Av. Eduardo Mondlane.

RESTAURANTE DIOGO. Getting there involves a 15-minute ferry trip over the bay to Catembe. Prawns are their speciality and you won't have to mortgage your air-ticket to pay for the meal. (Continued on page 81.)

The Natural History Museum in Maputo houses a display of stuffed animals and the only collection of elephant foetuses representing each stage of the animal's 22-month gestation period.

A view of Maputo, showing Botanical Gardens (foreground) and (from l. to r.) Praça de Independência, Câmara Municipal, Catedral de Nossa Senhora de Conceição (dating back to 1781), and Hotel Rovuma.

The pool area and tropical gardens in front of the gracious Hotel Polana. Built in the 1920s, the Polana is reputed to be the best accommodation available in Maputo.

The entrance to the Mercado Municipal, Av. 25 de Setembro, Maputo. This market is a maze of stalls, where you can buy anything from fresh fish to curios and handicrafts.

River taxis on the Incomáti River near the ferry crossing between Marracuene and Macaneta, which is just north of the capital of Maputo.

Rusty, ancient coasters in Maputo harbour, which currently generates a major source of income for the government.

Café Continental on the corner of Av. 25 de Setembro and Av. Samora Machel, Maputo. The Continental is a great place to have a snack and watch the passing parade.

Boarding the ferry to Maputo from the Catembe pier. Restaurante Diogo in Catembe serves excellent, inexpensive prawns.

A traditional Portuguese crab meal at Lucas' Restaurant, Inhaca Village.

Dried fish and coconuts on sale at Xai-Xai market. Xai-Xai Caravan Park is a ski-boater's mecca, and is filled with holiday-makers during South African school holidays.

Dhows in Inhambane Bay. Dhows are a traditional means of transport in Mozambique.

Fishing boats and locals on the beach on Inhaca Island, which is well known for its water sports, diving off the shallow coral reefs and spear-fishing.

Inhaca Hotel has recently been taken over and refurbished by a reputable Mozambican company.

Mozambicans proudly display their catch after an afternoon's spear-fishing off Inhaca Island.

Women selling tomatoes at Macia market. Macia is on the way to Xai-Xai, inland from Bilene, formerly known as San Martino.

Hotel and beach at Tofo near Inhambane. Tofo Bay is well known for its big-game fishing and surfing.

Early morning on Bazaruto Island, the largest island in the famous Bazaruto Archipelago. The entire archipelago was proclaimed a national park in 1971.

A ski-boat off Benguerra Island, the second largest island in the Bazaruto Archipelago.

An aerial view of sand banks on beautiful Benguerra Island. A range of water sports is available.

Guests enjoying a drink in the lounge at the popular Benguela Lodge on Benguerra Island. The lodge is famous for its traditional Mozambique dishes, seafood buffets and tropical fruits.

The attractive Benguela Lodge on Benguerra Island. Because the Bazaruto Archipelago is a national park, overnight visitors have to stay at one of the lodges.

Some of the comfortable A-frame chalets at Bazaruto Lodge on Bazaruto Island.

Sunset on the beach on Benguerra Island.

Saltwater fly-fishermen find a paradise on Magaruque Island, part of the Bazaruto Archipelago.

BEIJO GELADO, at 1858 Av. 24 de Julho, is a squeaky-clean fast food outlet with the best ice cream in town.

CLUBE NAVAL (yacht club) on the Marginal is a 'members only' establishment but, if you are prepared to pay a nomimal temporary membership fee, the breeze is fresh, the bar menu reasonable and the pool is clean and inviting.

More expensive choices

If you've been roughing it for weeks on end and want to splurge in Maputo, here are a few choices:

RESTAURANT 1908, situated on Av. Eduardo Mondlane next to the Central Hospital, is definitely worth a visit for the pizza! (See page 63, Dining in Style, for more details.)

RESTAURANTE TAJ MAHAL on Av. Filipe Samuel Magaia, three blocks up from the Central Market, offers authentic Indian cuisine and vegetarian meals at a reasonable price. Why not get a group together and mix and match your orders?

COSTA DO SOL on the far end of the Marginal (Marine Drive). Plenty of taxis (chapas) allow you to escape from town for a meal with a view and jazz on Sundays.

Nightlife and entertainment

Wish to mix with the locals? Remember that Maputo only wakes up at 11 at night. Leave your valuables behind, and try the following pubs, discos and nightclubs:

MINI-GOLFE. Great atmosphere. Entrance Mt10 000, but ladies get in free!

CLUBE ZOZO. At the Feira Popular (funfair), Av. 25 de Setembro.

TCHOVA XITA DUMA. 287 Rua Sansão Mutemba. Live jazz Wednesday to Saturda;y.

KOWHANA. Tropical beat under the intense African sky, near Mercado Xipamanine in Mafalala district.

QUINTA JAZZ. To be found in Matola, which is five kilometres out of Maputo on the road to South Africa and Swaziland.

CLUBE MATCHEDJE. 3785 Av. 24 de Julho. African dance shows. Live 60s music and jazz. Tel. 40 2153.

Something a bit more upmarket?

More expensive than the above and you'll have to wear longs and a shirt with collar. Beer could cost up to U.S.$3.

COMPLEXO SHEIK. Located at 67 Av. Mao Tsé Tung. Bar, restaurant and disco. Cover charge for disco. Takes place from Friday to Sunday. Tel. 49 0197.

ZAMBI. 8 Av. 10 de Novembro. Nice setting under palm trees overlooking the bay.

CENTRO DE ESTUDOS BRASILEIROS. At 1728 Av. 25 de Setembro. There is live entertainment on Friday evenings.

Movies in Maputo

It is worth visiting one of Maputo's cinemas just to marvel at the grandeur, excess, space and architecture from days gone by. Films on offer are generally either of the violent kung fu type, or heroic soppy Indian love stories.

At **Cine Africa** (Av. 24 de Julho) during October 1993 *Rambo 2*, *Mapantsula* and *Bloodsport* were showing! Try **Cinema 222** in the baixa (downtown) area or **Cinema Xenon** on Av. Julius Nyerere. **Cinema Gil Vincente** on Av. Samora Machel near the Conselho Executivo has been known to show Japanese soft-porn movies with subtitles in Chinese and Portuguese! **Cinema Scala** at 1514 Av. 25 de Setembro has been revamped and offers better international films. Tel. 42 2901.

Jazz

COSTA DO SOL RESTAURANT. Saturday evenings 5 p.m. to 8 p.m.

NAFTAL LANGA ART GALLERY. Friday nights.

RESTAURANTE PRINCESA. Av. 24 de Julho, on Sunday evenings.

SALON ARCO-IRIS (rainbow). Bairro Indígina – patronized almost exclusively by locals.

Theatre

Locally written and produced shows of a high standard are on offer in many theatres around Maputo – from 'someone's front room' to larger, more formal venues. Try the **Teatro Avenida** on Av. 25 de Setembro and the **Casa Velha** (old house) on Av. Patrice Lumumba, with its outdoor amphitheatre.

Two one-day walks

Walking is the best way to experience Maputo, but remember that as a tourist you may become a target for pickpockets, conmen and muggers, so don't flaunt anything of value. Wear a money belt under your clothes and hold your camera close to your body. Never leave your possessions unguarded or with a stranger at any time. It is highly advisable to start before 7 a.m. to give yourself enough time to appreciate the sights and scenery fully, without being in a rush to get back before dark (which is essential).

Route one (seven kilometres)

The downtown (baixa) walk starts and finishes at **Hotel Rovuma** (Rua da Sé), where there is safe parking. The hotel is next to the huge, white **Catholic cathedral**, one of Maputo's unmistakable landmarks.

Walk up from the hotel entrance to Av. Ho Chi Min, turn left and you will see the neo-classical **City Hall** and **Civic Centre** (Conselho Executivo) which was completed in 1945. Although imposing from the outside, it is the interior of the building that is of real interest. There are magnificent chandeliers and Louis XIV fittings and furniture, while the entrance hallway contains intricate scale models of the historic buildings of old Maputo. Enquire at the entrance on Av. Ho Chi Min for permission to enter the building.

From the front of the City Hall, walk down to the **Praça da Independência** (Independence Square, which is ironically a circle), turn right onto Av. Josina Machel and walk four blocks down to the **Louis Tregardt** (sic) **Trek Memorial Garden**, commemorating the disastrous attempts by the Boer Voortrekkers to secure a port for the Transvaal Republic during the nineteenth century.

From this monument, walk back to Independence Square and Av. Samora Machel, passing on your left the remains of the original **Lourenço Marques Club**, which has been rebuilt and is the new French Cultural Centre. The **Parque Tunduru Botanical Gardens** and the **Casa do Ferro** (designed by Gustav Eiffel who built the Eiffel Tower in Paris) will also be passed on your left before you reach the high-rise buildings which line Av. 25 de Setembro.

Cross 25 de Setembro to the **Continental Café** and turn right, walking two blocks until you see the **Mercado Municipal** (Central Market) across the road to your right. Inside is a maze of stalls selling anything from colourful fruit and odorous fish, to handicrafts, curios and spices. Purchase something if you are prepared to carry it for the rest of the day, or make a note to come back another time. The Mercado is a favourite haunt of pickpockets and con artists.

From the main entrance to the market, cross over Av. 25 de Setembro into Rua da Mesquita (Mosque), carry on down past the **Mosque** on your left and on two blocks to the notorious **Rua do Bagamoio** (nicknamed the 'street of sin') and the celebrated Victorian style **Hotel Central**. You are now in the baixa (downtown) Maputo.

The Hotel Central formed part of the original buildings of Lourenço Marques, many of which are over 100 years old, and has been renovated. Turn right into Rua do Bagamoio and one block away is **Praça dos Trabalhadores** (formerly Praça Mac-Mahon, named after the French President who arbitrated in the dispute over the territory to the south of Maputo in 1875), in the centre of which is the First World War Memorial Statue, built entirely of stone imported from Portugal. Adjacent to this square is the attractive copper-domed **C.F.M.** (Caminho de Ferro de Moçambique) **Railway Station** built in 1900.

From the railway station, walk back down Bagamoio past Hotel Central, **Pub Mundo** (the unofficial South African club), **Luso Nightclub**, the dilapidated historic **Carlton Hotel** and many other period buildings, towards the leafy **Praça 25 de Junho**. One street before the praça, turn right and on your right will be one of Maputo's magnificent cinemas – take a look inside and marvel at the size and grandeur. Walk past the Praça 25 de Junho, which is a colourful curio market on Saturdays and Sundays, to the **Fort of Nossa Senhora da Conceicão**, dating back to 1781, and around which the first small settlement of grass huts sprang up. The Museum of Military History used to be located inside the fort, but at the moment it is not open to the public.

From the fort, carry on along Av. Mártires de Inhaminga parallel to the docks past an open field on the left to the imposing new **Ministry of Finance** building.

Turn towards the bay here and walk to the nearby ferry jetty, from which boats depart to Catembe across the bay as well as to Inhaca Island. Catch a ferry to Catembe, which used to be a desirable residential area and is a 10-minute trip costing Mt500. A suggested stop for lunch is **Restaurante Diogo** in Catembe, which is a five-minute walk from the left of the terminal. The owner is originally from Goa and his establishment is famous for its prawns.

After lunch, catch the ferry back across the bay and turn right along Av. 10 de Novembro. A few hundred metres along the bay, turn left into the **Feira Popular** and wander amongst the cheerful pubs, clubs and eating places, before coming out on the opposite side into Av. 25 de Setembro. Turn left and make your way back towards Av. Samora Machel, but turn right up Av. Vladimir Lenine, on the corner of which is a half-completed 33-storey building. Climb up this edifice (the lifts don't work) if you have the energy for the best views of Maputo. One block up Av. Vladimir Lenine enter the **Parque Tunduru Gardens** (Jardim Botânico) and walk up to Av. Patrice Lumumba on which the old L.M. Radio, now Radio Moçambique Studio, is located. Turn left and then almost immediately right back up to the Hotel Rovuma for a well-deserved cup of tea.

Route two (seven kilometres)

The uptown (cima) walk starts and finishes at the **Hotel Polana** (Av. Julius Nyerere), where there is safe parking. The Polana reflects the gracious 1920s era of opulence and luxury and is well worth looking over, either at the beginning or end of your walking tour. From the Polana parking area, turn right into Av. Julius Nyerere, and cross the street. After about 50 metres you will encounter two stately houses from the colonial era on your left. The first is still occupied by the original owners, while the second has been transformed into **Ungumi Restaurant**, which is Maputo's most exclusive dining establishment. Ask the doorman to show you the Ungumi's magnificent entrance hall which is hung with works by favoured Mozambican artists (see page 62).

From here carry on 20 metres down Av. Julius Nyerere and turn left into Av. Kwame Nkrumah, one block along which the **Church of Santo Antonio da Polana** stands on the right. Enormous stained-glass windows extend high up into the soaring 'lemon squeezer' type spire. At the next intersection, turn left into Av. Mártires da Machava and walk five blocks further to the wide Av. Eduardo Mondlane with its four lanes.

To your left on the corner of Mártires da Machava and Eduardo Mondlane is the **B.I.P.** or Bureau de Informação Pública (Public Information Bureau), which offers videos, magazines and books relating to Mozambique, as well as maps, posters, stickers and T-shirts, which are on sale to the public.

From the B.I.P. turn right into Av. Eduardo Mondlane and carry on past the **Central Hospital** to the **Restaurant 1908**, housed in an Edwardian house which was the original Lourenço Marques hospital, built in 1908. The club welcomes guests for tea or lunch and serves Italian dishes as well as bar snacks.

From the Centro Social, cross over Av. Eduardo Mondlane and walk four blocks down Av. Salvador Allende towards Maputo Bay.

When you reach Av. Patrice Lumumba, turn left and enjoy the view over the bay on the way to **Praça da Travessia do Zambeze**, a traffic circle in front of the **Natural History Museum**, housed in an ornately sculpted building in the Manueline style of architecture.

The museum boasts a collection of world-renowned stuffed animals, as well as the only collection of elephant foetuses representing each stage of the animal's 22-month gestation period. The director of the museum, Dr Augusto Cabral, is a fund of information regarding Mozambique's history and wildlife.

Leave the museum and walk back around its front facing onto the praça, and turn left into Rua de Mateus Sansão Muthembe on which you will see the **Clube dos Empresários** on your left. This is a good, shady place to stop for a cool lunch or a drink on the terrace overlooking the swimming pool. From the Empresários, carry on down the road, watching out for the **Associação Cultural Tchova Xitaduma** on your right about two blocks before the intersection with Av. Julius Nyerere. This cultural centre often features exhibitions by local painters, sculptors and craftsmen.

Continue further on and at the T-junction turn left into Av. Julius Nyerere, the road on which the Hotel Polana is situated. It is now a two-kilometre stroll back to your starting point along a leafy avenue lined with gracious homes, interesting shops and varied restaurants. Pause for an ice cream, stop for lunch, watch the passing show over a pot of tea, and support the curio-sellers under the trees on the right-hand side of the avenue just before the Polana.

Availability of goods and services

The prices quoted below were accurate in October 1996.

PETROL. Mt7 500 per litre. **DIESEL.** Mt5 000 per litre. Available throughout the country, but shortages may occur in remote areas away from the main centres of Maputo, Inhambane, Beira, Tete, Quelimane, Nampula, Lichinga and Pemba. Diesel is more likely than petrol to be available in remote places. Petrol can generally be bought at markets throughout the country but is more expensive than at service stations.

ALCOHOL AND COOL DRINKS are widely available at slightly higher prices than in Zimbabwe, Malawi or South Africa, but it may not be a good idea to try to bring in all your requirements by car, due to customs duties. Get your liquor and wine from Keybee Lda, Rua Antonio Volaro, tel. 42 5154.

Another interesting place to buy alchohol is the 'thieves' market', called Ndaba neng, a Shangani expression meaning 'to run away'. A visit to Ndaba neng is not for the faint-hearted. You will be amazed at the spectacle of cases of whisky, wine, spirits and beer piled up high in the open air. Wine costs about Mt100 000 for five litres, beer Mt200 000 per case. Refill your L.P. Gas at Moçacor on Av. Filipe Samuel Magaia, on the right-hand side going up the hill, between Av. Josina Machel and Av. Ho Chi Min.

MAPUTO LIBRARY is on Av. 25 de Setembro. It used to house the C.C.F. (French Cultural Centre), which has excellent publications on Africa as well as French magazines. The C.C.F. has now moved to the premises of the old L.M. Club on Av. Samora Machel. Be warned that the toilets at the library (as in many public buildings) are quite disgusting.

COMPUTER REQUIREMENTS. Computec, 290 Rua Consiglieri Pedroso. Tel. 42 5900.

BOOKINGS for hotels, tours, and Avis and Hertz hired cars can be arranged through Nkomati Safaris in Maputo (telephone Colette at 49 2612).

Alternatively, bookings can be made through Empresa Nacional de Turismo, telephone Johannesburg (011) 339 7275. They can also be contacted in Maputo at 1023 Av. 25 de Setembro, tel. 42 5011. The Mozambique Tourist Board can be contacted at the same number in Maputo.

HARDWARE, TOOLS AND PAINT can be bought at Ferragens, tel. 42 6401, or from Radio Técnica Moçambiquana, 444 Av. Filipe Samuel Magaia, which has an excellent selection of specialist tools, screws, nuts and bolts.

BUSES AND TAXIS around town or to places away from Maputo can be found at the Central Market on Av. 25 de Setembro, the hospital on Av. Eduardo Mondlane or at Petromoc near the zoo on the road to Marracuene and Xai-Xai.

PASTELARIA G. VERDE. Fresh bread, rolls, pies, pastries, cakes and biscuits are available from this bakery (among many others), at 595 Av. de Karl Marx, as well as at the **CONTINENTAL CAFÉ,** which is situated on Av. 25 de Setembro.

FISHING EQUIPMENT, YACHT AND BOAT SPARES and accessories are sold at Fibreglass Sundlete, on Av. Vladimir Lenine.

ROAD AND REGIONAL MAPS of Mozambique can be bought at a stationery shop on the corner of Sekou Touré and Lenine.

AGRICULTURE AND FARMING. People interested in agriculture can contact Lomaco (Lonrho Moçambique), 1509 Av. 25 de Setembro. Tel. 42 2126.

MEAT can be bought at a butchery called Com Carne on the corner of Filipe Samuel Magaia and 24 de Julho. Tel. 43 0839.

PHOTOCOPIES (Mt500 per A4 sheet) can be done at Rank Xerox, Av. Revolução de Outubro, and Minolta, Av. 25 de Setembro.

More information and advice

TIME OUT magazine is published in English in Maputo. It is full of invaluable advice for the visitor to Mozambique. This twice-yearly periodical has a distribution of 15 000. Tel. Maputo (01) 3 3445.

B.I.P. (Bureau de Informação Pública), corner of Av. Eduardo Mondlane and Francisco Orlando Magumbwe. Maps, books, brochures, postcards, T-shirts and videos available. Tel. 49 0200, fax 49 2622, telex 6487. E-mail geo2@bip.moz.

NATIONAL DIRECTORATE FOR TOURISM. Situated at 1203 Av. 25 de Setembro. Tel. 43 1527.

HOTEL CENTRAL, Rua da Mesquita, has a notice board for travellers' messages as well as for anyone buying, selling, offering a service or looking for someone.

Vehicle repairs, spares and accessories

For advice on service and repair stations, contact BP Moçambique, 170 Av. Mártires de Inhaminga. Tel. 42 5021.

SPARES AND AUTO ACCESSORIES are obtainable at Acauto, 682 Av. Guerra Popular, tel. 42 2612, Trem Auto Lda, 2570 Av. 24 de Julho or Midas, 98 Av. Olaf Palme, tel. 42 1989. Swiss Auto on Av. Patrice Lumumba, just up from the British Embassy, has got a good reputation locally.

Posts and Telecommunications

The **Main Post Office** (correio) is in an attractive colonial-style building situated on Av. 25 de Setembro in the centre of town. Services here include E.M.S. (Expedited Mail Service), Poste Restante, a fax, telex and telegram service, as well as normal postal services. 'Post office box' or 'P.O. Box' in Portuguese is caixa postal or 'C.P.' Letters to South Africa, Namibia and Zimbabwe cost Mt4 000. (See page 30 for opening hours.)

Faxes to South Africa, Zimbabwe and Namibia cost Mt50 000 for the first page and Mt25 000 per page thereafter. Faxes to Europe cost Mt120 000 for the first page and Mt50 000 per page thereafter, while faxing to Asia and America costs Mt152 000 and Mt62 900 respectively.

Public phones (Telefone Publico) are advertised around town, but, if you want to make international calls, use the six phones on Av. Zedequias Manganhela, behind the post office. These are controlled by two telephonists who speak English (it is still a good idea to write down your number). The minimum rate is for three minutes. Local calls cost Mt600 for three minutes; calls to South Africa, Swaziland, Zimbabwe, Namibia and Botswana cost Mt45 000 for three minutes. Calls to other parts of the world range from Mt55 000 to Mt200 000 per three-minute period. Faxes to the Marisat network of Satcoms (Satellite Communications) cost Mt288 500 for the first page and Mt105 500 for every page thereafter.

Curios, art and museums

The Makonde people have amongst their number carvers of world renown. These folk live in isolated areas on the northern border between Mozambique and Tanzania and produce most of their work in ebony.

Although many curio sellers in Maputo claim to be selling Makonde work, the best way to judge if it's 'the real Makonde' is to look at the style. Makonde carvings are typically intricate, often bizarre, perhaps nightmarish and sometimes considered to be 'satanic' or 'surreal'. Curios are expensive in Maputo, but, if you don't plan to make the trip north, go to Makonde Artesanato, 114 Rua Consiglieri Pedroso, which features the genuine article. Alternatively, look at the good selection being sold on the pavement next to the Continental Café on Av. 25 de Setembro, as well as on the Marginal near the Campismo Municipal and on Av. Julius Nyerere near the Hotel Polana.

Maputo has fascinating museums including the Natural History Museum (on the Praça da Travessia do Zambeze), which houses the world's only collection of elephant foetuses representing each of the 22 months in its gestation period; Museum of the Revolution (Av. 24 de Julho), basically dedicated to glorifying Frelimo victories; Art Museum (Av. Ho Chi Min); the Museum of Geology (Av. 24 de Julho) and the Museu de Moeda (Av. Revolução de Outobro) which is a currency museum housed in what is probably the oldest intact building in Maputo.

North of Maputo

Buses (machimbombos) leave from the terminus near the big circle at the beginning of Av. 24 de Julho in Maputo. Transportes Oliveiras offer a reliable service right up to and beyond Beira for around Mt140 000. Cheaper, more rickety buses, minibuses and trucks can be caught outside the zoo.

Minibus taxis (chapas) are cheaper, more crowded and, while quicker than some buses, are certainly less safe. These leave from the Central Hospital, Mercados Central and Xipamanine and the zoo, as well as other locations around town.

Transport trucks load up near the harbour in front of the railway station and you may be able to find one going your way. Alternatively, make your way to the turn-off to Marracuene and Xai-Xai three kilometres past the end of Av. 24 de Julho and stick out your thumb. Hitching on boats is worth a try, but there are no regular passenger services and you may have to wait for weeks before you strike it lucky.

Taxis to the airport can be arranged by asking at the desk of your hotel, or by stopping one in the street (not easy). If you find a taxi, a reasonable fare to the airport will be Mt45 000. Otherwise catch a chapa to Praça dos Heróis (Heroes' Acre) for Mt1 000 and walk the last two kilometres to the airport (don't attempt this at night).

Addresses and telephone numbers

AIRPORT. Tel. 46 5029/30/74/79, 46 5834/9.

APIE (State Estate Agent). 2185 Av. Eduardo Mondlane. Director Mr Joaquim Manuel Mauricio. Tel. 40 0454/458/770, fax 40 0342.

BANCO STANDARD TOTTA (exchange rates and foreign exchange). Av. 25 de Setembro. Contact Mr Carlos Carvalho. Tel. 42 9082, fax 42 6967.

B.I.P. BUREAU DE INFORMAÇÃO PUBLICA (Public Information Bureau). Corner of Av. Eduardo Mondlane and Av. Francisco Orlando Magumbwe. Tel. 49 0200, fax 49 2622.

CHAVEIRO ECONOMICO (locksmith). 205 Av. Zambia. Tel. 73 3218.

CLUBE NAVAL (Yacht Club). Av. Marginal. Tel. 41 2690, Comodore 49 7674, 74 4484, Secretary 3 4098.

C.P.I. Centre for the Promotion of Investments (formerly G.P.I.E.). 2049 Av. 25 de Setembro, Director Dr Augusto Sumburane. Tel. 42 2454/7, fax 42 2459.

DINAGECA Maps and Land Attribution. 537 Av. Josina Machel. Tel. 42 3217/376, fax 42 1460.

UNIVERSITY OF EDUARDO MONDLANE. Dept. of International Studies. Tel. 42 0354.

FIRE BRIGADE 197 (Maputo only).

HOSPITAL. Special Clinic 42 4663.

IMPAR INSURANCE. 625 Rua da Imprensa. Contact Arlindo Ubisse at tel. 42 9696, fax 43 0620.

INTERNATIONAL COMMITTEE OF THE RED CROSS. Mr Dominique Buff. Tel. 49 0545, 49 2475, 49 0152, 49 1994, fax 49 1652.

LOMACO (Lonrho Mozambique Agro-Industrial Company), 1509 Av. 25 de Setembro, Mark Lucas (Commercial Manager).Tel. 42 2126/9, 21831/4, fax 42 2634.

LUNAT CAMBIOS LDA. Secondary Foreign Exchange Market. 65 Rua Consiglier Pedroso. Tel. 31900, fax 42 8333.

MADAL (Cattle and Game Ranching). Tel. 42 1495, fax 42 1497.

MAPUTO JARDIM ZOOLOGICO (Zoo Fund). P.O. Box 122, Skukuza, 1350, South Africa. The zoo is in dire need of financial support.

MAPUTO PORT AUTHORITIES DIRECTOR (for ship and rail enquiries). Contact Carlos Bambo. Tel. 42 5368, fax 42 1740.

MOZAMBIQUE OPPORTUNITIES. Management Consultant Bulletin. Tel. 3 3445/56, fax 42 3414.

MOZAMBIQUE TOURIST BOARD. Mr Arlindo Langa. Tel. 42 5011/3, 42 1097.

NATIONAL DIRECTORATE FOR ROADS AND BRIDGES (Direção Nacional Estradas e Pontes). 1225 Av. de Moçambique. Tel. 47 5145, fax 47 5290.

NATIONAL DIRECTORATE OF FLORA AND FAUNA (Direção Nacional de Flora e Fauna Bravia). 333 Av. Zedequias Manganhela. Contact DrMilagre Cezerilo. Tel. 43 1789.

NATIONAL DIRECTOR OF TOURISM. Contact Mr Victor Zacarius. Tel. 42 5011.

POLANACOLOR PHOTOGRAPHIC STUDIO (processing and passport photos). 726 Av. 24 de Julho. Tel. 42 7106, fax 42 2182

POLICE Tel. 199 (Maputo only).

SOUTH AFRICAN RESIDENT DIPLOMATIC REPRESENTATIVE. Situated on the corner of Av. Eduardo Mondlane and Av. Julius Nyerere. John Sunde. Tel. 49 2096, 49 1614.

SYSCOM (Authorized computer sales and service). 1111 Av. 25 de Setembro.Tel. 42 4036.

Travel agencies and airlines

DANA. Av. Vladimir Lenine (extension). Tel. 416 241, 416 246, fax 416 238.

LINHAS AÉREAS FRANCESAS (Air France). Tel. 42 0337/8.

LUSOGLOBO. 1211 Av. 25 de Setembro. Tel. 42 3302/3/4, fax 42 1298.

MEXTUR. 1233 Av. 25 de Setembro. Tel. 42 8427/8/9, fax 42 8430.

MIAMI TRAVEL TOURS. Av. Eduardo Mondlane. Tel. 73 3506, fax 40 0968.

MOZAMBIQUE HOLIDAY SERVICES. 758 Av. Mao Tsé Tung. Tel. 49 3025/6/7, fax 49 3025.

NATAIR CHARTERS. 1350 Av. Armando Tivane. Tel. 491 811, 465 477/8/9, fax 49 1872.

NKOMATI SAFARIS. P.O. Box 784, White River 1240, South Africa. Tel. Maputo (01) 49 2612, fax 74 3139.
POLANA TOURS. Av. Julius Nyerere 1380, Hotel Polana. Tel. 49 3533/4, fax 49 3538 (ask for Colette Fair and Elena Trafalis).
PROSOL VIAGENS E TURISMO. 809 Av. Filipe Samuel Magaia. Tel. 3 4098, 2 9506, fax 42 1908.
RECIL. 114 Rua da Sé, Hotel Rovuma. Tel. 42 1801/2, fax 42 1804.
S.E.T. Av. 25 de Setembro, Prédio Carvalho, Hotel Turismo. Tel. 74 1035.

SOUTH AFRICAN AIRWAYS. Tel. 42 0740, fax 42 2481.
S.T.A. AIR CHARTERS. 161 Rua de Gorongosa. Tel. 74 2366.
T.A.P. (Air Portugal). Tel. 42 0635.
TROPICAL TRAVEL INTERFRANCA SUPERMARKET. Av. 24 de Julho. Tel. 42 5078, fax 42 5082.
T.T.A. Air Charters. Maputo Airport. Tel. 46 5292.
TURMOL TRAVEL AGENCY. 472 Av. Karl Marx. Tel. 42 0734/8975, fax 3 3788.

3

Southern Mozambique outside Maputo

NAMAACHA

If you take the Swaziland route from South Africa to Maputo, Namaacha will be the first town you reach in Mozambique. Although the town is sadly dilapidated, a four-star hotel and a cool, scenic picnic spot next to a mountain stream can be recommended.

Accommodation

HOTEL LIBOMBOS. This is an ideal place to break your journey with a pot of tea and a refreshing swim. Double rooms at the hotel cost U.S.$45 per night. The hotel also has a nightclub, ladies' bar, comfortable lounge and gracious dining room. Telephone Maputo (01) 96 2719/20.

Eating and drinking

On your way out of Namaacha, the **CASCATA** (cascades) picnic site can be found by turning left just as the town ends, where there is a grove of trees. A shady tarred road winds its way down to the stream where there is a paved area for picnics . A sign in Portuguese translates as: 'No swimming due to deadly danger'. (*See also* Accommodation above.)

INHACA & XEFINA GRANDE ISLANDS

To reach Inhaca from Maputo either catch the ferry (Mt40 000 per person) from the jetty off Av. 10 de Outubro – a three-hour trip – or phone Nkomati Safaris in Maputo at (01) 49 2612, fax 74 3139 and ask for Colette or Richard who will arrange a safe and swift ride by speedboat for U.S.$35 return (per person, minimum 6).

Nkomati Safaris arrange day trips to Xefina Grande Island with its beaches, old cannons and snorkelling, as well as to places north and south of Maputo. An unforgettable (but not cheap) way of getting to the island is on a chartered yacht. Call James Brewer in Pretoria at (012) 805 2472.

There are charter flights direct to Inhaca from Johannesburg, Maputo and Nelspruit. Contact Metavia Airlines: Nelspruit, (01311) 4 3141/2, fax 4 1226, Maputo (01) 46 5487, 42 5078, fax 46 5964 and Johannesburg, tel. (011) 394 3780/970 1887, fax 394 3726.

As August to October can be very windy, a visit in this period may be uncomfortable.

Accommodation

INHACA HOTEL. Pestana Hotels and Resorts have taken over and upgraded the Inhaca Hotel. In season a double room costs U.S.$80 per person sharing, single U.S.$95; double off-season U.S.$70 per person sharing, U.S.$80 single – dinner, bed and breakfast. Call Maputo (01) 49 0551 or the Inhaca post office, tel. (01) 74 3545/39, ask for number 1.

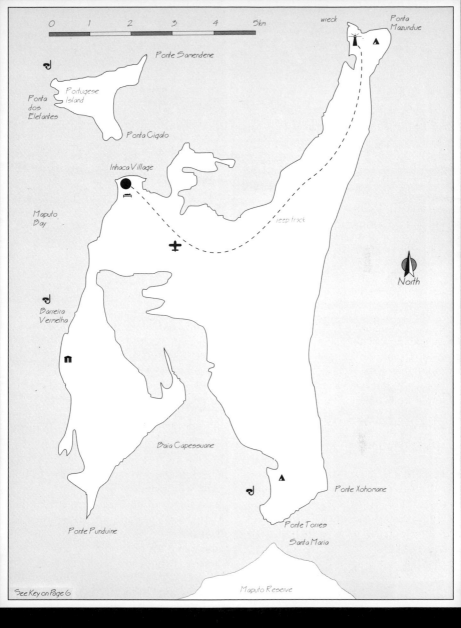

Inhaca Island

Camping on Inhaca

To find out about camping, call Direção Nacional Flora e Fauna Bravia in Maputo (01) 43 1789, or contact the Port Captain on arrival. Ask for directions to Coconut Village. RESTAURANTE LUCAS. A Mozambican institution. Lucas prepares excellent food and will cook your catch. In the village next to the market.

PORTUGUESE ISLAND

At low tide one can walk from Inhaca Island to the less developed Portuguese Island, with a camping site (Mt20 000 a day). You may struggle to find potable water.

MAPUTO ELEPHANT RESERVE

The abundant wildlife that once roamed the area has largely disappeared. In 1975 the 104 000-ha reserve was sanctuary to herds of antelope, 600 elephant and 65 white rhino relocated from Umfolozi in KwaZulu-Natal. Today perhaps 100 elephant and a few shy leopards and antelope remain. The elephant migrate along the Futi Channel to South Africa's Tembe Elephant Reserve. The sandy, acidic soils are fragile, so stick to worn tracks.

Msala Bush Camp accommodates 8 guests in tents. Nkomati Safaris offer packages including meals, game walks and drives, and turtle tours. Tel. Maputo (01) 49 2612.

MACANETA

Macaneta is about an hour's drive (including the ferry over the Incomati River) from Maputo. To get there, take the Xai-Xai road (the E.N.1) north. After 37 kilometres turn right at the small dilapidated town of Marracuene (not signposted), marking the turn-off to the ferry crossing point on the Incomati.

Turn right into Marracuene down a tree-lined, pot-holed double avenue and then left along the street overlooking the river. Another right turn down a sandy road takes you across the railway to the ferry terminal. If you are not in your own vehicle you can cross in one of the dugouts or rowing boats. There are chapas to Macaneta.

While waiting for the ferry over the Incomati River, buy some massive mangrove crabs. The five-minute crossing costs Mt50 000 per vehicle, Mt1 000 per person.

A half-hour drive (10 kilometres) on a sandy road (a 4x4 is not needed if you are prepared to push – there are plenty of local kids to lend a hand) leads to a restaurant and chalets on the sand spit between the river mouth and the sea. Remember to take the right-hand fork at the trading store selling cool drinks, beer and basic provisions.

The resort village of Macaneta has a trading store and a restaurant, and is favoured by local fishermen. On the banks of the Incomati, the remains of rice paddies are visible. These were cultivated by Chinese immigrants who also found the rich fishing waters irresistible, but initially did not have the means to exploit this resource. Their ingenious solution was a two-metre bamboo platform lashed together with reeds, a makeshift sail and collapsible hand-held mast resembling an organic, environment-friendly sail-board. The local fishermen inherited these craft from the now departed Chinese. They paddle them out every morning and sail back using the onshore afternoon winds, trolling for fish on strong handlines. The sea at Macaneta is ideal for fishing but not great for swimming or snorkelling. As it is the nearest clean stretch of beach to Maputo, it is popular over weekends.

Accommodation

INCOMATI RIVER CAMP. A gem of a secluded luxury river lodge. It's an adventure getting there; arrange to be met at the ferry by the owner/manager, Senhor Rodriguez. Contact Marisa in Pretoria at tel. (012) 343 2957 or Maputo (01) 42 5322, fax 42 1908.

CENTRO TURISTICO MACANETA (also called Campismo Macaneta). Tucked away in the dunes at Macaneta a secure, secluded and shady camp site with rustic ablution facilities has been open for a few years.

The turn-off may be difficult to find unless one has been there before. At Macaneta, turn right at the trading store and ask a local kid to direct you to Senhor Thomas (Gumede). Or contact George Gumede of the Centro Turístico Macaneta, in Maputo at tel. (01) 40 0747/8.

JAY'S CAMPING LODGE. Chalets and camping for folk looking for good amenities. Follow the signs from the Macaneta trading store. Call Nkomati Safaris in Maputo at (01) 49 2612, fax 74 3139 to book. Ask if the track is still for 4x4s only.

PONTA DO OURO

Ponta do Ouro is a small town with a few dozen inhabitants outside the tourist season. Swimming is safe with ideal surfing waves, and the beach is perfect to launch ski-boats. Scuba diving and big-game fishing are excellent, and fishing is possible from the rock shelves on the shore and miles of beach. The dunes have beautiful indigenous forest to explore, but ask locally about land-mines.

The 117-kilometre drive from Maputo to Ponta do Ouro definitely requires a four-wheel-drive vehicle and some patience. The route is not signposted and getting there is a matter of simply following the beaten track. Along the way there are a few unmarked turn-offs to the Maputo Elephant Reserve, which is open to day visitors. Do not try to camp in the reserve illegally as the Mozambican authorities take strong disciplinary action against trespassers.

Although the road from Maputo is initially passable, you need a 4x4 for the last 20 kilometres over very thick dune-sand. Where the

sand becomes thick, people have opened up 'detours' which are safe to use as they return after a few hundred metres to the main road. As a rule, it is very dangerous to leave the well-used tracks or to drive on the sand dunes due to the possibility of land-mines.

The border post between Manguzi (Kosi Bay) in northern Zululand, South Africa, and Ponta do Ouro is open 8 a.m. to 4 p.m. From South Africa take the road to Kosi Bay and turn left after the KwaNgwanase/Manguzi Kwiksave. From Kwiksave it is 18 kilometres to the border, from where it is 16 kilometres to Ponta do Ouro and 22 kilometres to Ponta Malongane.

For more information and bookings at Ponta do Ouro, telephone Benoni, South Africa (011) 849 5184. Bookings are essential as the Centro Turístico Ponta do Ouro (camping site) is very popular. Routes and road conditions are subject to change, so check on these when you make your reservation.

The best route to Ponta do Ouro from South Africa's northern provinces is via Komatipoort/Ressano Garcia, or Maputo where you take the ferry (Mt500 per person, Mt30 000 per car) from Av. 10 de Novembro across Maputo Bay to Catembe. The ferry leaves every hour, 5 a.m. to 7 p.m., and the trip lasts 15 minutes. From Catembe to Ponta do Ouro is 117 kilometres – a three-hour drive. Another route to Ponta do Ouro is to drive around Boane and Bela Vista to Catembe, which adds an hour to your trip.

There is no fuel at Ponta do Ouro or between Maputo and Ponta do Ouro. Two stores at Ponta do Ouro sell basic items such as firewood, charcoal, eggs, condensed and long-life milk, tinned food, potatoes, onions, tomatoes, cooking oil, flour, mealie (maize) meal, soap powder, sugar, candles, paraffin and paraffin lamps, matches, cigarettes, cool drinks, beer, wine and spirits, beans, rice and fresh bread (which arrives irregularly).

Accommodation

CENTRO TURISTICO PONTA DO OURO. There are fifty caravan/camping sites, two-, four- and six-bed bungalows and two luxury flats. The bungalows have beds (no bedding), tables, chairs, gas rings, cooking and eating utensils, fridges and electrical lighting. The flats are more comprehensively fitted out. The camp, set amongst the trees of an indigenous dune forest alongside a long and very beautiful beach, is sheltered from the wind.

Interesting, affordable drinks and meals are available at the restaurant/bar where ice is on sale. Ski-boats may be hired during peak periods (corresponding with the school holidays in Gauteng and KwaZulu-Natal).

Prices (per day) are: camping R20 per person; 2-bed huts R90; 4-bed chalets R200 per night; luxury chalets (up to six) R450. Tel. Benoni, South Africa (011) 425 2866.

MOTEL DO MAR, Ponta do Ouro. Four-bed cabanas U.S.$80 per night. Well-equipped kitchen, bedding, bath and shower. Excellent restaurant. P.O. Box 3564, Pretoria 0001. Tel. (012) 43 2846, fax 43 6659.

DIVING AT PONTA DO OURO. 5-dive packages R400; individual dives R85–R100. Full kit hire R70/day. African Water Sport Adventures, Umkomaas, tel. (0323) 73 2503/5, fax 73 2502.

PONTA MALONGANE

Ten kilometres north of Ponta do Ouro, this beautiful spot is set amongst the dune forests (see directions under Ponta do Ouro, page 93) facing onto a sheltered beach. Forty-five electrified campsites, U.S.$9 per person per night. Twenty-two rondawels: 2-bed U.S.$23 per night and 4-bed U.S.$80; 10 chalets: U.S.$92–U.S.$110 per night; shop, restaurant and bar. Well-equipped dive camp with its own tented accommodation.

DIVING AT MALONGANE. 5-dive package U.S.$110; individual dives U.S.$25; special dives U.S.$27–U.S.$33; air fill U.S.$5.50. Contact Intercontinental Explorers in Pretoria, tel. (012) 368 4262.

CATEMBE AND MAPUTALAND

The quickest way to reach Catembe on the southern side of Maputo Bay is the vehicle ferry from the pier on Maputo's Av. 10 de Novembro opposite the new Ministry of Finance building. Departures are at 5 a.m.; 6 a.m.; 7 a.m.; 8.30 a.m., after which expect a trip about every two hours until 9 p.m. The first ferry on weekends leaves at 6.30 a.m. and then reverts to the normal schedule.

Eating and drinking

RESTAURANTE DIOGO. A five-minute walk from the ferry terminal, Diogo serves good, cheap prawns. After Bela Vista (buy basic non-refrigerated provisions), cross the muddy Maputo River and pass through countryside that is part of the Maputaland ecosystem, stretching south to Sodwana Bay in South Africa.

BILENE (SAN MARTINO)

To reach Praia do Bilene with its fresh- and saltwater lakes and lagoons, turn off from the Xai-Xai road (E.N.1) at the village of Macia, 146 kilometres north of Maputo. It is then a 33-kilometre drive on a tarred pot-holed road to the fairly large resort town of Bilene. The 27-kilometre-long Uembje lagoon is an ideal family spot with long bright white stretches of sand for beach games and shallow, calm water for safe swimming. The mouth of the lagoon, usually blocked by a massive sand bank, is best reached by boat, but a long difficult track does allow access to the beach facing the open sea. Petrol and diesel are both available at Praia do Bilene.

Accommodation

HOTEL BILENE. On the traffic circle (praça) at the entrance to Bilene three kilometres from the lagoon, the hotel is clean and spacious. It has a restaurant, well-stocked bar and conference facilities. Shabby double rooms with bath go for Mt150 000 when the hotel is quiet and Mt200 000 when busy. Booking not possible.

Three camping/caravan parks with ablutions are functioning in Bilene alongside the lagoon. Standards are not reliable so check out all three when you arrive.

PARQUE FLORS. A really beautiful, shady caravan park with camp sites and chalets, situated alongside the lagoon. Among the facilities offered by Parque Flors are cold showers, firewood and charcoal, and a kiosk (quiosque) with basic food and necessities.

Bookings can be made through E.N.T. (Empresa Nacional de Turismo) who are in Maputo, at tel. 42 0324, 42 1794, 42 1797/8, fax 42 1795, or the Mozambique National

Tourist Company in Johannesburg, tel. (011) 339 7281, fax (011) 339 7295.

PALM TREE BILENE. Has 20 caravan sites; the rate is R25 per site per day, plus R15 per person. Also on the lagoon, it has four reed chalets overlooking the water, each sleeping four. Bilene (02) 2 2939 or Blackhill in South Africa (01351) 5 3996.

THE THIRD (UNNAMED) SITE is very basic and is situated close to Palm Tree Bilene.

CENTRO FERIAS DO BILENE (Complexo Martinho). Along the beach (praia) road, a right turn at the circle at the bottom of the hill leads to a dozen brightly painted cottages which were holiday cottages for Mozambique Railways (C.F.M.). Rooms cost Mt250 000 per single and Mt350 000 per double and the reception is the green building at the end of the tar. Tel. Senhor Pope in Maputo, (01) 42 6943.

LAGOA AZUL CHALETS (previously called Complexo Turístico Serra). Go past Centro Ferias do Bilene and turn right just before the road becomes gravel to reach this cluster of self-contained cottages which have everything except food. This is probably the most comfortable accommodation available in Bilene. Two-bedroomed chalets, which sleep four, contain fully-equipped kitchen, dining/sitting room, bathroom, fans, TV, bed-linen and other accessories.

Prices vary depending on the season and the day of the week, so contact Empresa Nacional de Turismo (E.N.T.) in Maputo at telephone (01) 42 0324, 42 1794, 42 1797/8, fax 42 1795. In Johannesburg, telephone the Mozambique National Tourist Company, at (011) 339 7281, fax 339 7295.

Eating and drinking

Hungry in Bilene? Try one of the following restaurants (note that prices are higher during busy periods):

RESTAURANT FERROVIARIO. Whole chicken (frango na brasa), Mt40 000.

TAKE-AWAY TCHIN TCHIN. On the beach road on the way to the camp sites. Good food in shady gardens.

RESTAURANT ESTRELA DO MAR. Medium prawns (camarão), Mt100 000.

RESTAURANTE BAR POUSADA PARADISO. Fresh fish, a speciality, costs around Mt30 000.

PAVILHÃO TAMAR. Close to the lake. Ask the chef to cook up something just for you.

Caravan, up the Limpopo with a gift of 1 000 rifles and 20 000 rounds of ammunition for the ruler. The Portuguese impounded the boat on its return to the river mouth and the result of the diplomatic row which ensued was that the steamer was returned and Rhodes ordered to abandon his interest in the area.

Once again in 1894 Gungunhana was deemed to be a sufficient threat to Portuguese interests to warrant the

XAI-XAI

Xai-Xai town is quite attractive with all the facilities needed by travellers and holiday-makers: hotels, restaurants, supermarkets, shops, ice, petrol/service stations, banks, public telephones and a hospital, amongst other things. Xai-Xai town is actually 10 kilometres inland from Praia do Xai-Xai and Praia da Supulveda, where all the holiday resorts are to be found. The cashew-processing factory is a fascinating place to visit.

The last 20 kilometres of the 224-kilometre drive from Maputo are a little bumpy, with some moderately sized potholes. This tarred road is likely to deteriorate due to the increase in heavy traffic. Once you cross the Limpopo toll-bridge (Mt2 500 per small car) you are in Xai-Xai town, the capital city of Gaza province.

The lower reaches of the Limpopo river were in the past host to a squabble between colonial powers. A hundred years ago Cecil John Rhodes had grand ambitions for the British colony, Rhodesia, and was looking for an outlet to the Indian Ocean for the landlocked territory.

In order to curry favour with Gungunhana, the powerful King of Gaza, Rhodes sent a 100-ton steamer, the *Countess of*

despatch of Governor General Antonio Enes on a mission to capture the king who had acquired the title 'The Lion of Gaza'.

So it was that the defiant King of the Shangaans was to take one last, lingering look at his beloved Gaza from the deck of a Portuguese gunboat on his way to exile in the Azores, where he died in 1906.

Accommodation

PENSÃO XAI-XAI. 1021 Av. Samora Machel. Tel. Xai-Xai (022) 2 2012.

COMPLEXO TURISTICO HALLEY. A large hotel situated on Praia do Xai-Xai. The revamped complex is right on a safe swimming beach (but there are no shark nets). It has a large bar, light-meal menu, dancing area and a

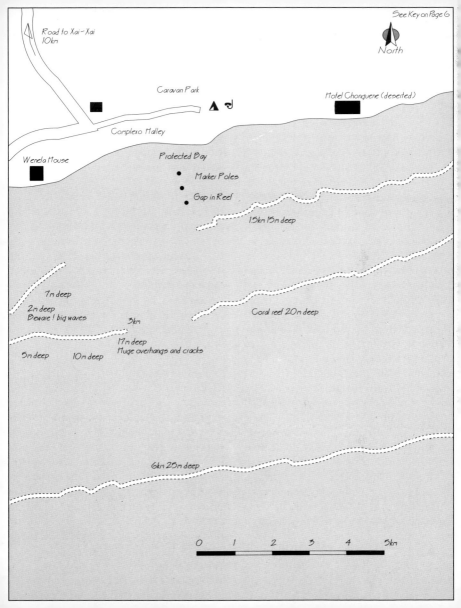

North

Road to Xai-Xai
10km

Caravan Park

Hotel Chonguene (deserted)

Complexo Halley

Wenela House

Protected Bay

● Marker Poles

● Gap in Reef

1.5km 15m deep

7m deep

2m deep
Beware! big waves

3km

Coral reef 20m deep

17m deep
Huge overhangs and cracks

5m deep   10m deep

6km 25m deep

0   1   2   3   4   5km

shop which sells all the basics. Rates (including breakfast) are Mt200 000 per single, Mt300 000 per double, and a four-bed suite Mt350 000. Meals cost Mt30 000 to Mt100 000.

XAI-XAI CARAVAN PARK. This is the South African ski-boaters' mecca and as a result is packed to bursting over South African school holiday periods, especially over Christmas and Easter.

Reasonably priced four-bed (R100/day) and two-bed (R80/day) bungalows and a rustic beachside bar add to the atmosphere. Expect to pay R20 per tent plus R12 per person for the privilege of using the brand-new ablution and laundry facilities. For telephone bookings, contact Johann in Xai-Xai, tel. (022) 2 2942.

XAI-XAI DIVING AND FISHING CAMP. In a section of Xai-Xai caravan park, Xai-Xai Diving and Fishing Camp offers accommodation, deep-sea fishing, snorkelling inside the reef, and excellent ski-boat fishing and, if you have all your own gear, scuba diving out to sea. Contact Mozambique Connection in Johannesburg tel. (011) 394 8727.

Along the beach road to the abandoned hotel at Chongoene there are unofficial places to camp which have no facilities. Although you may be tempted to set up here, there is an enterprising fellow, with an official receipt book and a friend who is a policeman, who will try to charge you Mt40 000 per tent. If you are camping right next to the hotel at Chongoene, befriend Vittorino who guards the building, as this is hotel property.

Public Transport

Transportes Oliveiras leave Maputo at 6 a.m. and arrive at Xai-Xai beach at 10 a.m. every day. The return trip departs at 1 p.m., arriving in Maputo at 4.30 p.m. (*See* page 87.)

Eating and drinking

GOLFINHO AZUL (the Blue Dolphin). This is an open-air restaurant located on the beachfront near to the Halley. Golfinho serves a plate of great chips for Mt10 000, while larger meals cost around Mt45 000. Beer and cool drinks cost Mt12 000. There are clean toilets here.

MERCADO MUNICIPAL. The market in Xai-Xai sells a fair range of fruit, vegetables, freshly baked rolls and bread, as well as traditional medicines and fish. A large loaf of bread should cost in the region of Mt3 000, a kilo of tomatoes Mt2 000, a kilo of bananas Mt10 000, a big papaya Mt5 000 (reputed to help prevent hepatitis and other infections), condensed milk Mt10 000, 2M (Dois Em) beer Mt10 000 and bottled water Mt14 000 per litre.

XAI-XAI CARAVAN PARK. Has a full restaurant and bar. Eat the best prawns and chicken peri-peri in Xai-Xai.

To do and see

WENELA. Named after a house belonging to the mine employment agency, Wenela is a tidal pool about two kilometres down the coast (i.e. in the direction of Maputo) – an interesting spot to visit. Wenela has a natural tunnel and blow-hole linking the pool to the sea. The locals call this place 'Jordan' as baptism-type ceremonies occur in the water. There are very treacherous rips and currents in the tunnel, so do not attempt to swim in it, even if you are a strong swimmer.

AN OPEN-AIR FURNITURE FACTORY is situated under a grove of cashew trees close to the mercado (market) in Xai-Xai town. The craftsmanship and beautiful, hardwood materials employed make this a place well worth a visit.

Facilities

CLEAN TOILETS can be found at the BP Service Station on your left as you enter the town from the south, at the Fairground and Golfinho Azul.

Shops

VULCANIZADORA EXPRESSO. Diagonally across the road from the BP station is a tyre-repair shop called Vulcanizadora Expresso, where you can get punctures repaired and have your tyres pumped.

CANTINHO DA MODA. Further into Xai-Xai, Cantinho da Moda sells everything from torch batteries and candles to mosquito coils and camera film.

CASA COELHO. For fishing tackle, hardware, vehicle spares, ropes, paint, brooms, padlocks, light bulbs, postcards and electrical wire, amongst other things, try Casa Coelho.

Money matters

THE B.C.M. (Banco Comercial de Moçambique), just off the main road near the city square, will probably give you a better exchange rate than you will be offered on the streets. Don't be put off by queues and crowds, as you will be ushered to the front.

PRAIA DO CHONGOENE

Two hundred and thirty kilometres north of Maputo, this town is reached by turning right off the E.N.1, 13 kilometres after Xai-Xai town, down a sandy road, making a 4x4 vehicle a recommendation. Unless the dilapidated hotel is renovated, you will have to camp and be fully self-sufficient.

CHIDENGUELE

The village of Chidenguele, 58 kilometres north of Xai-Xai, marks the turn-off to Lake Inhampavala, with one of Mozambique's most secluded camp sites on its southern shoreline. Ask for directions to the lake in Chidenguele; bring everything you need (fresh water is available from a spring).

QUISSICO

The next town after Xai-Xai is Quissico, which has a reliable supply of fuel and a clean, basic inn called Pousada de Zavala. This section of the E.N.1 has nasty potholes. The drive through Quissico affords magnificent views of a string of azure freshwater lagoons, 350 kilometres north of Maputo, stretching from Chidenguele in the south to Inharrime in the north. Although many are only a few kilometres from the road, access is difficult and facilities are non-existent.

The beaches and lagoons can be reached by turning right shortly after the town and following the 11-kilometre-long dirt track between the two largest lakes.

A few pot-holes and 44 kilometres north of Quissico you cross Lake Poelela with its turquoise-blue water. The 16-kilometre-wide lake is separated from the sea by a strip of beach dunes; it was probably here that Vasco da Gama first landed on the coast of Mozambique on 10 January 1498. He has often been incorrectly credited with being the first European to come to these shores, but apparently Portuguese explorer Pedro da Covilhã holds this dubious honour. In 1487 Covilhã was sent from Portugal to find a route to India via the Mediterranean, Egypt and Arabia. During his four-year journey he is believed to have reached as far south as Sofala, just south of Beira.

4

Inhambane and surrounds

INHAMBANE

You will know you are nearing Inhambane (the capital city of Inhambane province) when coconut palm trees by the thousand begin to dominate the landscape. Inhambane, 33 kilometres off the E.N.1 (Estrada Nacional 1) on the eastern side of the entrance to a large sheltered bay, is a sleepy, very neat and clean town of perhaps 50 000 inhabitants. The town is served by an airport suitable for jet aircraft and has port facilities capable of handling ships displacing up to 10 000 tons. Hotels, service stations, restaurants, banks, public telephones, cinemas, shops, markets, a bus terminus and an immigration office, where you can get your visa extended, are all to be found in Inhambane.

The dhows, coconut groves, spick and span streets and little Indian stores lend an oriental atmosphere to the town. Inhambane Bay was the southernmost penetration of Arab and Persian traders from around the 10th century until the mid-20th century. Slaves, ivory, gold and other metals from the African interior were exchanged for cloth, salt and beads.

During 1534 the Portuguese established a permanent trading post at Inhambane, making it one of the oldest European settlements in southern Africa. The 200-year-old Cathedral of Our Lady of the Conception, with its towering clock tower, as well as the former Palace of the Governor on the point near the cathedral, are two buildings of particular note.

Orientating yourself

If you arrive on the outskirts of Inhambane by road and carry on straight along the edge of the bay, you will reach the port (marked by tall cranes) where the Catholic cathedral and the jetty are obvious landmarks.

Av. Independência runs to the jetty, and on this wide, tree-lined avenue you will find Inhambane Hotel, Xiphefo Cultural Association, Garagem São Cristovão (vehicle repairs and fuel), a major bank and the municipal offices. On the opposite end of this avenue is a large traffic circle with a park (praça) in its centre, adjacent to which is Inhambane Railway Station.

Three avenues (apart from Independência) lead off this circle; one runs parallel to the railway line; another is Av. Revolução. If you turn right alongside the tracks, you will be heading for the beaches at Tofo, Coconut Bay and Ponta da Barra. In the same direction along Av. Revolução are Restaurante Tic Tic, Indian shops and the Central Market (mercado), next to which is the public transport (machimbombo) terminus.

From Inhambane jetty it is only 3.5 kilometres across the bay to the town of Maxixe (62 kilometres by road). Since Inhambane and Maxixe are important ports for local fishermen, a feature of the bay are the dhows, called ingalão or barcos de vela by the sailors (marinheiros) and fishermen. (pescadores). Ranging from a few metres to over 15 metres, these craft (and their crew) embody a noble tradition of proud self-sufficiency and ancient knowledge of the

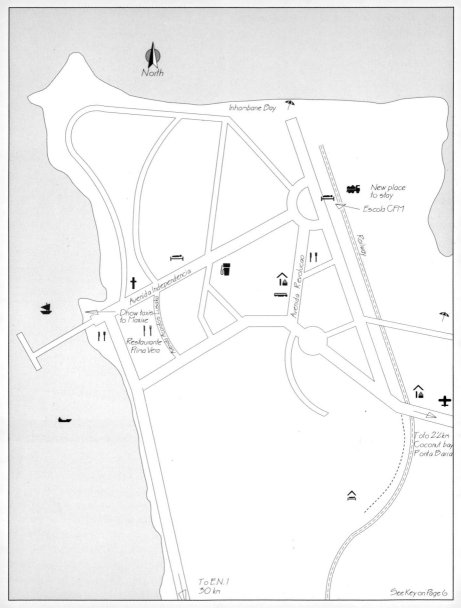

North

Inhambane Bay

New place
to stay

Escola CFM

Railway

Avenida Independencia

Dhow taxis
to Maxixe

Restaurante
Prima Vera

Avenida Revolucao

To F.N. 1
30 km

Tofo 22 km
Coconut bay
Ponta Barra

See Key on Page 6

secrets of the sea, unchanged for thousands of years. The return trip across the bay costs only Mt2 000 and the sailors will insist on carrying you to and from the boat so you won't even have to get your feet wet.

Accommodation

HOTEL INHAMBANE. Av. Independência. Very basic rooms range from Mt150 000 (double). Running water but uncomfortable beds. Lock-up garages. It appears as if no-one has stayed here for years. Tel. (023) 2855.
ESCOLA FERROVIARIO. Next to the station. Rooms for 4 cost Mt180 000. Tel. (023) 2822.

Eating and drinking

RESTAURANTE PRIMA VERA (Marianos Bar). Av. Acordos de Lusaka, close to the jetty. Not to be missed.
RESTAURANTE TIC TIC. 706 Av. Revolução. Best (very cheap) fish and chips in Mozambique.
QUIOSQUE JAMU (eating place and pub). Next to the jetty. Serves snacks. Good sundowner spot.
ENHICA. From November to March this intoxicating local brew is available. Try some!

To see and do

CORRIDA DE BARCOS A VELA. The Inhambane traditional boat race generally takes place every year during November.
GRAFICA SUL DO SAVE. An ancient printing press. next to Marianos Bar, Av. Acordos de Lusaka. A printing shop using 60-year-old presses. Every character is hand fixed on brass blocks and pushed into the manual press.
TOURIST INFORMATION. Palms Bazar near the central market organize beach trips.
OLD CATHEDRAL. Climb up into the bell tower for lovely views.

Addresses and telephone numbers

At the time of writing it was very difficult to call Inhambane from outside, but there is a local exchange in the town.
PUBLIC PHONE. International calls are possible opposite Quiosque Jamu.
TELECOMUNICAÇÕES (public phones). Av. Acordos de Lusaka.
INHAMBANE HOSPITAL. Tel. (023) 2211.
BANCO DE MOÇAMBIQUE. 97 Av. Acordos de Lusaka. Exchange currency here – you won't be able to use a credit card. Tel. (023) 2215.
GARAGEM SÃO CRISTOVÃO. 216 Av. Independência. Fuel and vehicle repair. Tel. (023) 2842.
T.T.A. (Air Charter company). Inhambane Airport. Tel. (023) 2842.
CINE TEATRO TOFO. Rua O.U.A.
TERMINUS (buses and taxis). Av. Revolução next to the Central Market.
MANUEL NUNES (general store). Av. Acordos de Lusaka.
GRAFICA SUL DO SAVE (stationery shop). 24 Av. Acordos de Lusaka. Tel. (023) 2534.
CAJU DE MOÇAMBIQUE (cashew wholesaler). 101 Estrada Nacional. Tel. (023) 2540.

PRAIA DE ZÁVORA

The unmarked turn-off to Závora is 196 kilometres north of Xai-Xai on the E.N.1. The half-hour journey to the modest camp, run by South Africans at present, can be managed by a skilful driver without a 4x4 vehicle. The friendly owner-cum-manager makes sure that his pastoral pub always has some of the coldest beer along the coast. Závora was previously (pre-1975) very popular with visitors from South Africa and (the then) Rhodesia. Fully serviced bungalows and houses for R45 to R60 per day. Comfortable camping sites and a new ablution block with flushing toilets and hot and cold water; R20 per person per day includes access to 220V power points (should you want to use an electric razor or a hair-drier). Meals of your choosing are prepared on request and served under the shade of the coconut-frond bar. Závora boasts excellent sheltered snorkelling and superb all-round fishing. The management does not allow spear-fishing or crayfishing in a designated area. Tel. Johannesburg (011) 455 4046/7.

PRAIA DOS COCOS

The turn-off to Coconut Bay is opposite the fish factory, situated next to the bay on the southern outskirts of Inhambane. The half-hour drive through the coconut planta-tions is difficult to manage without a 4x4 vehicle. The camping site was once an established family tourist resort, as evi-denced by the gutted cottages complete with tile murals of octopus and angelfish overlooking the magnificent bay. A small, hard-working and honest community of fishermen live a little way back from the beach. Along with the local manager and his staff, who are full of good humour, this makes for a secure and relaxing stay.

Cocos is for those who think life is too short to play golf. You will pay R15 for site and security; no facilities apart from a well with dodgy water – bring a can of drinking water or buy bottled water, sodas and beer from the manager. Tel. Senhor Armindo in Maputo (01) 41 5603, fax 40 0471.

PANDANE BEACH

Praia do Pandane (also called Jangamo), about 12 kilometres south of Coconut Bay along a 4x4 track, is an absolute snorkeller's

heaven. Cold showers and a 'long drop' pit toilet for R20 per day. This is perhaps the best inshore coral snorkelling along the entire southern Mozambique coastline.

PRAIA DO TOFO

Chapas to Tofo leave from the Inhambane market (Mt20 000). The last five kilometres of the 22-kilometre road from Inhambane is very pot-holed but negotiable with a two-wheel-drive car. Turn right at the 'circle' 19 kilometres from Inhambane, and you

will soon be at a magnificent beach with spectacular reefs less than 100 metres off-shore. This former holiday village echoes with the ghosts of past raucous big-game fishermen. The hotel has reopened and there is an unofficial camp site with no facilities, where you may be accosted by an official demanding money.

When the wind stops blowing, squadrons of mosquitoes move in. As theft is rife around here, it would be wise to employ a guard when you just have to take to the sizzling surf. Tofo Bay is renowned for its big-game fishing and is also one of the few places along the coast which offers a bit of good surfing.

103

As the sea bed dips steeply away from the land, allowing the formation of large waves and strong currents, Tofo beach can at times be less than ideal for launching ski-boats. Experienced skippers should have few problems and, if the weather does turn nasty once you are out at sea, there is always Inhambane Bay for a safe refuge. Snorkellers and divers should be wary of the waves and currents, and limit their trips to just after low tide. Bathers are warned to swim and surf only directly in front or to the right of the hotel (facing the sea).

Independent travellers can camp under the casuarina trees (remember that these exude and drip a mild gum), but no outdoor facilities whatsoever exist at present. There are no shops at Tofo, but fish can be purchased fresh on the beach at about noon every day, and you can eat at the hotel (reasonable prices) as long as you give the manager or chef a day's advance warning. Also try Alan's Restaurant in the dunes and Clube Ferroviário. Surfing is excellent at Tofinho between Tofo and the monument.

Accommodation

COMPLEXO TURISTICO DO TOFO MAR. The constant, fresh sea breeze keeps away mosquitoes and makes air-conditioning less necessary. There are ten double rooms with private bathroom, hot and cold water. Luxury suites with two beds U.S.$50. Double rooms (facing the ocean) U.S.$45, (facing inland) U.S.$30.

Restaurant (excellent lobster or crayfish), bar and covered outdoor patio area – ideal for sipping cold drinks away from the tropical heat. Tel. Maputo (01) 42 7352 after hours to book.

CLUBE FERROVIARIO. Basic rooms for 3 or 4. Cold water only, cooking facilities. Mt400 000 per room. Tel. C.F.M in Inhambane (023) 2453.

PONTA DA BARRA

Seventeen kilometres from Inhambane, go straight at the junction (a right turn leads to Tofo). The sandy road leads 8 kilometres to the beach where there is a fishing lodge and camp site up the coast to the left.

BARRA LODGE BEACH RESORT. Self-catering cottages, backpacker bunkhouse, camping, beach bar and restaurant. Scuba gear and dive course. Trips to places of interest. Tel. Johannesburg (011) 314 3239.

MAXIXE TOWN

Maxixe (pronounced 'Masheesh') is the only point where the main road (E.N.1) meets the coastline. Consequently Maxixe is a natural stopover if you are heading further north or south, or if you want to get to Inhambane or Linga Linga by boat. The E.N.1 passes between the town and the bay and thus, apart from Campismo Maxixe, all the facilities will be to your left if travelling north, and right if travelling south.

There are three reasonably priced hotels in Maxixe (for the desperate) and an excellently run and equipped camp site next to the jetty where, for Mt1 000, you can take a dhow for 3.5 kilometres to Inhambane.

Maxixe has a good exchange telephone which you can use to call anywhere in the world at Maputo's rates (see page 87).

Accommodation

POUSADA DE MAXIXE (hotel and restaurant). Upstairs double rooms Mt70 000 with bath, downstairs double rooms Mt45 000. There is no running water.

HOTEL GOLFINHO AZUL. Double rooms with bath Mt80 000 to Mt120 000, no running water.

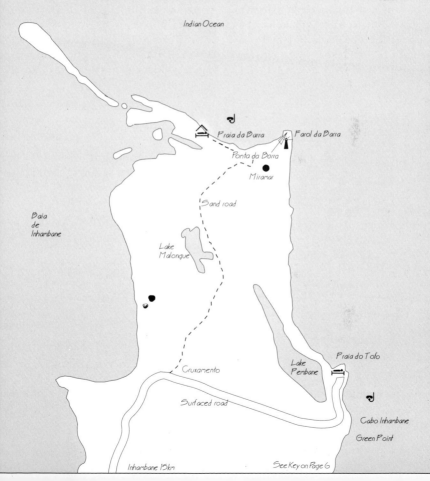

O 1 2 3 4 5km

North

Indian Ocean

Praia da Barra   Farol da Barra

Ponta da Barra

Miramar

Sand road

Baia
de
Inhambane

Lake
Malongue

Praia do Tofo

Cruxamento   Lake
Pembane

Surfaced road

Cabo Inhambane

Green Point

Inhambane 15km   See Key on Page 6

HOTEL PALMAR. Primitive facilities are available at Mt25 000 for a double room.

CAMPISMO DA MAXIXE. Contact Erwin Jakes, P.O. Box 149, Maxixe, tel. (023) 2351. Just 20 metres away from the main road, 200 metres from the jetty, a five-minute walk to Maxixe town. Secure, shady camping sites, bungalows and beach houses. Clean ablutions with hot/cold showers.

Ski-boat permits (required by law) can be arranged and there are launching facilities, and a boat for hire. Tuck-shop and takeaway food (Erwin Jakes, who owns and

Ponta Linga Linga is 12 kilometres by sea north of Maxixe. The boat-sheds and bungalows are due for completion at the end of 1997. Driving to Linga Linga is not practical, but its location adjacent to a deep water channel (two metres deep at low tide) makes it perfect for ski-boats. Hiring a dhow from Maxixe to Linga Linga will cost roughly Mt100 000.

Campismo da Maxixe, with its secure parking, is the base and central reservations office not only for bookings for Linga Linga, but also for trips by boat to Linga Linga. Dugongs are sometimes spotted by snorkellers off Linga Linga.

Eating and drinking

RESTAURANTE DOM CARLOS. One block behind Golfinho Azul. The best restaurant in town.

HOTEL GOLFINHO AZUL. Acceptable food; if you insist it is served hot (quente).

QUIOSQUE O VELEIRO. Pub and take-away on the beach next to the jetty. Watch the dhows over a cold drink at sunset from the quiosque for an elemental experience.

STOP. Next to the main road, overlooking the jetty. Really quaint.

Facilities in Maxixe

MOBIL 24-HOUR SERVICE STATION. Fuel, oils, puncture and basic mechanical repairs. Very limited selection of spare parts available.

MERCADO CENTRAL (Central Market). Turn down the road between the Pousada and the Golfinho Azul.

BOAT LAUNCHING AND FISHING PERMITS. Permits cost Mt72 800 for a two-engine boat (three days); single-engined and sailing boats, Mt36 400. Processing of double-motor permits may be delayed, while those for single-engined craft are issued immediately.

runs Campismo da Maxixe, is a former chef of note). There is safe parking for travellers heading for Linga Linga; overland safari trucks are welcome. Prices: R10 (or Mozambican equivalent) per tent (backpacker size), R50 per caravan site. Double bungalows (en-suite bathroom) available for R110 per day. 2-bed beach houses R80. Breakfast available if ordered the night before. Lockup parking for people taking their own boat to Linga Linga, price negotiable.

PRAIA DE MORRUNGULO

The turn-off on the E.N.1 is 11 kilometres to the north of Massinga and the road is suitable for two-wheel-drive cars.

Accommodation

MORRUNGULO RESORT. The Nelson family own and run this camping site, favoured by the Zimbabwean beach set in school holidays. R30 per day gives access to cold showers, pit latrines, safe drinking water and a secure, clean well-run camp site. Tel. Meridian Travel in Johannesburg (011) 783 7116.
SELF-CATERING CHALETS. 2 furnished bedrooms, well-equipped kitchen, bathroom with hot/cold water. R345 per chalet but prices vary according to season – Christmas and Easter are the most expensive.

Facilities

MORRUNGULO DIVE CENTRE. Comfortable chalets and full diving equipment and facilities. Dives cost R70–R110, depending on where you dive and what gear you hire. Snorkelling trips are also on offer for R25. There are plans for a swimming pool and diving courses to be available in the future. To book for Morrungulo Dive Centre, contact Jacques or Heidi at Marine Safaris in Pretoria, tel. (012) 998 9989. Snorkelling from the shore is only recommended for strong swimmers, as there is not a protected bay.

MASSINGA TOWN

The significance of Massinga will probably only be brought home to you if you damage part of your car somewhere near this sleepy little village. As this section of the E.N.1 has truck-eating pot-holes, you will be glad to learn that there is an excellent workshop that does wonderful welding. The workshop is behind one of the two filling stations; fear not if you have to wait for repairs – right next door is one of Mozambique's finest restaurants (see Eating and drinking below).

Eating and drinking

RESTAURANTE DALILO. One beaming Rashid owns Dalilo and his pub offers 11 different brands of ice-cold imported beer at remarkably reasonable prices. Rashid serves fine soup and a memorable, extremely hot peri-peri chicken. Well worth a visit.

POMENE/PONTA DA BARRA FALSA

Pomene and Ponta da Barra Falsa can be found 52 kilometres from the E.N.1. on a very sandy, almost impassable road (even in a very rugged 4x4). There are plans afoot to rehabilitate this area, but, until the road is repaired, very few will be able to get to Pomene.

This deserted spot (plans for a lodge are on the table) offers excellent fishing and tales to tell of folk catching sailfish off the point 'in the good old days'.

PONTA SAO SEBASTIAO

At the point of an isolated wild peninsula, Ponta Mingo Lodge, accessible only by air or boat, is aimed at game fishermen. Contact Ricky Jacobs, Durban, South Africa, tel. (031) 368 1947, cellphone 082 446 6493.

Central Mozambique

In the central region the Mozambican Plain (Planície Moçambicano) narrows considerably, giving way to the Gorongosa, Chimanimani and Vumba ranges in places. While mangrove swamps still occur sporadically along the coast (as in the southern region), a widening of the continental shelf and the influence of massive deposits of silt at the mouths as well as to the north and south of the Save, Púngoè and Zambezi rivers forms a habitat hostile to the formation of corals. The occurrence of coral reefs decreases considerably, apart from around the Bazaruto Archipelago. Consequently there are no significant coral islands (the Bazaruto Archipelago is sand and rock) off the coast of the central region.

The acacia and mopane savannas which cover the interior of the southern region give way to the temperate miombo woodland and semi-deciduous humid forests of the central region's interior. Coastal vegetation alters from the open broad-leaf dune forests and dense scrub of the south to the extensive alluvial meadows and savannas of the Zambezi, Púngoe and Búzi river valleys and deltas. Mozambique's most extensive remaining mangrove (mangue) swamps occur between Beira and Nova Mambone and in the Quelimane region.

The population density of the central region is higher than the southern, especially in southern Zambezia province. The predominance of the Shangaan (Changana) tribe and language gives way to Shona, Sena and Nyanja, making the cultural diversity in the central region greater than in the south. Following the general trend of the entire east African coastline, the influence of Islam along the shores of Mozambique increases the further north one moves. While Beira may still exhibit a predominantly Christian character with regard to dress and architecture, Quelimane's population has a Muslim appearance and mosques instead of churches and cathedrals begin to dominate the city skyline.

Mozambique's central region is bounded in the south by the Sabi (Save) River and in the north by the Zambezi (Zambeze) River. Machipanda on the border with Zimbabwe and the Zambezi River delta are the western- and easternmost reaches respectively. The provinces of Sofala and Manica comprise the central region which (for the purposes of this guide) includes the towns of Vilankulo, Inhassoro and the Bazaruto Archipelago. The central region's highest point (and indeed that of Mozambique) is Monte Binga (2 436 metres) in the Chimanimani range, while Gorongosa mountain as well as the Goronguè and Choa ranges reach altitudes above 1 800 metres. Sofala province (named after the site of the first fort built by the Portuguese on the southern African coastline) has a largely flat and featureless coastline (apart from sand dunes and extensive mangrove swamps) which is nearly 400 kilometres long. Manica province's boundary with Sofala corresponds vaguely with the 300 metres above sea level contour, making it one of Mozambique's highest and most temperate regions. Apart from the Rio Save in the south and the Rio Zambeze in the north, the central region is bisected by three other significant rivers, namely the Búzi, Púngoè and the Luaua.

The towering granite domes, inselbergs or monte ilhas so characteristic of the landscape of northern Mozambique first make their appearance in Manica and Sofala provinces. These intrusive volcanic formations contrast with the ancient surface lava flows which have formed the hills in the Espungabera region. This unique combination of varying geology, relief, altitude and precipitation have produced a habitat unique to the region with corresponding fauna and flora. In fact, the birds such as the whitebreasted alethe and Gunnings robin, found only in and around Mozambique's lowland forests in the Beira region and northwards, have in the past drawn bird enthusiasts from all over the world.

5

Vilankulo, Inhassoro and Bazaruto Archipelago

VILANKULO

Vilankulo town (formerly Vilanculos) is over 700 kilometres from Maputo, 404 kilometres from Inchope on the E.N.6 (Estrada Nacional) between Chimoio and Beira, and 21 kilometres from the turn-off on the E.N.1. It is well supplied with service stations, markets, Indian shops and a clinic with competent doctors. Electricity is generated by means of natural gas, and telephones are not reliable. A tarmac airstrip allows access by air, and this with the road makes Vilankulo one of the mainland's gateways to the Bazaruto Archipelago. The approach road to Vilankulo meets a circle after a BP Service Centre on the left. A right turn leads to the central market and business centre (one kilometre away). Four kilometres after a left turn you reach the harbour, beach and the Hotel Dona Ana.

Accommodation

HOTEL DONA ANA. Twenty-three comfortable rooms, 33 separate annexes along the beach. The camp site has basic facilities but is due to be upgraded. Restaurant and bar with views across to Magaruque. Secure parking for visitors to the islands. The hotel is in radio contact with the islands and will arrange for you to be picked up if you have a booking at one of the lodges. Day trips to Magaruque cost about Mt20 000 for the dhow. A room at the hotel will cost R50 per person per night (special group rates are available). Overlanders are welcome; it is recommended that you book. Write to C.P. (Caixa Postal) 2, Vilankulo.

CASA DO SENHOR JOSEF. Comfortable reed and thatch house. Two double rooms; you can pitch a hiking tent in the garden. The clean bathroom has running water; meals served by prior arrangement. Mt180 000 per bungalow for three. To get to Senhor Josef, walk two kilometres down the beach road; it is 100 metres past Quiosque Tropical on the right.

SIMBIRE LODGE. Authentic Mozambican fishing village with 2-bed huts and camping. Turn left where the road meets the bay and follow a sandy track for about 2 kilometres.

THE LAST RESORT. On the beach across the bay from the Dona Ana (near Simbire). Reed and thatch huts and camping sites.

Eating and drinking

PEROLA DO MAR and **QUIOSQUE TROPICAL**, on 3 de Fevereiro (the beach road to the right of the hotel). Cool drinks and beer; give them a few hours' warning if you intend eating, or bring along something for them to prepare.

Transport

Buses out of town leave at 7 a.m. daily from a store 500 metres up the road from the Dona Ana. There are regular taxis (chapas) from the same point into town. A 'disco' and traditional market exist close to the hotel.

INHASSORO

Inhassoro is a small, sleepy fishing village 94 kilometres north of Vilankulo and 15 kilometres off the E.N.1 where there is a fuel station. The pumps regularly run dry so don't rely on filling up here. Inhassoro has a camp site, two hotels, bus terminus, a couple of restaurants, general store, market, health post, police station and short grass airstrip, only 100 metres from the village.

Trips from Inhassoro

During the South African school holidays scuba diving, snorkelling, island trips and gamefishing are offered by Hutnic Adventures, based at SETA. Tel. Tzaneen, South Africa (0152) 309 9842.

Accommodation

HOTEL SETA is one of the neatest and most peaceful places to stay in Mozambique. The dining and entertainment complex and pub have been refurbished throughout in hard woods, reed and thatch. Huge mahogany trees provide shade on a patio overlooking the beach, while the camping site is secure and constantly cooled by the sea breeze.

Self-contained two-bed chalets are available for Mt150 000 per night, while campers are charged Mt25 000 per person. Dishes on offer at the restaurant range from Mt35 000 for fresh line-fish to Mt100 000 for prawns.

HOTEL INHASSORO has nice views over the sea to Bazaruto Island, but it is very run-down. At Mt50 000 for a double room, it is still a shoddy second choice to the Seta.

COMPLEXO SALEMA MUFUNDISSE CHIBIQUE (Complexo Inhassoro) – shop, restaurant, lodgings and sometimes fuel. Just after the Seta and just before the beach, turn right into Inhassoro and you will find this establishment (after one kilometre) on your right. The bus terminus is also located here. Tel. Maputo (01) 72 2846.

BAZARUTO ARCHIPELAGO

The islands of (in descending order of size) Bazaruto, Benguerra (Ilha de Santo Antonio), Maqaruque and Santa Carolina

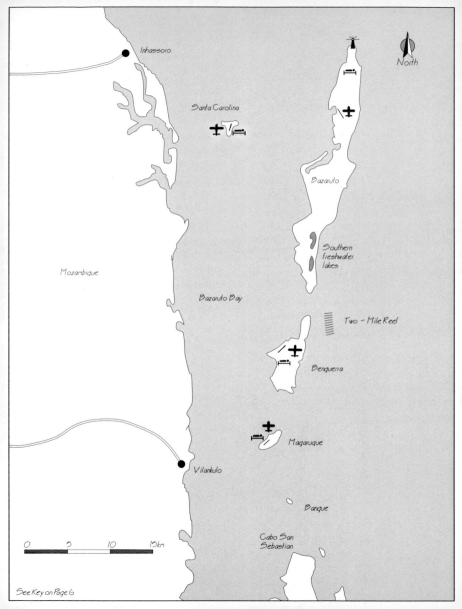

North

Inhassoro

Santa Carolina

Bazaruto

Southern freshwater lakes

Mozambique

Bazaruto Bay

Two – Mile Reef

Benguerra

Vilankulo

Magaruque

Banque

Cabo San Sebastian

0   5   10   15km

See Key on Page 6

(Paradise Island or Ilha do Paraíso), along with a few other tiny rocky outcrops, make up the Bazaruto Archipelago. Declared a national park in 1971, the archipelago boasts among its wildlife 180 species of birds, endemic butterflies, Suni antelope and freshwater crocodile. The protected reefs and beaches support dolphin, dugong, game fish, giant lobster and several species of marine turtle.

Community-orientated conservation projects on Bazaruto are funded by the World Wildlife Fund, the South African Nature Foundation and the Endangered Wildlife Trust. Only people staying at a lodge may overnight on the islands of the Archipelago .

The three larger islands were part of an extensive sand-spit peninsula, once attached to the mainland, but separated as the continent dipped into the Indian Ocean over millions of years. Only Santa Carolina is a true rock island and is consequently surrounded by deeper water than the other three.

All the islands support populations of fishermen and their families, many of whom are not permanent residents and may migrate between the archipelago and the mainland in their pursuit of good fishing waters.

Magaruque and Santa Carolina islands are nearest to the mainland; Magaruque is situated 10 kilometres due east of Vilankulo town, and Santa Carolina a similar distance from the coast. Benguerra and Bazaruto are due north of Magaruque, and the latter 30 kilometres due east of Inhassoro. The eastern seaboard of the islands (apart from Santa Carolina) faces onto the deep waters of the restless Mozambique Channel, rich in game fish. To avoid the occasional high winds and powerful currents, tourist facilities are all located on the landward (lee) side of the islands.

Access

By air

Although all the islands have airstrips, the only tarmac surface is on Magaruque, where aircraft can land, even after heavy rain. Flights to the other islands are sometimes diverted to Magaruque, where transfers by boat are available. All the hotels

and lodges offer fly-in packages, but trips can usually be guaranteed only during the high season (April– December). An alternative is to get a group together and charter a plane from Harare, Johannesburg, Nelspruit or Maputo. (See page 50 for details on charter companies.)

By road/boat

From the south via Maputo and Inhambane, the road to Inhassoro and Vilankulo is in good condition, apart from a few potholes on the 250-kilometre section between Maxixe and the turn-off to Inhassoro. From the north via Chimoio, Inchope and Rio Save the road is in poor condition for 100 kilometres before the Rio Save but passable. Secure parking is available in Inhassoro at the Seta Hotel and in Vilankulo at the Hotel Dona Ana.

Hutnic Adventures at SETA has radio communications between the Archipelago and Inhassoro, and the Hotel Dona Ana in Vilankulo is in radio contact with all the island lodges. You can either arrange with one of the lodges to be collected by speed-boat from the mainland, or hire a dhow if you don't mind the exposure to the sun, discomfort, (small) danger of sinking and have plenty of time – there may be delays due to unsuitable winds or no wind at all.

ILHA DO BAZARUTO

The island has an 800-metre-long grass airstrip (being upgraded) which may be unusable just after the rare thunderstorms in the area. In this event, guests are transferred by boat from Magaruque which has a paved strip. The lodge is about one kilometre from the landing strip close to the north-western point of the island, a pleasant ride in an open Land Rover. Unless you arrive at high tide, your boat will only be able to beach some distance from the lodge and thus a transfer by vehicle will be necessary.

Accommodation

BAZARUTO LODGE overlooks a small coral-fringed, palm-lined bay across which Santa Carolina is a small dot and the mainland a shimmering blur. The neatly thatched, luxuriously appointed A-frame chalets fit in unobtrusively against forest-covered sand dunes with a 100-year-old lighthouse perched on top. Contact Pestana Hotels and Resorts, tel,. Johannesburg (0110 368 1947.

Built by the Portuguese, the Farol do Bazaruto last flashed its beam out to sailors at sea more than a decade ago. Its rehabilitation has formed part of the development plans for tourism on the island.

While the individual chalets on Bazaruto are spread out along the beach for privacy, a central complex next to a swimming pool contains a bar, games-room, lounge, dining hall (which serves excellent food) and conference room. The cross bar, on which catches of the day can be hung up to be weighed and photographed, was a central feature of the Bazaruto experience in days gone by, but today's more environmentally conscious fisherfolk generally tag their trophies and release them back into the depths alive and kicking.

Conservation of the environment, particularly marine life, is always uppermost in the minds of the management, a fact that is reinforced during an introductory talk and slide show on the corals presented by the resident dive msaster.

During recent times, Bazaruto has attracted increasing numbers of salt-water fly-fishermen, while the island boasts an endemic species of butterfly which has led to scenes of grown people rushing about with flimsy nets. Of further interest to ecologists are the freshwater lakes which are populated by crocodiles, attesting to the fact that the island separated from the mainland no more than a few thousand years ago.

Prices range upwards from U.S.$120 per person per day. Scuba and fishing gear can be hired at extra cost, as well as boat and Land Rover trips. Contact Mozambique Island Tours in Johannesburg. Tel. (011) 447 3528, fax 880 5364. Alternatively contact Pestana (Hotel Rovuma) in Maputo tel. (01) 42 0525, fax 42 0524.

ILHA DE BENGUERRA

Benguerra Island, although only about a quarter of the size of Bazaruto, is structurally very similar.

Accommodation

BENGUELA ISLAND LODGE consists of a central dining and socializing area and 13 thatched bungalows, tucked away underneath the trees of a natural indigenous forest. The lodge is famous for its cuisine of fresh tropical fruits, seafood buffets and traditional Mozambican dishes. A full range of saltwater sports are on offer and day trips by motorboat to scenic Vilankulo town on the mainland can be arranged. The price of U.S.$100 per person per night includes full board and 23% tax. Hire of scuba gear and ski-boats is at extra charge. A fully equipped six-berth dive catamaran is also available for charter.

Contact Benguela Island Holidays either in Johannesburg, at tel. (011) 483 2734/5, fax 728 3767, or in Maputo, at tel./fax (01) 32846.

ILHA DE MAGARUQUE

Accommodation

In keeping with its postage-stamp size, the ambience on the island is relaxed and intimate. Magaruque has the advantages of a tarred airstrip, superb snorkelling/scuba diving on a reef a few metres from the front of the hotel, and ease of access from the mainland. Transfers to and from Vilankulo will set you back only U.S. $50 for the boat, which can take six persons with their luggage. Alternatively, there are always dhow rides for the adventurous. A leisurely walk around the coast of the island will take three hours.

The price for a double room in high season is U.S.$110 per person per day, and U.S.$88 in low season. A beach bungalow costs U.S.$88 in high season, and U.S.$72 in low season. Contact Barracuda Safaris, Harare, Zimbabwe. Tel. (09263 4) 79 6411, Fax (2634) 70 6148. Alternatively, book through PROSOL, tel. (01) 2 9606/3 4096 or SABINAIR, tel. (01) 46 5108, both in Maputo.

ILHA SANTA CAROLINA

Also known as Paradise Island and sometimes referred to as the 'Pearl of the Indian Ocean', this charming piece of rock is a mere three kilometres long and 500 metres wide. The airstrip and hotel have been renovated and fly-in packages are available.

Full water-sport and scuba facilities take advantage of the calm seas and unspoilt reefs which surround the island. Contact Maccon International in Johannesburg. Tel. (011) 447 3216.

6

Beira and surrounds

BEIRA

Beira is an important port city at the mouth of the Púngoè River. It lies about halfway up the Mozambican coastline. The distance by road from Harare is 600 kilometres and from Johannesburg (via Komatipoort/Ressano Garcia and Maputo 1 800 kilometres).

Anyone entering this area by road should be equipped for all eventualities. Apart from the E.N.1, roads between Inhassoro and Beira are in very poor condition and impassable after rain due to mud and damaged bridges. There are presently no facilities and the ferries which cross the mouth of the Save and Buzi rivers are not operational.

Stone from the ruins of the fort at Sofala (the first European-built structure in southern Africa, constructed in 1501) have been used to build a cathedral in Beira.

Getting to Beira

HITCHHIKING. The busiest road to Beira is from Mutare in Zimbabwe. Your best bet may be Zimbabwe-registered pick-ups and minibuses. Approach the drivers at the border post or hitch with an up and down motion of the open hand, which is used to flag down drivers in Mozambique.

TAXIS. The Mutare/Beira taxis (chapas) are often yellow Peugeot minibuses or Toyotas.

PRIVATE CARS. Some roads in Mozambique had little maintenance during the civil war. The Mutare/Beira road is good tarmac, and others are being upgraded. Important

bridges have been destroyed and it may be prudent to plan trips north of Beira in the dry season (May–November), even in a 4x4.

BOAT AND SHIP. Try hitching lifts on private sailing boats at the Mombasa, Dar es Salaam, Richards Bay and Durban yacht clubs. Passenger ships arrive irregularly at Mozambique's ports. Most are cruise ships, making this route potentially very expensive. If you are stuck in an East Africa's port, look out for *Dimini* II and III, *Polana*, *Lugenda*, *Afriquia* and any Transmaritima de Sofala boats.

TRAIN. Trains run at present from Harare to Mutare, and Mutare to Beira. The schedule is erratic between the border and Beira, and it may be better to use a chapa. Beira station's telephone number is (03) 32 1051.

Accommodation

Don't always be put off by appearances. Some decent hotels in Beira look awful but are acceptable once inside.

HOTEL EMBAIXADOR. Rua Major Serpa Pinto. Booking essential. Double from U.S.$40 to U.S.$60. Tel. (03) 32 3121/3, fax 32 3785.

HOTEL MIRAMAR RESTAURANTE E ALOJAMENTO. 157 Rua Vila Boas Truão, on the beachfront, lock-up parking, air-conditioning. U.S.$20 double per night. Tel. (03) 32 2283.

HOTEL RESIDENCIAL DO INFANTE. 218 Rua Jaime Ferreira. Mt200 000 per double room. Tel. (03) 32 3042.

HOTEL MOÇAMBIQUE. 3 Rua Bagamoyo. U.S.$65, double with private bath. Satellite TV. Tel. (03) 32 5175.

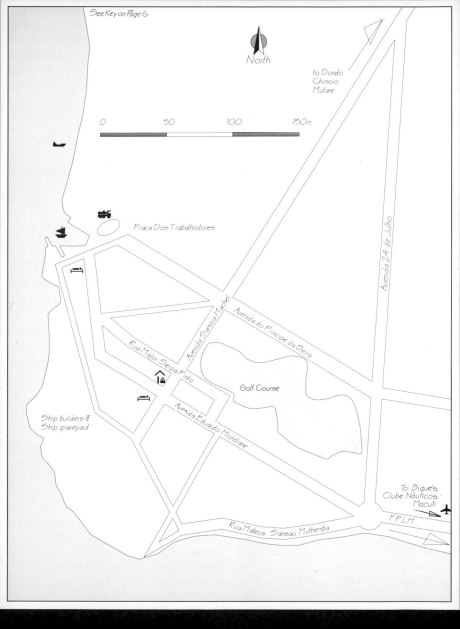

Beira

HOTEL SAVOY. 297 Rua Pedro Alvares Cabral. Mt120 000 per double – clean rooms, dodgy toilets. Tel. (03) 32 6855.

HOTEL BEIRA. 92 Rua Luís Inácio. Mt150 000 double. Recently renovated. Tel. (03) 32 3045.

Inns (pensões)

PENSÃO SOFALA. 544 Av. Bagamoyo, opposite Take-Away 2+1. Tel. (03) 32 2375.

PENSÃO BEIRENSE. 65 Rua Luís Inácio. Filthy, but cheap at Mt80 000 per double room. Tel. (03) 32 5089.

Backpackers, campers, etc.

BIQUE'S (Beeky's). Catch the Estoril chapa to Beeky's, 10 kilometres north on the Av. das FPLM, halfway between Clube Náuticos and the lighthouse. Chalets being built; excellent pub/restaurant. Camp site and space for overland trucks. Look after your belongings. Tel. (03) 31 2853.

CLUBE NAUTICO. This is primarily a restaurant club with a pool, but the management does allow camping on a sandy, windswept spot. The toilets and showers (cold water only) are clean. Petty theft is common at night. Tel. (03) 31 3093.

Eating and drinking

CLUBE NAUTICO (Restaurante O Zequinhas). On Av. das FPLM. Excellent seafood and other Portuguese food. Tel. (03) 31 3093.

RESTAURANTE DOS C.F.M.-C. Inside the railway station off Praça dos Trabalhadores. Bewildering array of Mozambican and Portuguese dishes. Tel. (03) 32 8280.

MIRAMAR. Rua Mateus Sansão Muthemba (near the Oceana). The chicken peri-peri at Miramar is strongly recommended. As at the Náutico, there is a good view of the beach from the restaurant.

TAKE-AWAY 2+1. One of the best in the city. A good place to have lunch. Reservations are recommended. Tel. (03) 32 9883.

RESTAURANTE CLUBE DO GOLFE. At the golf course. Very popular. Don't miss 'Mozambique Night' every Thursday. Tel. (03) 32 9533.

MINERVA. Near the small boat harbour (Mananga) and **ARCADIA (JOHNY'S PLACE)**, 2000 Rua Poder Popular. For a taste of real Portuguese cuisine.

ALI BABA'S, near the black market (marquinino) and **PIC–NIC**, 115 Rua Costa Serra. Both places have central air-conditioning and a romantic atmosphere.

CENTRO HIPICO, on the Dondo road next to the airport flyover. Watch horses being trained while you are eating your meal.

Buying food

Food and other items purchased at the informal open-air markets will be cheap (as long as you are a decent bargainer). Supermarkets are expensive and thus it may be advisable to bring the basics (such as powdered milk) along with you.

A colourful variety of fresh fish, fruit and vegetables is available from the central produce market (Mercado Central) near the square (Praça do Município). Many Portuguese bakeries operate, while South African produce is available everywhere. Fresh milk is sold near the market (boil before use).

Get your prawns (camarão) for around U.S.$2 per kilo from the fishermen on the beach north of the lighthouse (farol). Bring your own scale as theirs over-read drastically.

Cashew nuts (castanhas de caju), as well as car batteries, can be bought at Organizacões Palmeiras opposite the military barracks on Av. Eduardo Mondlane off Praça do Município.

Yoghurt can be bought at the Take-Away 2+1 near the taxi rank. Buns and delicious coconut tarts are available at the Riviera Café on the square.

Nightlife and entertainment

CLUBE OCEANA. Sophisticated yet relaxed Latin American atmosphere. Gets going after 11 p.m.

CENTRO HIPICO. Situated just off the E.N.6 (to Dondo) on the airport road. Fridays and Saturdays. This is where Beira's beautiful people meet to dine, dance and swim in the pool.

GRUTA CEM HORAS. Hotel Moçambique. For the adventurous – watch out for people slipping something into your drink.

CLUBE DO GOLFE. Best-known Beira disco on Friday and Saturday nights.

Cinemas

There are many cinemas in Beira, three of which operate regularly:

NOVOCINE. Violent American action movies.

NACIONAL. Movies in Portuguese.

OLYMPIA. Chinese kung fu.

Avoid ...

MILITARY AREAS. Beaches five kilometres north and just south of Beira are controlled by the military. Do not bring your camera to these areas!

PROSTITUTES. Many attractive, well-dressed Beira women (red hair dye is popular) are prostitutes who may mistake male tourists for sailors.

BEIRA BEACHES. Those close to the Púngoe River mouth are not safe after dark.

LEAVING YOUR CAR UNATTENDED. Lenses, side mirror, hubcaps, windscreen, etc. are removed in seconds.

Things to see

GRAND HOTEL. The ruins of the (once) Grand Hotel near the mouth of the Púngoe River.

Note the trees growing from balconies and the goats in the lobby.

THE CITY SQUARE (Praça do Município) is surrounded by colonial architecture, curiosity shops, tea rooms (salões de chá) and government buildings. This is a good spot to orientate yourself and to meet the Beira 'tourist guides' and confidence tricksters.

THE MARBLE MUNICIPALITY BUILDING on the south-east side of the municipal square which has a tile mural of the historical Sofala castle in its entrance hall.

THE CASTLE-LIKE JAIL on the northern side of the square.

THE HUGE CHAOTIC INFORMAL BLACK MARKET (T'Shungamoyo) near the golf course, where almost anything (mostly stolen) is available.

THE LIGHTHOUSE (farol) and the shipwrecked *Macuti*, north along the beach road (Av. das FPLM) nine kilometres from Beira centre.

THE PALM-LINED BEACH north of the lighthouse, where the fishermen bring in their catches.

THE SHIP-GRAVEYARD is situated to the south of the city on the muddy banks of the Púngoe River.

THE MAIN HARBOUR close to the main railway station (comboio). Obtain permission at the gate first.

SAVANE (Rio Maria) is 20 kilometres north of Beira; 4x4 vehicle recommended.

Curios

Look around for the intricate, bizarre 'torture art' that is produced by local painters and carvers belonging to the Makonde tribe in the north.

Rhino horn, ivory and animal skins will be offered to you on the street.

MAKONDE CARVINGS. There is a co-operative next to the Swedish housing block on the Av. das FPLM. The prices are high as the carvers sell most of their work to well-paid aid workers.

TAM TAM. On Praça do Município.

COROAS DE MOÇAMBIQUE near Scala Café.

Things to do

BOAT/SHIP RIDES. Enquire at the small boat harbour (Mananga port) or phone Port Control at (03) 7 8264 and ask for Feliciano. Trips by trawler to the southern islands (Santa Carolina/Paradise and Bazaruto) are common. The northern coast islands (Mozambique Island and Archipelago das Querimbas) are less visited but well worth the wait for a boat, if you have time.

EXCURSIONS TO GORONGOSA NATIONAL PARK. Take a self-drive day trip (if you have a 4x4), or contact Safrique, tel. (03) 32 3686.

GOLF. Founded in 1907, the 18-hole course has clubs available for hire. Tel. (03) 32 9533.

Medical help

Conditions at the Beira Central Hospital are far from ideal. If you need urgent medical attention, contact the International Red Cross who may fly you to Johannesburg. There is a clinic operated by foreign doctors between the Hellenic Community Church and the Hospital Ponte Gea. Some pharmacies sell prescription drugs over the counter, while homeopathic and herbal remedies are available from Lopes e Ramos Ervanaria, near the Scala Café (salão de chá).

Media

Beira's newspaper is Diário de Moçambique.

Facilities

Beira toilets are generally disgusting. However, these places usually have clean toilets: **BIQUE'S** (Beeky's). Macuti beach near the lighthouse. Beeky's boats the most beautiful toilets in Africa!

PISCINA (swimming pool). Opposite Hotel Moçambique.

JOHNY'S RESTAURANT (Arcadia) is situated near the small boat harbour.

FATIMAR QUIOSQUE is located on the beach in front of the Beira Corridor Group's compound.

MONACO RESTAURANT. Rua da Madeira.

CLUBE NAUTICO DA BEIRA. Situated on Macuti beach near the Central Hospital.

Visa extensions

For U.S.$15 you can extend your visa at 209 Rua Artur Canto, which is opposite Infogest LDA.

Telephones

Mozambique has a satellite telecommunications network. Go to the green and white telegraphic office (telecomunicações) north-west of the square (Praça do Município). The operators here usually speak English.

Money changing

Bank and black market rates are similar. However, as changing money at a bank is a laborious process, it may be more convenient to use the semi-official money changer at Dragão shop, facing away from the square to the south.

Apart from U.S. dollars, South African rands and Zimbabwe dollars are in demand in Beira. Note that transactions in pounds sterling attract an automatic £20 commission. Be very wary of changing money on the street, where the rate of exchange will be lower than what you will get from the banks or semi-official changers.

Useful addresses & telephone numbers

BEIRA CITY COUNCIL. João Zandamela. Tel. (03) 32 2125/32 4123 (w), 32 2422 (h).

BEIRA AIRPORT. Tel. (03) 30 1071.

HERTZ CAR HIRE. Av. Armando Tivane. Tel. (03) 32 2315, fax 32 2415.

AVIS CAR HIRE. At Beira Airport. Tel. (03) 30 1263, fax 30 1265.

MARINERS. Ask Bonny about Gorongosa and the Caia ferry. Tel. (03) 32 9071.

CAMINHO DE FERRO DE MOÇAMBIQUE (C.F.M.). Mozambique Railways. Tel. (03) 32 1051.

GORONGOSA NATIONAL PARK

This former showpiece of colonial Mozambique's conservation effort, one of the sad casualties of past conflict, is being rehabilitated. An aerial survey made by the authorities during 1996 indicated that, though the wildlife has been decimated by hungry rebels and soldiers, all previously occurring wildlife is still found, albeit in very small numbers. The rehabilitation of Gorongosa (Parque Nacional de Gorongosa) has been initiated using a grant from the International Monetary Fund (I.M.F.).

The task of rehabilitating Gorongosa is one of the many challenges for the new government. Don't expect to see much game (except for elephant), but it is still interesting to drive through the reserve by turning right at Nota, 22 kilometres before Gorongosa town. Carry on down the 100-kilometre scenic track through Chitengo Camp to Muanza on the Beira–Inhaminga road. Initially Gorgongosa will remain open only to special interest groups, such as ornithologists and botanists. For the latest information on the park contact (011) 726 6467 in Johannesburg. Mount Gorongosa is outside the park, to the north-west.

7

Manica Province

Along with the provinces of Tete and Niassa, Manica is one of Mozambique's landlocked provinces. Its border with Zimbabwe to the west corresponds with a range of high mountains called the Planalto de Chimoio consisting of Mount Binga which, at 2 436 metres, is the highest point in Mozambique, the Choa Range and Mount Goronguè (1 887 metres). The Gorongosa Range rises on Manica's eastern border with Sofala, and the combination of high- and lowland vegetation, as well as tropical latitudes, make the unpopulated

areas of Manica province an ideal habitat for upwards of 500 different bird species, many endemic to the area.

Most of Manica is covered by miombo woodland, while there are herbaceous zones on the mountains. Nearly 90% of the province's population are engaged in subsistence agriculture, with some small-scale open-pit gold mining and commercial forestry. Chimoio town is strategically located on the important trade, rail and fuel pipeline corridor between Beira harbour and Zimbabwe. With an estimated population of 80 000, Chimoio is Mozambique's fifth largest town and is an important commercial centre. Manica province was in the past one of Mozambique's principal citrus-producing areas.

Three major rivers form the northern and southern boundaries of the province, namely the Luenha and Zambezi to the north and the Sabi to the south. In addition the province is crossed by the Búzi, Revúè (with its Chicamba Real dam) and Púngoè rivers. Two border posts allow access from Zimbabwe, one at Mutare/Machipanda and the other at Mount Selinda/Espungabera. Both are open from 6 a.m. to 6 p.m., with Espungabera being a quieter, cheaper and more scenic entry point into Mozambique.

The road from Espungabera to the E.N.1 (Estrada Nacional or National Road) via Gogói and Dombe traverses stunning highlands and deciduous forests. A four-wheel-drive vehicle is a recommendation during the wet season (October to March).

Manica town, between Machipanda and Chimoio, is a busy coffee-growing centre and is worth a stopover to buy fresh coffee beans (change money at the bank or the open-air market), and to look at the chaotic open-pit gold mines (ask for the minas do ouro). A track leads from Manica to a mineral water (Água Vumba) bottling plant from where you can walk into the scenic Vumba hills (there are no pathways yet).

CHIMOIO

While Chimoio, the capital city of Manica province, may not be of specific importance to tourists and travellers, it is situated on the busiest road route in Mozambique.

It is a logical stopover for people who enter the country late in the afternoon, as well as being suitable as a base for visits to the Chimoio highlands (50 kilometres away), the Chicamba Real Dam (60 kilometres away) and the Gorongosa area (120 kilometres away).

Due to its altitude above sea level, Chimoio experiences mild winters and warm summers, enjoying temperatures that rarely drop below 20 °C or rise above 30° C.

December and January are the wettest months, during each of which Chimoio receives approximately 200 mm of rain. Chimoio is 100 kilometres from the Machipanda frontier with Zimbabwe, and 200 kilometres from the important Indian Ocean port city of Beira.

Note that, in central Mozambique, Zimbabwe dollars are the preferred currency, with South African rands following closely behind. The once flourishing black market has virtually disappeared, although you might still find the informal (quasi-legal) money changers convenient, as bank bureacracy and queues can be rather daunting.

Accommodation

MOTEL MOINHO, named after a mill-shaped building, is situated on the outskirts of Chimoio on the Beira side.

If you are coming from Machipanda on the E.N.6, carry on around the circle which marks the beginning of Chimoio, and follow the signs to Beira on the right. This road skirts the town and, to reach the motel, take left turn shortly after a turn-off to Chimoio, which is down a 500-metre-long tree-lined road.

Accommodation costing Mt120 000 for a double room and Mt200 000 for a suite is clean and comfortable. The restaurant serves wholesome meals, but it is advisable to give the chef plenty of notice. This is a good place for a break if you are on your way to Beira in the afternoon and want to avoid driving at night.

HOTEL CHIMOIO. Located on the same avenue as (and between) the white high-rise government building and the post office. Double rooms without running water cost Mt85 000.

Eating and drinking

BAZAR. Mercado Municipal. Open-air market that is situated close to the high-rise apartments which stick out like an oil rig in the Sahara Desert.

Put on your bargaining cap and you will be able to eat well for Mt15 000.

CHAPACEM BAZAAR. Opposite the Railway Station and the taxi (chapacem, pronounced 'shaapa-sem') rank. Get your live chickens here.

LE CLUBE SPORT on Av. 25 de Setembro next to the soccer stadium (where concerts take place over the weekend). Reputedly the best restaurant in Chimoio (reasonably priced too).

RESTAURANTE BAR CHICATECO. Two kilometres before you reach Chimoio from the Zimbabwe side, there is a signposted turn-off to the right down a sand track. Five hundred metres along this sand track is a clean and cool restaurant and pub, which serves excellent food at around Mt60 000 per meal.

PADARIA (BAKERY). Fresh bread and rolls are sold here every day. On the left-hand side of Av. 25 de Setembro just before you reach the road that leads over the railway line back to the Beira road.

RESTAURANTE KANIMAMBO. Situated at the railway station; turn right and follow the street parallel to the tracks. Turn left after two blocks.

CAFÉ CHIMOIO and **CONCORD CAFÉ.** Alongside and opposite the Montalto Movie Theatre where one of America's unsung exports – violent films – are on show.

Other important places in Chimoio

SERVICE STATIONS (GARAGEMS). Three are operational. One is on the left just before the circle as you enter Chimoio on the Zimbabwe side, the second is in town on the road which crosses the railway tracks and the third on the right as you bypass Chimoio on the E.N. 6.

PROVINCIAL HOSPITAL which has trained foreign doctors on its staff and facilities for malaria testing.

VEHICLE ENGINE AND TYRE REPAIRS are undertaken in makeshift workshops on opposite sides of the E.N.6.

VEHICLE SPARES AND ACCESSORIES are obtainable (but expensive) at Casa R.E.C.H.I. – the fanciest shop (loja) in town.

VARIOUS BANKS are located on Av. 25 de Setembro, where you can change money. There is also an unofficial money changer operating next to the chapacem depot, but be careful!

POST OFFICE AND TELECOMUNICAÇÕES. Just off the Central Square, these public telephones allow you to get in touch with anywhere in the world.

L.A.M. (Linhas Aéreas de Moçambique), the domestic airline, has an office on the left, just up the road from the level crossing.

LIBRARY & MUSEUM. Opposite soccer stadium.

IMIGRAÇÃO, where you can extend your visa for a month at a time, is located in the neighbourhood of the Conselho Executivo and the Topocadastro (Map Office).

CABEÇA DE VELHO (OLD MAN'S HEAD). Two kilometres out of Chimoio, this outcrop is visible from the Central Square. The bald granite rock formation, hundreds of metres high, commands panoramic views and should be climbed if at all possible.

CHICAMBA REAL DAM

Coming from Zimbabwe, pass through Manica town. After 17 kilometres you will encounter a stone wall with 'Casa Msika' embedded in it.

This wall indicates the turn-off to the resort. Turn right onto a good gravel road leading a further eight kilometres to the site, which is almost an island when the dam is full. Chicamba Real Dam is fast gaining a reputation as an excellent bass and bream fishing spot.

To reach Chicamba village and the dam wall, turn right one kilometre after the hamlet of Bandula which is 54 kilometres from Machipanda. The road to the village is in a fair condition.

After eight kilometres either turn right up to Chicamba, perched high on a hill overlooking the dam, or carry on straight and cross the Revué River on a bridge just below the dam wall. About 500 metres from the bridge, you will come to a steel container (the sort of thing normally seen piled on container ships) next to the water.

This container houses a small shop and bar and bears the legend 'Protector de Pesca em Chicamba' inscribed upon it, which means 'Protector (self-proclaimed) of the fish in Chicamba'. Cold beer and cool drinks are available here, as well as rice, bread, candles, tinned food and other

staples. Just after this kiosk you will see a shady parking area with a grass hut next to it for the guard.

Fortunately for those who don't lug a boat about wherever they go, one might be available just below the parking area for the price of the petrol you use, which amounts to about a tankful or 20 litres. The lake water is drinkable after boiling.

Accommodation

CASA MSIKA, Lake Chicamba. This quiet lodge has a central complex with bar, restaurant and swimming pool. Six-bed chalets with bedding, toilet and shower en suite. Electricity for lighting and fridges is supplied by generator. About R240 or Z$500 per six-bed chalet.

A comfortable camping site is available. Tel. Chimoio (051) 2 2675, fax 2 2701.

The manager, Peter Thornicroft, also runs a crocodile farm which used to supply meat to the Frelimo soldiers. His land-mine logic can be summarized as follows: The places most likely to have been mined are basically anywhere that traffic is forced to slow down or stop – possible ambush points – for example, sharp bends, intersections, bridges and cuttings.

MOUNT BINGA

At 2 436 metres, Mount Binga is Mozambique's highest peak and is part of the Chimanimani mountain range.

Binga is best approached from the Zimbabwe side via the Chimanimani National Park, which will cost you Z$100 for a week's permit with free camping in the wilderness area.

From the Mozambique side, get to Chimoio and ask for the Sussundenga or Rotunda road, which is suitable only for four-wheel-drive vehicles. Once you have travelled 70 kilometres from Chimoio, start asking for directions to Monte Binga or get to Rotunda and plan your trip from there. This route is for experienced, adventurous mountain walkers only, as there are no formal pathways or route markers.

8

Quelimane and surrounds

QUELIMANE

The capital city of Zambezia province, Quelimane (pronounced 'Kilimani'), is an important river port with a population of approximately 250 000. Situated on the Rio dos Bons Sinais, which is tidal and navigable for more than 50 kilometres upstream, Quelimane lies only a few metres above sea level amongst vast mangrove swamps, allowing little relief from the intense, humid heat.

Despite its strategic location halfway up the coast of Mozambique, Quelimane has remained cut off from the rest of the country, due to the barrier formed by the Zambezi river 120 kilometres to the south, as well as the lack of good roads and a rail linkage to other centres.

Prior to the civil war in Mozambique, Quelimane was the point of export for the extensive cashew nut, coconut, citrus, tea and sugar plantations which represent the main economic potential in Zambezia Province. Today this port remains a busy business hub with a regional airport, comfortable hotels, reasonable restaurants, well-stocked supermarkets, friendly people and millions of coconut palms.

With the advent of the exploitation of the region's rich resources of titanium, asbestos, granite and precious stones, as well as the upgrading of the road link south to Beira, Quelimane's importance is sure to be boosted. The area experiences up to 1 800 mm of rain annually, 70% of which falls from December to April.

Temperatures reach the mid-40s (Celsius) from October to December and seldom drop below the 20s from May to July. Humidity is high throughout the year due to the inland location – especially so during the wet months.

Zambezia has the highest population of all of Mozambique's ten provinces, and over 90% of the labour force is active in the subsistence agricultural sector.

Due to the variations in its elevation, ranging from sea level to nearly 2 500 metres above sea level, Zambezia province has great natural scenic beauty, with landscapes ranging from mountains and gorges to thorn-tree savanna and mangrove swamps. Bird-watching conditions are consequently similar to those in the Gorongosa area.

Significant hot springs are to be found at Lugela, Mocuba and Gilé (which were mined during the civil war), while the 2 419-metre-high Mount Nimule (the second highest point in Mozambique), east of Gurué, contains fascinating caves used for mysterious rituals.

The crocodile-infested Chire and Zambezi rivers form the western boundary of Zambezia Province.

There is still a fair amount of big game present in the swamp region of the Zambezi Delta between the villages of Luabo and Micaune.

Zambezia's coastline is rich in fish, prawns, lobster and coral, with the islands of Silva, Fogo, Coroa, Casuarina and Epidendron being especially good diving and snorkelling areas.

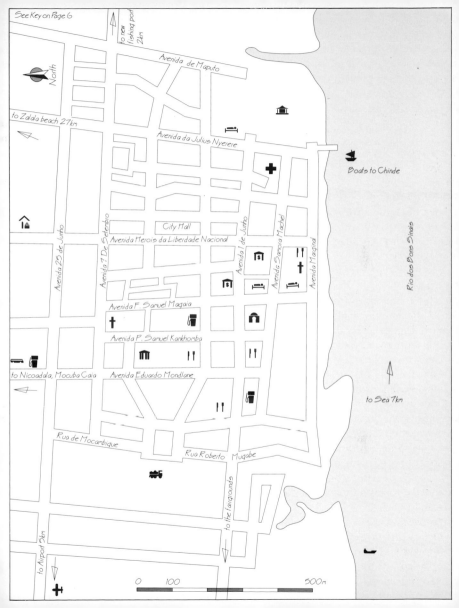

See Key on Page 6

North

to new fishing port 2km

Avenida de Maputo

Avenida da Julius Nyerere

to Zalala beach 27km

Boats to Chinde

Rio dos Bons Sinais

City Hall

Avenida Heróis da Liberdade Nacional

Avenida 25 de Junho

Avenida 1 De Setembro

Avenida 1 de Junho

Avenida Samora Machel

Avenida Marginal

Avenida F. Samuel Magaia

Avenida P. Samuel Kankhomba

to Nicoadala, Mocuba Caia

Avenida Eduardo Mondlane

to Sea 7km

Rua de Moçambique

Rua Roberto Mugabe

to the Fairgrounds

to Airport 5km

0   100   500m

A mineral exploration company called Modrill is based at Moebase on the mainland adjacent to these islands. You may be able to arrange a lift to the area on a Modrill truck if one of their representatives happens to be in Quelimane at the time (try at the Hotel Zambeze). Ask for Julio Pinho de Sousa or Herbie Carlson.

Getting to Quelimane

By air
L.A.M. (Linhas Aéreas de Moçambique) offers a domestic service from Nampula and Maputo to Quelimane. Phone L.A.M. in Maputo at (01) 46 5810 or Johannesburg (011) 331 6081.

By road
Overland travellers from the north can enter Mozambique only from Malawi, as there is at present no bridge or ferry over the Rio Rovuma, which forms the boundary between Tanzania and Malawi. Rumour has it that you may be able to cross the Rio Rovuma near Negomano at the height of the dry season (tempo da seca). Visas are available from the Mozambique offices in Lilongwe and Blantyre; a photocopy of the first two pages of your passport and two passport photographs are required. Visas are usually valid for 30 days, and can be extended. Processing visa applications may take up to a week.

The two main road routes from Malawi to Zambezia province are via the Namwera/Mandimba and Mulanje/Milange frontier posts. At present the route of choice may be via the Namwera/Mandimba border post; follow the railway line to Cuamba and Mutuáli where you turn right to Gurúè; follow the road south to Errego, Mocuba, Namacurra, and then turn left at Nicoadala for the 30-kilometre stretch to Quelimane.

The Mulanje/Milange option is the most direct. The road has been cleared of mines, but don't walk in the bush on the side of the road. This route may be impassable during the rainy season but is being upgraded and will be the route of choice in future.

Crossing the Zambezi
From the south the road is open, as there is now an operational ferry over the Zambezi River, and bridges in the area have been repaired.

Up until 1996 the only road bridge over the Zambezi in Mozambique was at Tete. However, the reconstruction of the Sena

rail bridge and its adaptation for road traffic has been completed. Approach roads on either side of the river are being upgraded. Transportes Cocorico run 4x4 passenger vehicles between Beira and Quelimane. Contact Senhor Brandão at Pensão Moderna, Beira. Tel. (03) 30 1174.

Options for backpackers

Those travellers who are cycling, relying on public transport or hitching to make their way through Africa may decide to attempt one of the following ways of entering Mozambique at places that are not open to vehicles:

From Malawi, get your Mozambique visa in Blantyre or Lilongwe and take the ferry from Nkata Bay, Nkhotakhota or Monkey Bay on the shores of Lake Malawi, to the Likoma Islands, a Malawian enclave inside Mozambican territory, five kilometres from the Mozambique shoreline.

From Likoma Islands, arrange a ride on one of the dhows (ingalão) or dugouts (kanoa) to Cóbuè on the lakeshore and from there make your way along the coast to Metangula. After Metangula you should hitch as far as Lichinga, which is the capital of Niassa province, to get your passport stamped at Imigração (Immigration). Another option is to cross the lake from Salima in Malawi to Meponda in Mozambique (a distance of 60 kilometres, so choose a reliable boat) and then make your way to Lichinga.

From Tanzania, get your visa in Dar es Salaam, and then catch a bus or hitch south to Mtwara, a large town on the border with Mozambique. Due to the flood period of the Rufiji River (in Tanzania) this road may be closed between April and July. There are also internal flights between Dar es Salaam and Mtwara.

Catch a dhow (ingalão) from Msimbati near Mtwara or get to Mwambo on the north bank of the Rio Rovuma and cross to Quionga in Mozambique. Dhows are common along this stretch of coast (you will sail amongst the incredible coral islands of the Querimba Archipelago), while the road is in a fair condition to Palma, Mocímboa da Praia (you can have your passport stamped here) and Pemba.

Accommodation

HOTEL CHUABO. Av. Samora Machel, opposite the deserted cathedral in Quelimane. There are 68 rooms, some with air conditioning, U.S.$45/person. Tel. (04) 3181/2.

HOTEL ZAMBEZE. Rua Francisco Manyanga. Thirty rooms, some with bathroom and air conditioning. Mt50 000/person. Disco busy most nights.

HOTEL 1 (PRIMEIRO) DE JUNHO. On the river end of Av. Paulo Samuel Kankhomba. Very clean. Helpful, friendly staff. There are fans in the rooms and shared ablutions, and water is provided in buckets. Reasonable food. Mt80 000 per person. Tel. (04) 21 3067.

PENSÃO IDEAL. Av. Filipe Samuel Magaia, close to the cathedral. Meticulously maintained, air-conditioned rooms, some with bathroom en suite. Famous for its prawns. Mt120 000 for a double room. Tel. (04) 21 2739.

Eating and drinking

RESTAURANTE AQUARIO. Situated on the corner of Av. 1 (Primeiro) de Julho and Av. Heróis da Liberdade Nacional. Restaurante Aquario is air-conditioned with a shady outside patio area. Frango Zambeze (chicken) can be recommended. Beer from Malawi is served. Tel. (04) 21 2870.

RESTAURANTE REFEBA. On Av. Marginal, overlooking the Rio dos Bons Sinais. Excellent place to sip a cold drink while watching the sun setting over the water.

NICOLA SALÃO DE CHA. On Av. 1 de Junho just past the mosque on the way to the railway. Tea, cakes and chamuças (samoosas) are their speciality.

PENSÃO IDEAL. On Av. Filipe Samuel Magaia close to the cathedral. Spotless, comfortable restaurant with air-conditioning. Excellent prawns are to be had, but advance arrangements are recommended.

HOTEL ZAMBEZE. On Rua Francisco Manjanga. Fish and chips (batata frita) a speciality.
MERCADO CENTRAL has many small stalls offering a cooked meal for under Mt5 000. Pineapples the size of beach balls, papaya as sweet as strawberries and enough coconuts to float an ocean liner.

Cook your own traditional dish

Mukwane (or Matapas in Portuguese), which is made with varying ingredients, is the staple diet of the Chuabo people, especially as their cattle herds are virtually non-existent at present. Three varieties are favoured in Zambezia province: Mukwane de mandioca (cassava leaves) Mukwane de nyemba (leaves from the nyemba tree) and Mukwane de nyewe (a variety of bean).

Ingredients

Nyemba, mandioc or nyewe leaves
Garlic
Peri-peri
A pinch of salt
Mature coconuts with milk and water (coconut water is the juice inside the coconut; if you squeeze the flesh of the coconut, milk comes out)
Small prawns (locals eat them uncleaned)

Method

- Strip leaves from stalks.
- Crush leaves with garlic, peri-peri and a little salt.
- Boil leaves or beans for about one hour (until grassy green smell disappears).
- Soak the grated coconut in water for a few minutes.
- Take fistfuls of the grated coconut and squeeze the milk into the pan.
- Add the coconut water.
- Add bay leaves and the prawns.
- Cook for ten minutes. Serve hot.

Things to see and do

The bairros or suburbs which surround Quelimane are a maze of humanity and traditional dwellings and crafts. Find yourself a guide and take an early morning walk amongst the real people of Mozambique.

Nightlife

HOTEL ZAMBEZE boasts a nightclub which hops on most nights.
CLUBE DE DESPORTOS ESTRELA VERMELHA ZAMBÉZIA. Situated on the corner of Av. Samora Machel and Av. Filipe Samuel Magaia. Lambada, salsa, rumba, macarena, you name it. Friday and Saturday nights.
CINE ESTUDIO is air-conditioned and shows English movies with subtitles.

Excursions from Quelimane

PRAIA DE ZALALA. Complexo Kass-Kass, P.O. Box 212302, Praia de Zalala, Quelimane. Consists of a restaurant and individual, fully-equipped houses which sleep between four and six people and cost from Mt35 000 to Mt100 000 per day. The beach (Praia de Zalala) is flat, hard enough to land a jumbo jet and goes on for miles. There are good surfing waves at high tide. An ethno-jazz band called Thulrúka plays on weekends (say 'hi' to Renato, Ibraimo and Belmiro for me). Revel in prawns the size of your arm, and loads of fish.
CHINDE PORT AND THE ZAMBEZI DELTA can be reached either by chartering a T.T.A. light plane (for U.S.$500 per hour) or by catching a ride on one of the boats ferrying food aid down the coast. Contact T.T.A. at the airport or go to the jetty (cais de embarque) and ask for boats going to Chinde. The cost should be around Mt60 000 each way.

HOT SPRINGS (fontes quentes) surface around the towns of Mocuba, Lugela and Gilé. It is likely that these were mined during the war, so it is advisable that you speak to the locals and find out what the current situation is. The hot spring between Chipanga and Pinda (on the Sena–Morrumbala road) is a personal favourite.

THE ROAD TO NAMPULA

As far as Cuamba, the surface is fairly good, but, from Mocuba onwards, beware! Between Mocuba and Alto Molócuè (188 kilometres) there are frequent deviations around poorly filled-in trenches, as well as two places where the tarmac road leads to a river where there is no bridge. Eighty kilometres from Mocuba, start looking for detours onto badly rutted roads down to the old bridge.

ALTO MOLOCUE. A friendly, picturesque little town. Stay at the charming Pensão Tambe Uone just off the square.

NICOADALA AND MOPEIA

Nicoadala is situated 30 kilometres from Quelimane. Turn left at Nicoadala, carry on along the trans-Mozambique 'highway' and ask for the turn-off to Mopeia. On the way to Mopeia, you may pass young boys with their belongings on top of their heads and one of them will be carrying a live chicken. The chicken is used as a bribe to get through the border into Malawi where the children work, buy soap and sweets and then return to Mozambique to sell them.

Mopeia was formerly a centre for the sugar plantations in the area, and a ferry once chugged across the Zambezi River nearby, providing a vehicle route to the south. At present, although the ferry is nowhere to be seen, travellers cross the Zambezi by dugout and then continue on to Beira and other towns in trucks or chapas. Since the re-commissioning of the ferry at Caia, this route has lost its importance.

To get to Mopeia, make inquiries in Quelimane about Senhor Americo's machimbombo.

Northern Mozambique

Northern Mozambique is naturally divided by Malawi into two distinct regions: the north-east and the north-west. The north-eastern region consists of the provinces of Zambezia, Nampula, Cabo Delgado and Niassa. Extending from Chinde on the Zambezi delta in the south to Namuiranga village at the mouth of the Rovuma, and from Cobuè near Lake Malawi's Likoma Islands in the west to Mozambique Island in the east, this is a vast area of mysterious mountains (Namúli and Unango), historic settlements (Angoche, Mozambique and Ibo islands), idyllic islands (Ilhas das Querimbas) and wildlife (Niassa Reserve).

The coastline is over 1 000 kilometres long. Tiny coral creatures that thrive in the warm tropical water have produced about one hundred coral isles and islets. The main island grouping off Zambezia is the Moebase Archipelago. The Angoche Archipelago lies adjacent to Nampula Province, while the remote Ilhas das Querimbas lie between Pemba and the Rovuma. Deep, vast inland bays are also a notable feature of this seaboard, with Nacala harbour among the world's deepest and Pemba Bay one of the world's largest natural ports.

Mozambique's coastal flats, hundreds of kilometres wide in the south, are at their narrowest in this region, where the Mozambican Plateau replaces the Mozambican Plain as the dominant relief feature. This is the result of an underlying geological structure, composed of immense volcanic batholiths exposed by erosion throughout Nampula, Zambezia and Niassa provinces, in the form of obelisk-shaped granite domes. Mounts Namúli (2 419 m) in Zambezia, Mitucué in Nampula and Jeci in Niassa are all examples of granite domes. Apart from these enormous basalts, metamorphic rocks occur widely and marble quarries operate at Montepuez in Cabo Delgado province. Minerals and semi-precious stones such as tourmaline, aquamarine and morganite occur around Nampula town, Nacala and Morrua.

Major rivers in this region include the Zambezi; the Rovuma, forming the boundary between Mozambique and Tanzania; the Lugela, rising on the Malawi border near Mt. Mulanje; the Molócue, which has its source on Mt. Namúli; the Lúrio, which forms the boundary between Nampula and Cabo Delgado; and the Lugenda, draining lakes Chiuta in Malawi and Amaramba in Mozambique. Yet another major freshwater feature is Lake Malawi, with a 250 kilometre-long coast alongside Niassa Province.

The north-western region comprises the province of Tete. Resulting from the penetration by Portuguese explorers and traders up the Zambezi valley as far as Zambia's Luangwa River, this remote region is different and very distinctive from the rest of the country. The Cahora Bassa dam and hydro-electric scheme is located on the Zambezi River in the heart of Tete Province, and the resultant 270-kilometre-long lake is both a fishing mecca and a highway to wilderness areas otherwise inaccessible. Tete, the province's capital city, dates back 300 years and has long been a hub of trade in southern Africa. Today the suspension bridge spanning the Zambezi at Tete is still on the trans-African highway and is the only crossing point for vehicles downstream of Chirundu on the Zimbabwe/Zambia border.

The western border is formed by the Luangua River. Biri-Biri village on the Malawi frontier lies on the eastern extremity, while Missale is the northernmost town and Chindio on the junction of the Shire and Zambezi rivers is the southernmost point. Although the Zambezi drains the entire area, major tributaries such as the Luangua, Luia, Luenha and Revúbué have carved deep valleys in Tete province before flowing into the Zambezi. From the bottom of the Zambezi valley, to the tip of the Angónia plateau's Mt. Domué (2 095 m) on the Malawi border, this area of Mozambique exhibits many landscape and climatic variations.

Geologically, this region is a complex mix of volcanic, sedimentary and metamorphic rocks. Tete province is rich in minerals such as coal, gold, copper, iron and nickel, as evidenced by the coal mine at Moatize and the alluvial gold diggings around Chifumbazi. Lava flows surface as hills on the Zimbabwe border around Nyamapanda, and intrusive granite batholiths surface as domes around Muende on the Angónia Plateau. Large areas of erosion occur within the boundaries of the Zambezi drainage basin and depositional flats formed by the flooding Zambezi are present on its banks, where it joins the Shire River.

9

North-Eastern Mozambique

NAMPULA

Nampula, the capital city of Nampula province, is 680 kilometres by road north-east of the Zambezi River (from the town of Caia), 505 kilometres east of Mandimba on the Malawi border, 172 kilometres west of Mozambique Island (Ilha de Moçambique) and 728 kilometres south of the Tanzanian border (at the mouth of the Rovuma River).

Access

By air
Nampula is served by L.A.M. and a few private charter companies. Its airport, five kilometres from city centre, has a canteen and gift shop. Hired cars may not be on offer, but it is easy to get a taxi or lift into town.

By road
Most travellers arrive from Malawi to the west via Mandimba and Cuamba. The gravel road is eroded and rocky and negotiable only by vehicles with a high ground clearance or 4x4 vehicles. Until some low-level bridges are repaired the road may be impassable during the rainy season.

Nampula is accessible from the south by car – the ferry is working and the bridge at Sena has been repaired. From the north there is no bridge or vehicle ferry (and never has been) over the Rio Rovuma. Hitchhikers can get a ride to a point on the banks of the Zambezi or Rovuma rivers, and then cross by boat and continue on the other side.

By rail
A passenger train runs to no fixed schedule from Cuamba to Nampula, and Nampula to Nacala. The 350-kilometre trip takes one day; if you take the goods train, you may be competing for space with potatoes, livestock and thousands of local travellers (the ride is free). Not recommended for the squeamish.

Geography

Set between two major rivers, the Ligonha and Lúrio, Nampula is perhaps the most scenically beautiful of all of Mozambique's ten provinces. The endless flat plains and swamps of southern Mozambique give way to deciduous miombo woodland and magnificent towering granite domes and towers. Nampula province is a very densely populated region and is an important maize and cashew nut growing area. Almost 90% of the population are engaged

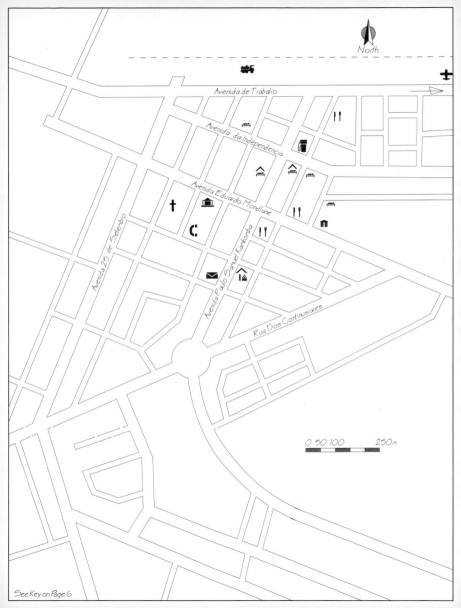

in subsistence agriculture, while feldspar and semi-precious stones are also an important source of income.

Rock climbing

The sheer sides of the peaks dotting the route between Cuamba and Nampula are a climber's paradise. Before approaching rock faces by car or on foot, find the local 'administrador' or 'secretário' and ask about a mine-free path. Some of the highest faces in the world are apparently in the area.

Facilities

The largest city in northern Mozambique, Nampula offers a range of accommodation, restaurants, shops and interesting places to visit. The electricity and water supply (the water is not potable without boiling) is reliable, while a satellite link ensures clear telecommunications.

Accommodation

HOTEL LURIO. 12b Av. Independência. Clean, secure, friendly staff. Running water (cold), some beds need replacing. Mt180 000/ double room with private bath. Excellent breakfast for Mt15 000. Tel. (06) 21 2520.
HOTEL TROPICAL. Behind the Cinema Moçambique. The Tropical is presently occupied by the United Nations. U.S.$80/double room. En-suite bathrooms. Recently renovated. Tel. (06) 21 2232
RESIDENCIAL A MARISQUEIRA. 20 Av. Paulo Samuel Kamkhomba. Suites with TV, video, fridge, air conditioning. Mt175 000 for two people. Luxury double rooms Mt250 000, normal double rooms Mt120 000. Private bathrooms. Tel. (06) 21 3611 or 21 2093.

HOTEL NAMPULA. Corner of 4 Av. Francisco Manyanga and Av. Primeiro de Maio. Comfortable rooms: Mt80 000 single, Mt140 000 double. Coffee shop. Tel. (06) 21 2147.
PENSÃO MARQUES. Av. Paulo Samuel Kankhomba. Mt40 000 per person, popular with backpackers and budget travellers. Tel. (06) 21 2527.
RESIDENCIAL MONTE CARLO. Rua Cidade de Moçambique, diagonally opposite the post office. No running water. Mt120 000 double with private bath. Tel. (06) 21 2789.

Eating and drinking

CLUBE C.V.F.M. Rua 3 de Fevereiro, one block away from the Hotel Lúrio towards the railway tracks. Swimming pool, patio bar and air-conditioned restaurant. Excellent seafood dishes from Mt30 000 to Mt120 000.
RESTAURANTE LORD. Rua Daniel Napatima. Cosy pub serving Carlsberg beer from Malawi and excellent prego rolls (prego no pão). Meals from Mt25 000 to Mt120 000.

RESTAURANTE CLUBE DE TENIS. Av. Paulo Samuel Kamkhomba, in the shade of trees behind an office of the Electricity Department. Prawns Mt90 000, sandwiches a speciality.
RETIRO DISCO AND RESTAURANT. Just out of town on the left-hand side on the road to the dam (barragem). Relaxed atmosphere.
PETISQUEIRA. Next door (to the left) to the entrance of the Hotel Lúrio. This is a cool retreat away from the midday heat. Beer,

cool drinks and snacks, lulas (calamari) for Mt30 000, galinha (chicken) for Mt25 000 are all available here.

TAKE-AWAY XITENDE. Close to the airport. Xitende is an ideal place to drink, watching the setting sun and whiling away those long, humid evenings.

TAKE-AWAY EXPRESSO. Av. Eduardo Mondlane (on the same block as the Lúrio, but on the opposite side). There is no cooked food here, but a tempting selection of imported confectionary will save 'chocoholics' from the sanatorium.

MERCADO CENTRAL. On the corner of Rua Monomotapa and Av. Paulo Samuel Kankhomba. From cashews to cornflakes, it's all on sale here.

Places of interest

CRAFT MARKET. On the park (Praça Feminina) in front of the Conselho Executivo near the cathedral. Furniture, fabrics, carvings, reed mats and baskets, and a wide variety of edibles. Not to be missed. Sundays only.

THE MAIN STREET. This wide tree-lined one-kilometre-long avenue runs parallel to the railway line and is named after Eduardo Mondlane, the first president of Frelimo.

NAMPULA CATHEDRAL. With its twin towers and massive dome, the cathedral is an unmistakable landmark in the middle of town.

NATIONAL MUSEUM OF MOZAMBIQUE. Situated on the lower end of Av. Eduardo Mondlane. Tel. (06) 21 2129. Varied exhibits provide fascinating insights into the diverse cultures that have contributed to the Mozambican society. Watch the famous Makonde sculptors at work in their co-operative behind the museum. Their carvings are on sale.

PUBLIC TELEPHONES (telecomunicação). Located on Rua Monomotapa, one block down from the cathedral.

Calls to Europe cost from Mt125 000 to Mt250 000, Africa from Mt75 000 to Mt120 000. Calls to Oceania, Asia and North America are all charged at Mt150 000 for the minimum initial three-minute period.

POST OFFICE (correios). On the corner of Rua Cidade de Moçambique and Rua Paulo Samuel Kankhomba.

IMMIGRATION (Imigração). Attractive old building on the corner of Rua Monomotapa and Av. Francisco Manyanga. Visas can be extended here; price negotiable.

BP SERVICE STATION. On Av. Independência, diagonally opposite the Hotel Lúrio. Open from 8 a.m. to 5 p.m. Some spares available.

L.A.M. OFFICE (DOMESTIC AIRLINE). At the railway end of Av. Francisco Manyanga. Tel. (06) 21 3311.

SUPERMARKET. Adjacent to the Hotel Lúrio. Selection of imported foodstuffs, drinks and condiments. Frozen-fish market.

J. FERNANDES VEHICLE SPARES (acessórios do carro). On Rua 3 de Fevereiro, next to Pensão Nampula.

NAMPULA RAILWAY STATION (Caminhos de Ferro de Moçambique or C.F.M.). Tel. (06) 21 2032. The tracks run parallel to Av. do Trabalho, which leads to the airport (if you turn right) and to Cuamba and Quelimane (left). A passenger service has been implemented. Hitching a free ride on the goods train to Cuamba or Nacala is only for those who aren't afraid of pain! The old steam engines on the railway sidings are worth a look.

BUS AND TAXI TERMINUS. Minibuses, trucks and buses to far-off places. Located on Av. de Trabalho near the railway station.

MAKONDE STATUE SHOP. Ask for Senhor Abdul Abakasamo, who lives across the road from the Mercado Central and has a large stock of the ebony carvings.

PARAISO DA MODA. Indian clothing shop on Rua Daniel Napatima next to Restaurante Lord. Advice on changing foreign currency into meticais is available here.

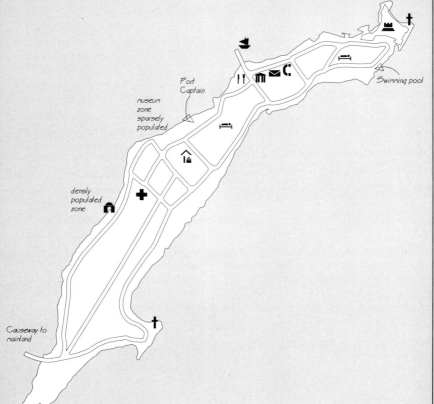

North

Chapel of our Lady of Baluarte

Swimming pool

Port Captain

museum zone
sparsely populated

densely populated zone

Causeway to mainland

0 100 200 300 400 500m

See Key on Page 6

CIVIC CENTRE (Conselho Executivo). A very attractive example of Portuguese colonial architecture is found across the Praça Feminina (Women's Park) from the cathedral. CINÉMA MOÇAMBIQUE. Av. Eduardo Mondlane next to the museum. See why the children in Nampula think that Americans are people who have the biggest guns and solve their differences by kicking each other to pieces! May have been converted into a church.

ANGOCHE

One hundred and ninety-eight kilometres from Nampula (via Liupo, where there is a guest house owned by Zé Padero) on a reasonable gravel and sand road lies the historic town of Angoche, with its associated archipelago made up of the islands of Mequeli, Quilua, Mafamede, Puge-Puge, Nejovo and Caldeira. Due to its relative isolation, the residents of Angoche reflect the influence of centuries of contact with traders from Arabia and India more markedly than do the citizens of Mozambique Island.

Coti is the language spoken around Angoche. Only a small percentage of the population is able to communicate effectively in Portuguese.

Getting to Angoche

Chapas to Liupo leave at 6 a.m. from the road out of Nampula. Angoche–Liupo costs Mt40 000, Liupo–Quinga Mt 30 000. Fuel is available at Angoche, and there is an adequate pensão (Oceânia), a few restaurants and a well-stocked market with fresh fish aplenty. Angoche is at least a two-day dhow ride from Mozambique Island, while the road down the coast to Moma, Pebane, Olinga, Namacurra and Quelimane (the capital city of Zambezia province) is very scenic, but negotiable in 4x4 vehicles only (and then only during the dry season).

Places of interest

QUINGA BEACH. Angoche boasts some of southern Africa's finest untouched beaches e.g. Quinga (pronounced Kinka) (access from Liupo); the islands and coral reefs are a tropical wonderland. At Quinga ask for Senhor Nic, who has a camp and boat on the shore.

NACALA

Nacala, 80 kilometres from Mozambique Island, is possibly the deepest natural harbour in the world; it is an important outlet for goods from Malawi and Zambia as well as from Mozambique. Although there are no tourist facilities aside from a large hotel, there is a long beach with restaurants and hotels at Minguri, 20 kilometres around the bay from Nacala. The road is in a fair condition for the 190-kilometre stretch between Nampula and Nacala (pedestrians can be a hazard, as grass huts line the road in many places). Fuel is available at Nacala. Money can be changed at a shop called 'Classica'.

Just before Nacala, turn right and carry on 15 kilometres to Fernão Veloso, a magnificent beach with excellent snorkelling just 50 metres offshore.

THE ROUTE TO THE NORTH-EAST

From Nampula to the turn-off at Namialo the road is good, after which there are stretches with bad pot-holes as far as Montepuez and Pemba.

The road north to Macomia (Estrada 243) is suitable for two-wheel-drive vehicles with a high ground clearance, after which four-wheel-drive capability is a recommendation during the wet season. The coastal sand road between Pemba and Mocímboa da Praia should only be used after careful consultation with the local population, but it has been upgraded as far as Mucojo, 170 kilometres from Pemba.

ILHA DE MOÇAMBIQUE

The name Mozambique is apparently a corruption of 'Mussal A'l Bik' (or perhaps 'Mussa Ben Mbiki'), the name of an important Arab sheik or political chief living on the island at the time of the Portuguese arrival. The settlement on Mozambique Island owes its initial importance to its use as a secure refuge and port, as well as its convenient position in relation to the monsoonal trade winds. Mozambique Island is also aptly referred to as the ponto de encontro de civilizações (meeting point of civilizations).

This small island, 2 500 metres long and 600 metres at its widest, is a microcosm of the country, encapsulating all the major cultural and linguistic influences which have contributed to today's rich Mozambican society. Sailors from Persia and Arabia in their open-decked dhows were the navigational pioneers of the Indian Ocean, with Arab trading vessels first appearing along the coast during the eighth century.

Commercial activities initially centred on the exchange of ivory, gold and slaves from Africa for beads, spices and cloth from India and Arabia. Eager to break the Arab and Indian domination of the trade in spices, silk cloth and exotic perfumes from the East, the Portuguese explorers rounded the Cape of Good Hope and, under the leadership of Vasco da Gama, anchored off the island in 1498. Da Gama carried on to India with the help of an Arab pilot recruited in the port of Melinde (Malindi).

In 1507 the Portuguese occupied the island, building a small fort and leaving behind just fifteen men to protect their trading post.

Construction of the fortress of St Sebastian (Fortaleza S. Sebastião) began in 1558 and had not been completed when the Dutch besieged the island between 1607 and 1608.

Mozambique became a town in 1763 and was renamed a city by Portuguese authorities in 1810, a period in which the colony existed basically on the export of slaves.

With the abolition of the slave trade in the nineteenth century , a new liberalism developed which allowed permanent settlement on the island by African people, and more freedom of movement into the interior by white people. The island's status as the capital city of the Portuguese province of Mozambique was lost to Lourenço Marques in 1886, partly due to the threat from the British in Natal, and the boers of the Transvaal Republic seeking an outlet to the sea.

The Bairro Museu (museum district) section of Mozambique Island (about two thirds of its area), was declared a World Heritage Site by UNESCO in 1992.

Location

Mozambique town ('Ilha') is located some 175 kilometres from Nampula. The road is in good condition as far as the turnoff two kilometres from Monapo; after this it becomes badly pot-holed. The island is the point at which Mozambique is closest to Madagascar (where the Mozambique Channel is narrowest).

Access

A single-lane toll bridge of three and a half kilometres (which has passing bays at 500-metre intervals) links the southern point of the island to the mainland. A channel to the north allows small boats to sail into the sheltered bay on the mainland side of the island. Dhows sail between Mozambique Island and Nacala, Mogincual as well as Angoche. The nearest landing strip, situated five kilometres away at Lumbo, was Mozambique's first international airport. Daily chapa rides serve the Nampula-Ilha road.

Places of interest and facilities

CAMPING. This is strongly discouraged as tents are slashed regularly. Rather pitch your tent on a balcony of the Pousada.

ENGLISH-SPEAKING GUIDES. English teachers at the Escola Secundária (secondary school), situated on the mainland side of the island near the fortress, are happy to act as interpreters and guides for a small fee.

FORTALEZA S. SEBASTIÃO (fortress of St Sebastian). When it was built during the 16th century, this stronghold was the largest structure in central and southern Africa. It is in a good state of preservation and its underground cisterns are still the only source of permanent water on the island. Guided tours through the fort (conducted in Portuguese) can be arranged at the Museum.

PALACIO DE S. PAULO (St Paul's Palace). Close to the port and jetty, the palace and the Chapel of St Paul are now a museum. Noteworthy pieces of Portuguese and Indo-Portuguese art, decoration and furniture have survived the centuries and a leaking roof. Museum visiting times are as follows: Wednesday to Friday, 8 a.m. to 12 noon and 2 p.m. to 5 p.m.; Saturday, 9 a.m. to 12 noon and 2 p.m. to 5 p.m.; Sundays and holidays, 9 a.m. to 3 p.m. The museum is closed on Mondays and Tuesdays.

BEACHES AND CORAL REEFS. Since Mozambique Island's beaches are also the toilet for upwards of 15 000 people, they are no place for visitors. However, a small picturesque beach at the back of the fort, which is difficult to get to, is charming at low tide. Swimmers, snorkellers and divers can catch a dhow ride to Goa Island, Snake Island (Ilha das Cobras) or the superb beach at Chocas-mar on the mainland.

These pristine places are all no more than a couple of hours' round trip by dhow, unless the wind stops blowing, of course.

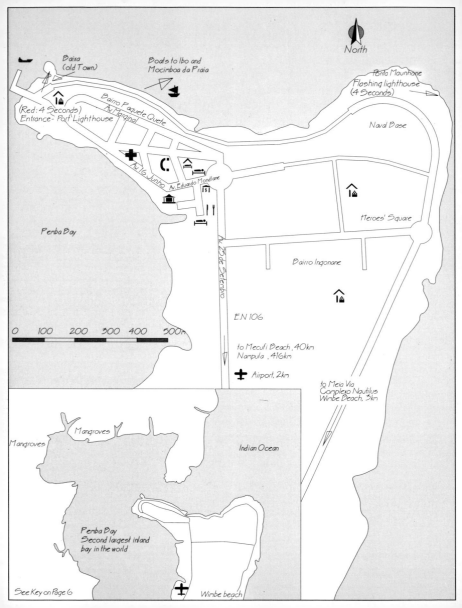

North

Baixa
(old Town)

Boats to Ibo and
Mocimboa da Praia

Ponto Maunhone
Flashing lighthouse
(4 Seconds)

Naval Base

Bairro Paquete Quete
Av. Marginal

(Red: 4 Seconds)
Entrance- Port Lighthouse

Av. 16 Junho

Av. Eduardo Mondlane

Heroes' Square

Pemba Bay

Bairro Ingonane

Av. 3 de Setembro

E.N 106

to Mecufi Beach, 40km
Nampula, 416km

Airport, 2km

to Meia Via
Complexo Nautilus
Winbe Beach, 3km

0   100   200   300   400   500m

Mangroves

Mangroves

Indian Ocean

Pemba Bay
Second largest inland
bay in the world

Winbe beach

See Key on Page 6

PRINCIPAL MOSQUE (Mesquita). In the old Arab quarter of town overlooking an anchorage for fishing boats on the mainland side of the island. There are many smaller mosques dotted around – the oldest of which is situated close to the Palace Museum.

POUSADA MOÇAMBIQUE. A clean, airy, dilapidated building in the northern, museu (museum) sector. The staff are friendly and helpful, but beds and mattresses are collapsing and water in the bathrooms is supplied by the bucketful. Mt75 000/double room. Bring your own mosquito net. Meals are adequate, but expect a long wait.

COMPLEXO PISCINA (swimming pool and restaurant). On Sundays the pool is filled with sea water. The restaurant serves lobster (crayfish) and fish and chips – place your orders well in advance. The patio is always cooled by a fresh sea breeze and is an ideal vantage point from which to watch the dhows slip across the water. There is a curio market here on Sundays.

ASSOCIAÇÃO DOS AMIGOS DA ILHA (Assocation of the Friends of the Island). This organization was formed to promote the island as a living monument to the cultural heritage of Mozambique. The office is next door to the meticulously restored Banco de Moçambique building.

BANCO DE MOÇAMBIQUE. From the museum, walk to the police station (P.P.M.), take the right fork and four blocks down you will find the attractive Banco de Moçambique building. Change your foreign currency here.

CAPITANIA DO PORTO (Port Captain). Housed in historic buildings near to the police station. Report here if you arrive in your own yacht.

HINDU TEMPLE. Attesting to the Indian influence, a small Hindu temple and garden are hidden away amongst the stone houses adjacent to the Mercado Municipal.

MERCADO MUNICIPAL. As no food is grown on the island, the market usually has a very limited range of produce on offer. Purchase your food requirements before you arrive.

BIBLIOTECA (library), in the Council Chambers (Conselho Executivo). Contains the island archives and books of historical interest.

TELEFONE PUBLICO (public telephones). Microwave and satellite technology make worldwide communications possible. Located on the same block as the museum.

BOMBAS DE GASOLINA (petrol pumps). Petrol and diesel available 100 metres from the causeway linking the island to the mainland.

BAR ESCONDIDINHO (restaurant and pub). Take the left fork at the police station down to a small square on which there is a cosy restaurant with a name which means 'hide-away'.

RESTAURANTE ANCORA D'OURO. Straight down the road from the jetty next to St Paul's Chapel. Meet the locals here, but don't expect to eat unless you order your meal a few hours in advance.

CORREIOS (POST OFFICE). One block down from the Ancora d'Ouro towards the causeway side of the island.

HOSPITAL. Situated on the boundary between the densely populated bairros and the Museum sector. It has one doctor and very basic facilities.

PEMBA: PAPAYA PARADISE

Anyone spending more than a week in Mozambique should definitely get to Pemba. Anyone who spends more than a week in Pemba will probably fall in love with the place.

This section is dedicated to all those travellers who take its contents to heart and take the time to discover that there is far more to Pemba than the palm-lined beach, Praia de Wimbe.

Getting to Pemba

From outside of Mozambique, there are no regular or scheduled flights or ships direct to Pemba. There is no rail link to this magnificent natural harbour, while the town can be reached by road via Nampula and Namialo, the road being in a fair condition. Note that the road from Malawi (Mandimba) to Nampula is suitable for 4x4 vehicles only.

By air

Get yourself to Maputo, Quelimane or Beira. Reliable scheduled internal Linhas Aéreas de Moçambique (L.A.M.) flights from all of these towns to Pemba depart on Sundays, Tuesdays and Fridays. At the time of writing a single from Maputo to Pemba cost Mt1 256 000. Inquire about the substantially reduced excursion fares.

Owing to the lack of alternative reliable forms of public transport (specifically passenger boats), planes are usually fully booked, especially during December, so prior booking is essential.

Items of value are regularly stolen from baggage that is placed inside the hold, so make sure that you always take money, jewellery, cameras, electronic goods, etc. with you as hand luggage.

By boat

Since Pemba is at the end of the run for local ships plying the Mozambique Channel, it is not wise to consider this angle of approach unless you have plenty of time,

Benguerra Island is a national park with freshwater pools and a turtle breeding area.

Hotel Dona Ana in Vilankulo is spacious and the restaurant and bar have stunning views of Maguruque Island across the sea to the north.

The view from the top of Hotel Dona Ana in Vilankulo, situated on the mainland, a short trip by dhow from the Bazaruto Archipelago.

A young boy on Bazaruto Island with his share of the catch. The rich harvest from the sea compensates for the general poverty of the region.

The Bazaruto Lighthouse on Bazaruto Island was built about a hundred years ago, but has not been in operation for over a decade.

A magnificent coral shelf in the Indian Ocean. The warm Mozambique current and clear waters attract diving enthusiasts to the magnificent 2 500-km-long coastline.

Anemone and clownfish, part of the Indian Ocean's colourful marine life that is found offshore on the many coral reefs.

Beira harbour in the mouth of the Púngoè River; the city centre area can be seen in the background. Situated about halfway up the Mozambique coast, Beira is an important port city.

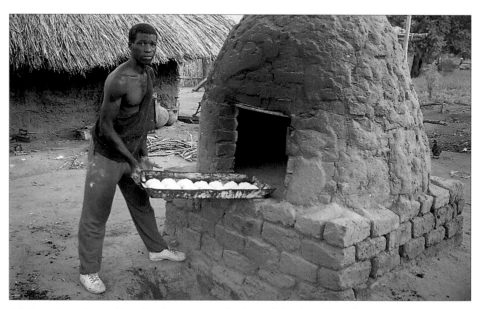

A baker using a charcoal-burning clay oven to make the traditional pão *(bread) in Mopeia, roughly mid-way between Beira and Quelimane.*

Shona women on a wooden bridge over the Púngoè River in Manica province, central Mozambique.

A sidewalk tailor in Quelimane. A few metres above sea-level, set amongst huge mangrove swamps, Quelimane is extremely hot and humid.

In the bairro *(suburb)* on the outskirts of Quelimane.

The road from Quelimane to Praia da Zalala passes through some of the most extensive coconut plantations in the world.

A man with dried oysters at the beautiful, unspoilt village of Pangane in northern Mozambique.

The Catholic Church on Mozambique Island. The island boasts some of the most beautiful architecture to be seen in the whole country, showing Portuguese, Arab, Indian and African influences.

A Macua girl wearing a natural skin softener, a paste made from the ground bark of the nciro tree. The paste is washed off at night.

The courtyard inside the Palace Museum on Mozambique Island. The museum has some interesting Portuguese and Indo-Portuguese art on display.

Bairro Unidade, Mozambique Island. Poverty is rife throughout the country and the people rely on subsistence agriculture and fishing to eke out a living.

Cannons on the ramparts of the Fortaleza de S. Sebastião, Mozambique Island. Construction of the fort began in 1558 and was not complete when the Dutch besieged the island between 1607 and 1608.

The palm-lined beach at Praia de Wimbe in Pemba is one of the most beautiful spots in Mozambique.

Fishermen on Lake Cahora Bassa survive on their catch of bream and tigerfish. Any surplus is used for barter, usually in exchange for maize meal.

A temporary camp in the Messenguezi basin at Lake Cahora Bassa. In the 1960s damming of the Zambezi began, as a means of providing hydroelectric power.

Sena women, Tete province in north-western Mozambique. Although poverty is rife throughout the country, people make the best of scanty resources.

Cahora Bassa dam wall and gorge. The name Cahora Bassa is said to be derived from the Chewa term 'Kebrabassa' which means 'the end of the work'.

and have fallen in love with Maputo, Beira, Quelimane, Mozambique Island, Nacala, Durban or wherever you end up after stumbling around south-eastern Africa for a while. Waiting for a boat might be frustrating, expensive and futile. On the other hand you might just meet up with a swashbuckling skipper of a sport fishing boat on its way up to the fabled, unexplored islands north of Pemba, who needs extra crew for the voyage.

Apart from the odd elusive fuel tankers (Pemba is sometimes without either diesel or petrol) which blot the bay at increasingly irregular and lengthy intervals, vessels to look out for if you are in Durban, Richards Bay, Maputo, Quelimane, Nacala or Vladivostok, are the small coasters captained by very helpful fellows who don't mind giving you a free ride, but are unfortunately unable to say just when their little boat will be leaving for anywhere.

Perhaps the best shipping line to contact is Navique E.E., based in Maputo, Beira and Quelimane, which operates the following ships: *Save* (with a Portuguese captain called José), *Dimini* II, *Dimini* III, *Lugenda* and *Afriquia*. Approach also Transmaritima de Sofala E Estrela do Mar.

This section of seaboard is also becoming increasingly popular with the South African yachting fraternity. If you are in the neighbourhood of a port in South Africa, try contacting the yacht club to arrange a lift.

Accommodation

Pemba has two acceptable tourist-standard hotels. Cabo Delgado is in the new town or cima at the junction of the Nampula road and Complexo Nautilus on Wimbe beach (Praia de Wimbe). Both are considered amongst the best in Mozambique, mainly because they are clean, reasonably priced

and well-maintained. There are other less expensive places to lay down your weary head, which range from pretty good to cockroach corner:

HOTEL CABO DELGADO. From Mt150 000 to Mt250 000 per double room; all rooms air-conditioned with bathroom en suite. Situated on Av. Eduardo Mondlane at the corner of the road to the airport and Nampula. Transport to the beach (five kilometres away) provided. There is a fair restaurant; the hotel may be noisy at night. Tel. (072) 2558.

COMPLEXO NAUTILUS. Mt370 000 (four-bed, self-catering chalet), Mt420 000 (six beds). Air-conditioned with bathroom en suite. On Wimbe beach, which is reached by turning right (if you're coming in from the airport) at the concrete world globe opposite the dilapidated old military barracks. The Nautilus has a conference centre, reasonable restaurant, boat hire, windsurfing and snorkelling on shallow coral reefs. They hire out speed boats for Mt250 000 per hour plus fuel. Ask at the hotel about the compressor (owned by a Dane) which is in town. Transport to the town and the airport is available. Booking is absolutely essential. Tel. Pemba (072) 3520 or Johannesburg (011) 339 7275, fax 339 7295.

HOTEL PEMBA. Rua Forças Armadas, tel. (072) 3442. Mt75 000 per double with bath, but don't expect running water. Clean and quiet with a flat roof for braais (barbecues) from where there is a stupendous view. To get there from the airport, turn left at the circle near the Hotel Cado Delgado, left again and then first right up the hill. Currently being upgraded.

The restaurant will prepare meals if they are given plenty of warning. The pub may not be well stocked.

PENSÃO BAIA. Situated on Av. 1ᵉ Maio Pemba, tel. (072) 3435. Mt85 000 per double – clean, communal ablutions. This is probably the best place to stay if you want to meet the movers and shakers of Pemba. Tables outside under huge, shady trees are a cool refuge during the heat of the day. Serves the best food in town (great burgers can be had for Mt9 000). Situated one street up from the airport/Nampula road circle opposite Telecomunicações de Moçambique, where there are public phones .

HOTEL RESIDENCIAL LYS. Rua Forças Populares, tel. (072) 3432. Clean rooms with bath and running water. Close to Hotel Pemba, before the left turn up the hill.

MARITIMO. Mt30 000 per person. Cheap and pretty nasty, but the closest accommodation to the harbour. Maritimo is situated in the old town or baixa on the main, dual carriageway road, on the right-hand side just after the circle near the Mercado Municipal (fruit and vegetable market). Meals can be arranged.

Eating and drinking

If you stay at **COMPLEXO NAUTILUS** on Wimbe beach, you will probably end up taking most of your meals there. Prices are reasonable, but the fare gets monotonous after a few days. There are other options, on the beach and in town. These are certainly well worth the extra effort. Standards and availability of what's on the menu vary from day to day, so my impressions may not be your own on any particular day. If you don't want to eat in restaurants, buy your food at one of the local markets – it's 90% cheaper! While in Pemba, be adventurous and try all of the following restaurants:

PENSÃO BAIA. See Accommodation above.

RESTAURANTE BOITE WIMBE (also called the Aeroclube). At the far end of Praia de Wimbe, this restaurant serves meals and is fairly popular with the locals. This is the place to be on a Saturday night after eleven.

Halfway along the beach there is a café called **QUIOSQUE TROPICAL**. It has thatch umbrellas and serves tasty snacks (good prego rolls). Generally only operational over weekends and during school holidays. Good place to sip sundowners.

RESTAURANTE CABO DELGADO. Not to be confused with the tearoom on the corner. Walk into the hotel entrance and turn right up the stairs. The food can be excellent.

ESTRELA VERMELHA. In the downtown part of town, two-thirds of the way along the main road to the bay. I had an excellent meal

here while watching a video of the 1992 Olympic Games and contemplating whether the restaurant's boxing ring would ever be used again. Prices are low and portions huge. There are generally good Portuguese wines; however, the choice may be limited to one item. Get a group together (warn the owner) and make a night of it. Intricate Makonde carvings are on sale here.

VICE VERSA. Inside the Mercado Municipal – seats ten. A meal for two costs Mt10 000. The couple who run it are very helpful and will prepare whatever you ask for, as long as they are given a day's notice.

TAKE AWAY. Run by folk who prepare excellent food at a reasonable price. As you come in from the airport or Nampula, in a house on the left 100 metres before the circle. The only place in town to buy pizza. Try the local dish, matapas or mukwane in the Mukua language.

Markets and stores

In line with the general rule that applies in Mozambique, supermarkets in Pemba sell goods imported from South Africa, making them pretty expensive if you are on a tight budget. Stores do not usually stock any fresh produce, but there are plenty of fresh vegetables, fish and fruit available at the traditional markets in the bairros (suburbs).

Traditional markets

The traditional markets (bazares) can be found in the bairros Natite, Cariaco, Ingonane, and Paquite Quete. Ask locals for directions. The difference in cost between restaurants and preparing your own food is a factor of about ten. Fresh bread is sold outside the Hotel Cabo Delgado – croissants and doughnuts are baked on Wednesdays.

Shops and banks

A variety of shops are listed below according to the sequence in which they are reached after turning left up the hill onto Av. Eduardo Mondlane at the circle near the Hotel Cabo Delgado:

BANCO DE MOÇAMBIQUE (on the left). Change money here if you don't want to risk the slightly better rate offered at some of the shops operated by Indian people.

VIDEO CLUBE (left). Hires out English movies.

SUPERMARCADO (on the right). This fancy store is divided into three sections: food, clothing and stationery (buy your camera film here), and hardware. Prices high but you will probably never need anything here.

DRESS SHOP (on the left). Get your tailor-made outfits here, as well as the revenue stamps required on application forms for visa extensions.

SALÃO PEROLA (on the left). Hairdresser and perfumaria. About Mt50 000 for a hairdo.

ARMAZÉMS BOB (on the left). For buoys, fishing tackle and alarm clocks.

Old town

Details of shops down in the old town (baixa) near the harbour which may have something for you are below:

CASA CARIM KATCHI. Walk in with a $100 bill stuck to your forehead to be sure of a warm welcome! The owner is an unofficial money-changer.

NIASSA COMERCIAL. On the main street behind a tree. Good bottle store and hardware. Money exchanged at a poor rate.

REPARADORA ELÉTRICA. Motorcycle spares, fish hooks, glue, insulation tape, hacksaw blades, light bulbs and electric motors.

VARIOUS INDIAN-OWNED SHOPS. Sell items ranging from frilly underwear and bread flour to pots, pans and pirated cassette tapes.

VOLVO PENTA. On the road running past the port entrance. Keep going until you see a pile of cargo containers on the right.

MERCADO MUNICIPAL. Depending on the season and the inclination of the suppliers, this market usually has a fair variety and quality of fruit, fish and vegetables.

Food is usually sold by the kilo, but you can ask for half (meio). There are Muslim folk selling spices, and do investigate all the little stalls which surround the market. One kiosk, on the left before you enter, sells Mozambican rum for around Mt30 000. Mention my name for a discount.

There are also interesting shops on the right-hand side of the main road from the airport or Nampula on the way into town.

Fuel is readily available. Diesel costs about Mt2 000 per litre and petrol Mt3 800.

Nightlife

Pemba folk really enjoy their dancing Lambada style. Live bands sometimes play at the soccer stadium and the secondary school, but otherwise music is belted out via records and tapes.

AEROCLUBE. (or Boite Wimbe). Gets going after 11 p.m, Saturday nights most popular. Entrance Mt10 000. Beer and snacks. On the end of Wimbe beach. Best place in Pemba.
ARCO IRIS (RAINBOW). Coming from the beach, turn left 100 metres before the T-junction with the airport road. A dirt track leads to a shack resembling a barn. Mostly teenagers frequent this club, but they dance wonderfully. No food; entrance Mt10 000. The DJs will play your requests, if available. Bring along your own tapes.

PINJA PALJOTTA. Situated behind the principal mosque. Has a local atmosphere.
SHIVA. At the Sports Clube de Pemba. This is the club where the chefes grands, or top dogs, of Pemba meet.

To do, see and buy

Walk along the beach (Praia da Wimbe) to the lighthouse (farol), after which there is a restricted military area, so be careful. Trips take 45 minutes there and back if you are a super-fit hater of walking along beautiful coastlines, two hours if you are a normal city couch-potato, and a whole day if you are with someone you like, have a picnic lunch packed, and enjoy snorkelling.

Charter the cabin cruiser *Robi* (for sale) from the boat yard near the harbour for U.S.$200 per day. Go up the coast to the islands with friends for a few days. A big catamaran owned by 'Per' anchored near the jetty can be chartered for U.S.$170 per day.

Visit Chuiba beach (beware of petty thieving) by carrying on along the road past Wimbe beach through the cashew tree groves. Avoid the military area.

Buy bizarre carvings at the Makonde co-op just off the road to Wimbe on the left, 700 metres after the junction with the airport road. Mueda (the Makonde capital) has a clean, basic pensão (Mt50 000) with a sculpture commemorating the 1964 massacre of Makonde elders by Portuguese commandos. Buses go to Mueda and Mocímboa da Praia every week (Mt70 000 one way).

Reflect on the inscription 'Sacrificed for monarchical ambition' carved into one of the headstones in the cemetery on top of the hill overlooking the bay behind the governor's residence. Buried here are 122 Commonwealth troops, including 20 South Africans. A legacy of the campaign against the Germans in Tanzania.

If you want a shell collection, carry on past Complexo Nautilus and keep an eye on the right-hand side of the road where there is a legal shell shop just after the police station.

Violent American movies are screened at the cinema near the port.

Watch mahogany boats being built at the yard around the corner from the harbour.

It may be possible to hitch lifts on planes by chatting to the South African pilots who fly for STA or LOMACO.

Renew your visa (three months maximum) at Imigração, 200 metres down the road from the cinema. For U.S.$15 you will have it in five days, or U.S.$30 for one day.

Ask the manager of the Complexo Nautilus if you can pitch your tent in front of the hotel. Watch out for spring tides.

IBO, QUERIMBA AND PANGANE

The best way to reach the 40 islands of the Querimba Archipelago is by boat taxi from Pemba's bairro Paquite Quete. Haggle your way on to a dhow and go to Ibo, Mocímboa da Praia, Pangane, Palma or Tanzania. There are motor ferries (subject to availability of fuel and spares) to Ibo once a week, and to Mocímboa da Praia once a month. Ibo has a pensão (Ujamaa do Ibo) and a fortress, and nearby Querimba Island a guest cottage at the Gessners' house. The Gessners are third-generation (on the island) German settlers, who export copra from Querimba.

MOCÍMBOA DA PRAIA

This is a quiet, sheltered port that is suitable for small boats. The mangrove-lined bay, in the centre of which is a picturesque baobab-covered island, is an important dhow anchorage. The town has markets, shops, a post office and an immigration office to stamp you out if you are heading for Tanzania.

Accommodation

PENSÃO MAHOMETANA MAGID is clean and the roof doesn't leak. A double room costs Mt150 000. Shower by bucket. Basic meals are available.

MUEDA

Mueda, which is the Makonde capital, has a memorial to tribal elders who were massacred by the Portuguese in 1960. This sparked off the resistance movement (Frelimo) which eventually gained power in 1975. Mueda has a reasonable pensão and can be reached from Pemba by bus.

PALMA

Excellent mat weaving and an unpleasant pensão with reeking toilets. The rooms cost Mt20 000 per person.

CROSSING THE ROVUMA

In August 1996, there was still no bridge or ferry service over the Rio Rovuma, nor has there ever been. According to residents of the Negomane and Mocímboa do Rovuma areas, Portuguese farmers during the colonial period did cross the river in trucks at the height of the dry season (tempo da seca), i.e. July to October. Apparently bulldozers were used to create temporary drifts, making a crossing through years of accumulated mud a very challenging proposition during the foreseeable future.

NIASSA PROVINCE

Niassa is the least developed, least populated, most isolated and remote of all of Mozambique's ten provinces. Its northern border is the wild Rio Rovuma, across which lies Tanzania. There is no official road link between Tanzania and Niassa Province. To the west is the vast Lago Niassa (Lake Malawi) with its fringe of mountains forming a formidable barrier to access from that direction. From the coastline and Cabo Delgado province, a rough gravel road leads from Pemba through Montepuez to

Marrupa, Malanga and Lichinga. Presently the only practical way to reach Niassa, Lichinga and the Mozambique side of Lake Malawi is from Malawi via the Chipode/Mandimba frontier (open between 6 a.m. and 6 p.m.). This is also the route of choice if you are on your way to Nampula and the coastline via Cuamba.

Due to its altitude, Niassa is cool in summer and can be bitterly cold in winter (apart from the lake shore where it is warm all year). The province receives most of its rain from December to March, and the winter months may be totally dry. Maniamba, 100 kilometres north-west of Lichinga, is in fact one of the wettest places in Mozambique. Miombo (brachystegia) deciduous woodland dominates the landscape, apart from the lakeshore where tropical vegetation and coconut palm trees occur. Although there is a rail link from Nacala via Nampula and Cuamba to Lichinga, the stretch between Cuamba and Lichinga is used perhaps once a month and the lack of a paved (tarmac) link has left Niassa behind the rest of the country with regard to development and the people are very poor.

LICHINGA

The largest town in Niassa province, Lichinga, is nevertheless tiny with a population of approximately 40 000. Unless you are hitching or travelling in a sturdy car or truck, the sensible way to get to Lichinga is by air on L.A.M. from Maputo. Even then the town may become cut off during heavy rains and so, until the roads are upgraded (presently being undertaken), it is advisable to explore this area during the dry season. If you do own a four-wheel-drive vehicle and like to get far away from other overlanders, Niassa province is the place for you.

Apart from the accommodation and eating facilities detailed below, there is a petrol station, provincial airport, post office, hospital, police station, bank, immigration office (Imigração) and satellite public telephone system (under construction). Lichinga power station is only fired up from seven until ten every evening, after which it is very dark, so carry a flashlight.

Accommodation

RIVAL RESTAURANT AND HOTEL. On Av. Samora Machel close to the edge of town. No running water and the food is alright if you like eggs and potatoes. Prices for accommodation are negotiable, starting from Mt40 000 per double room.

POUSADA LICHINGA. Opposite the Post Office and next to a bank just off Av. Samora Machel. The best place to stay in Lichinga. Expect charges to be around Mt150 000 for a double.

HOTEL LICHINGA. Situated next to the Municipal Market. Only to be considered as an option if the Rival and Pousada are full.

Eating and drinking

Try all the hotels. The locals seem to favour the Rival. If you have your own cooking facilities, shop at the colourful Municipal Market where the variety and availability of food is seasonal.

MANDIMBA

Situated at the frontier with Malawi (border post hours 6 a.m. to 6 p.m.), Mandimba is a good place to spend your last few million meticais if leaving Mozambique. There is an

extensive market, and Restaurante/Bar/ Pensão Ngame (on the main road which goes to Lichinga or Cuamba) which offers good food, clean toilets and comfortable rooms. Secure parking.

LAGO NIASSA

Although the roads, especially the last few kilometres down to the shore of Lago Niassa (Lake Malawi), are definitely four-wheel-drive territory, a visit to the Mozambique side of the lake may just be an experience (at last!) of 'Real Africa', i.e. undisturbed by tourists. Accessible from Lichinga, there are three small fishing villages where the only thing available is ... yes, you guessed it – fish (and maybe coconuts): Meponda (42 kilometres from Lichinga), Metangula (138 kilometres) and Cóbuè (190 kilometres).

There is no public transport leading right to these hamlets, but chapas and trucks regularly go as far as Maniamba on the way to Metangula and Cóbuè, after which you will have to hope for a lift with a government truck or aid vehicle. Every few days a boat goes from Metangula to Cóbuè. Get your passport stamped in Cóbuè and take a boat to Likoma island, from where there is a steamer to mainland Malawi. The roads to the lake pass through picturesque scenery and so, even if you don't quite make it to the water, the trip will still have

been worthwhile! Note, if you are really sure of your 4x4 vehicle, an excellent expedition is tackling the 750 lonely kilometres from Lichinga to Pemba on the coast. You will pass through some of the wildest country in Africa, but if you break down you may just have to till the earth and raise a crop until someone else comes along! The destination is worth the arduous journey which may take three days in good weather and forever during the big wet (January to April).

IN TANZANIA

Sick of the tourist-trodden, overland, over-done routes? Try this ...

Get a Mozambican visa in Dar es Salaam. Take a bus from Dar es Salaam south to Mtwara on the Tanzanian/Mozambique border and then hitch to Msimbati at the mouth of the Rovuma river.

There is no bridge over the Rovuma, so hire a dugout or dhow and cross into Mozambique. If you are on a dhow, head south via the most beautiful, unspoilt, uninhabited coral islands (of which there are 40) to Mocímboa da Praia, Pangane beach and Pemba.

Note that the road south to Mtwara from Dar es Salaam is closed due to flooding from March to July. The ferry over the Rufiji River cannot run, but it is possible to catch a passenger boat or an Air Tanzania flight.

10

Tete Province and Cahora Bassa

TETE PROVINCE

While most of Tete province (pronounced 'teh-teh') is about 500 metres above sea level, and is very hot all year (temperatures in Tete town regularly top the 45 °C mark), areas of the Angonia and Maravia plateaux reach 2 000 metres and have temperate climates moderated by altitudinal influences.

The important 'Tete Corridor' between Malawi and Zimbabwe – known as the 'gun-run' during the civil conflict, since there were frequent armed attacks on vehicles using this route – bisects the province and has already become one of Africa's principal overland highways. Apart from a short stretch of potholes, the road is smooth, brand-new tar all the way from Blantyre in Malawi to Harare in Zimbabwe, and no-one shoots at you any more.

Border posts at each end of the 'Corridor' are open from 6 a.m. to 6 p.m. and, even though you may plead that you are only in transit, you will still have to pay 'border tax' (imposto da fronteira) and third party insurance (seguros) on the Mozambican side. Border tax ranges from ten Zimbabwe dollars (Z$) to ten pounds sterling (equivalent to Z$100!) per person, with charges for your vehicle depending on its size. Insurance charges (and others) appear to depend on whether or not the officials think that you are prepared to pay more.

Clearly it is in your interests to get your hands on a few Zimbabwe dollars before entering Mozambique at Nyamapanda or Zóbuè. Zimbabwe dollars are available from

the touts on the Malawi side of the border (you should get about Z$12 for U.S.$1). If the officials insist on U.S. dollars, point out that you carry all foreign currency (apart from Zimbabwe dollars of course!) in the form of traveller's cheques. **Be patient!**

Yet another option available to avoid the 'Zóbuè blues' is to enter Tete province from Malawi at Dedza (open from 8 a.m. to 4 p.m.), 85 kilometres south of Lilongwe. The Dedza–'Tete Corridor' road is scenic, in a fair condition and you may come across the odd antelope or leopard (if driving at night).

TETE TOWN

If you wish to visit Cahora Bassa, get your credencial (permit) to enter the dam wall area from Hidroelétrica Cahora Bassa (H.C.B. or 'ach seh beh') at the Emose office in Tete.

Tete town is 224 kilometres from Blantyre and 382 kilometres from Harare. Situated on the broad floodplain of the Zambezi River, 500 kilometres from the delta at its mouth, Tete used to be accessible by fairly large river boats before Kariba and Cahora Bassa dams moderated the annual floods. Historically, Tete was the farthest inland outpost of Portuguese influence and an important trading port for ivory, hardwood and slaves. Today Tete remains significant due to the fact that, apart from the bridge at Vila de Sena and the ferry at Caia, the bridge over the Zambezi at Tete is the only crossing point for 2-wheel-drive vehicles downstream

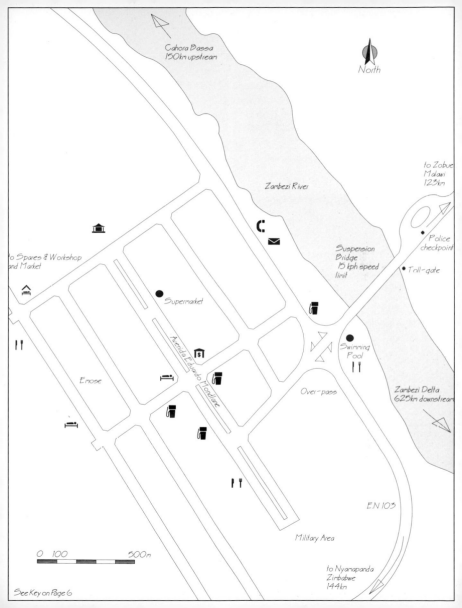

Cahora Bassa
150km upstream

North

Zambezi River

to Zobue
Malawi
123km

Suspension
Bridge
15 kph speed
limit

• Police
checkpoint

• Toll-gate

to Spares & Workshop
and Market

Supermarket

Avenida Eduardo Mondlane

Emose

Swimming
Pool

Over-pass

Zambezi Delta
625km downstream

E.N 103

Military Area

0   100   500m

to Nyamapanda
Zimbabwe
144km

See Key on Page 6

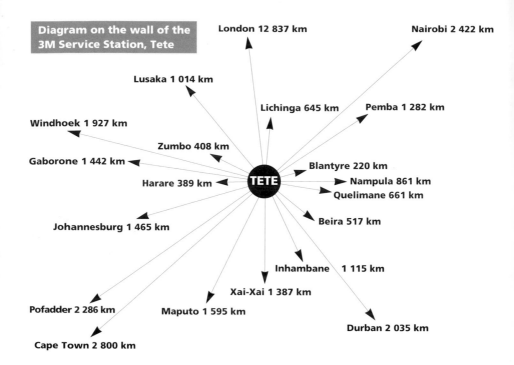

Diagram on the wall of the 3M Service Station, Tete

London 12 837 km
Nairobi 2 422 km
Lusaka 1 014 km
Lichinga 645 km
Pemba 1 282 km
Windhoek 1 927 km
Zumbo 408 km
Gaborone 1 442 km
Blantyre 220 km
Harare 389 km
TETE
Nampula 861 km
Quelimane 661 km
Beira 517 km
Johannesburg 1 465 km
Inhambane 1 115 km
Xai-Xai 1 387 km
Pofadder 2 286 km
Maputo 1 595 km
Durban 2 035 km
Cape Town 2 800 km

of Chirundu – a town on the Zimbabwe/Zambia border. Note the 15 km/h speed limit on the bridge is strictly enforced.

Accommodation

HOTEL ZAMBEZE. Fine views of the Zambezi (English spelling 'Zambezi', Portuguese 'Zambeze') at Mt120 000 to Mt500 000 per double room. Tel. (052) 2 3003.

HOTEL KASSUENDE. Av. 25 de Junho. The rooms are being upgraded; some have air conditioning, some private baths. Prices from Mt40 000 to Mt160 000 for a casal (for married couples only). Tel. (052) 2 2531.

PENSÃO ALVES. This is a friendly place, situated on Av. 25 de Junho just past Hotel Kassuende on the right. The prices are negotiable and range from Mt40 000 for a double room upwards. Tel. (052) 2 2523.

Eating and drinking

RESTAURANTE FREITAS. A good place to break a long, hot journey, tucked in on the river bank, next to the bridge on the downstream side. On a cool terrace overlooking the Zambezi. Comprehensive menu. Clean toilets

RESTAURANTE ZAMOÉ. On the road which extends directly from the bridge into Tete.

HOTEL ZAMBEZE. Staff are accustomed to serving foreigners; pricier than the others.

BAR RESTAURANTE À MARISQUERA. Situated on Av. Eduardo Mondlane; busy at night.

Facilities

Tete town is, according to the locals, 'the hottest place on earth' (personally I think Quelimane beats it). Add to this the high incidence of malaria and you have a picture

of a rather inhospitable place. However, should you need them one day, the following shops and services are available:
• On the right as you approach (from Zimbabwe) the flyover to the bridge over the Zambezi is Restaurante Freitas (see Eating and drinking on page 170).
• In the order reached (from the Zimbabwe side) passing under the flyover to the bridge, on the road running parallel to the river:
3.M. Service Station; Restaurante Djonino; Post Office (correio); Cinema 333; Telefones Públicos and Police.
• As reached if you drive up the road on the left after the flyover (straight up from the 3.M. Petrol Station):
BP Service Station (open Sundays); Hotel Zambeze; Mabor Tyres (pneus); Sonafel Spares; Imigração (visa extensions).
• Go straight up past the Hotel Zambeze to the T-junction with Av. 25 de Junho. Turn

right here and you will reach the following:
Hotel Kassuende; Padaria (bakery); Supermercado; Snack-Bar Restaurante 2002; Pensão Alves; Mosque; Mercado Municipal (open-air market); Tecnauto Landrover Agent; vehicle spares and repair shops.
• On Av. Eduardo Mondlane, starting from the Governor's House side and moving to the military garrison side:
Supermarkets; Indian shops; Hotel Zambeze; Banco Commercial de Moçambique; 3.M. Service Station; Bar Restaurante a Marisquera.

CAHORA BASSA

The turn-off to Songo town and the access road to the lakeside and dam wall are 24 kilometres from Tete on the way to Zimbabwe. The road is paved and the scenery alone makes this 130-kilometre diversion worthwhile .

The name Cahora Bassa (called 'Cabora Bassa' in colonial times) is apparently derived from the Chewa term 'Kebrabassa', which means 'the end of the work'.

Traders and travellers on the Zambezi, during the seventeenth, eighteenth and nineteenth centuries, were paddled and pulled up the river by locally 'recruited' slaves as far as a point around 100 kilometres upstream from Tete. At this point powerful rapids and short waterfalls effectively prevented further progress upstream and thus boats could only drift back downstream and the toil of the slaves came to an end at Kebrabassa.

In 1957 Mozambique was still a Portuguese province and the local government appointed a commission to investigate developing the Zambezi valley below Tete for agricultural and industrial purposes. Initially the idea of a dam arose because of the perceived need for flood control and irrigation. By 1960 the Portuguese government had firmly identified Cahora Bassa as a site for a formidable hydro-electric scheme and moves were afoot to obtain financing for the project.

The participation of South Africa's Electricity Supply Commission (ESKOM) was crucial from the outset, as South Africa with its extensive mining and industrial sectors would be the only significant market for the power which would be generated by harnessing the Zambezi at Cahora Bassa. ESKOM agreed to guarantee purchases of energy and the fact that the 1 400 kilometre-long twin power lines would have to carry direct current (D.C.) meant that power could not be tapped before it reached the Apollo Converter Station near Pretoria.

Separate A.C. lines have already been built to Nampula and Quelimane in northern Mozambique, while a line to Maputo remains on the drawing board.

In 1966 the ZAMCO Consortium was awarded the Cabora Bassa (as it was then called) contract; the agreement was signed in Lisbon on 17 September 1969. Despite attacks on supply routes by the Frelimo liberation movement, work forged ahead. The transmission lines were completed and the lake began to fill in 1974.

Ironically the power supply to South Africa was cut in 1986 when the Renamo resistance movement, a creation of the then Rhodesian and South African secret services, sabotaged hundreds of pylons in response to South Africa's terminating its support of Renamo, in terms of the Nkomati Accord.

At present no power from Cahora Bassa reaches South Africa and it is estimated that at least U.S.$150 million will be needed to rebuild the lines.

There are now plans to build yet another dam 40 kilometres upstream of Tete.

Specifications of Lake Cahora Bassa*

Dam type : Double curved concrete arch
Dam height : 160 metres
Dam crest altitude : 331 metres
Lake length : 270 kilometres
Capacity : 52 000 million cubic metres
Average inflow : 2 800 cubic metres per second (cumecs)
Flood inflow : More than 30 000 cubic metres per second
Area : 2 660 km^2
Catchment area : 1 200 000 km^2
Generating potential : 4 000 megawatts
*Source: *Damit* by Henry Olivier

Facilities on the lakeshore

Songo is in fact five kilometres away from the lake and, although roads do lead down to the water, getting permission to camp or launch a boat is likely to be a slow and laborious process.

SONGO FISHING AND CANOE SAFARIS. It's a good tar road all the way to Songo. The camp is near the dam wall; fishing is as good as Kariba in the sixties. All-inclusive 5-day packages including flight R2 800. Tel. Charles Norman Fishing Safaris, Johannesburg, South Africa tel./fax (011) 888 3168, cellphone 083 252 5149.

Chicoa is reached by turning left five kilometres before the police post on the edge of Songo, down an initially pot-holed 40 kilometre-long tarred road which later becomes gravel. Folk from Zimbabwe are busy developing a fishing camp at Chicoa, and I hear that the tigers are biting. No contact address or telephone numbers are available as yet.

SONGO TOWN

Songo was built to house the people who built Cahora Bassa dam and is now occupied by the staff needed to keep the generators well oiled.

The town (which is still a piece of Portugal in the middle of nowhere) perches on a plateau 500 metres above river level and a steep tarred road winds five kilometres down to the wall and huge subterranean generator chambers.

The gorge is truly magnificent and, although the dam is a brilliant engineering achievement, one cannot help wondering what it might have been like to shoot the wild water of the exciting rapids, which now lie dead under 100 metres of boringly still water.

Access to the lake shore

PIET HOUGAARD'S CAMP, Màgoé. Access via Shamva and Mount Darwin in Zimbabwe, through the Mukumbura/Mucumbura frontier (open 8 a.m. to 4 p.m.), after which it's two hours on a rough gravel road, which can become almost impassable during rain. R325 per person per night, road transfers from Mucumbura if required. Tel. Charles Norman Fishing Safaris, Johannesburg, South Africa tel./fax (011) 888 3168, cellphone 083 252 5149.

As the dam wall area is regarded as a security risk (encircling minefields were laid, firstly to keep out Frelimo, later to deter Renamo), prospective visitors are screened at a police checkpoint just before the town and are required to present written permission (credencial) from one of the the H.C.B. (Hidroelétrica Cahora Bassa) offices. These can be found in Tete, Chimoio, Maputo (all in Mozambique), Harare (in Zimbabwe) or Johannesburg (in South Africa).

In Tete, find out about a credencial at the H.C.B. (pronounced 'ach-seh-beh') office, next to EMOSE (Empresa Moçambique de Seguros), one street up from the Hotel Zambeze.

For further information, or to arrange a guided tour of the power station, contact the H.C.B. office in Maputo, located at 1132 Av. do Trabalho, tel. (01) 40 0647, fax. 40 0551 and telex. 6-467.

Accommodation

CAMPING (campismo). Although there is no formal site or facility, camping at the lakeside in the controlled area around Songo is permitted after consultation with the town administration (enquire at the police station). A fee may possibly be levied.

POUSADA SETE MONTES. Situated in the centre of Songo is this delightful oasis of greenery and peace in the heat and dry of Tete province. You will pay Mt220 000 for double rooms; casal (rooms for married couples) cost a mere Mt150 000. A full English breakfast will set you back Mt16 000.

Eating and drinking

CENTRO SOCIAL H.C.B. Take your evening meals (lunch as well on weekends) here by arrangement with H.C.B.'s Senhor Tonim – ask for directions at the police station. There is a swimming pool here as well.

POUSADA SETE MONTES. Good wholesome food, but you would be wise to order a couple of hours in advance.

RESTAURANTE PLANALTO (on the left). As you wind up the hill after presenting your credencial at the police post, watch out for Restaurante Planalto just where the road levels out.

SUPERMERCADO (SUPERMARKET). Various well stocked shops (high prices) are dotted around town. Try the one just down the road from the police station.

Facilities

Songo also boasts a paved airport, filling station, post office and a hospital.

Bibliography

Atlas Geográfico, Volume 1, República Popular de Moçambique, Ministério de Educação, Stockholm, 1986.

Axelson, Eric. *Portuguese in South-East Africa,* Cornelis Struik Publishers, Johannesburg, 1973.

Muller, Judith von D. *Art in East Africa,* Frederick Muller, London, 1975.

Newitt, Malyn. *History of Mozambique,* Witwatersrand University Press, Johannesburg, 1994.

Olivier, Henry. *Damit,* Macmillan South Africa, Johannesburg, 1975.

Skrodzki, Bernhard. *Guide to Mozambique,* Bradt Publications, Chalfont St Peter, England, 1994.

Index